Frank Crane

The Religion of Tomorrow

Frank Crane

The Religion of Tomorrow

ISBN/EAN: 9783337262587

Printed in Europe, USA, Canada, Australia, Japan

Cover: Foto ©Lupo / pixelio.de

More available books at **www.hansebooks.com**

The Religion *of* To-morrow

The Religion of To-morrow

By
FRANK CRANE

"LO, I AM WITH YOU ALWAY"
Matthew, xxii, 20

HERBERT S. STONE & COMPANY
CHICAGO & NEW YORK
MDCCCXCIX

TABLE OF CONTENTS

                                                                Page

CREDO vii

CHAPTER I. INTRODUCTION . . 3
Religion is the Personal Influence of God.

CHAPTER II. THE KINGDOM OF HEAVEN . 23
The Purpose of God's Personal Influence is Transformation, not Transportation.

CHAPTER III. DYNAMICS . . . 53
The Power of Religion Consists, not in Rewards and Punishments, but in God's Personal Influence.

CHAPTER IV. ETERNAL LIFE . . 81
Life Influenced by God's Personality Becomes Eternal in Quality.

CHAPTER V. THE SHADOW OF THE CROSS 101
The Central Doctrine of Christianity is not Based upon the Cross, but upon the Resurrection, and Salvation is not the Legal Consequence of the Dead Christ's Deed, but the Present Effect of the Living Christ's Immanence, Made Possible by His Death.

CHAPTER VI. DEFINITIONS . . . 129
Scriptural Terms for the Operation of Religion are Explainable only by Assuming It to be God's Personal Influence.

CHAPTER VII. THE LIGHT FROM THE CROSS 161
The Crucifixion is not the Atonement; It is but a Part of the Atonement, and It or Any Scheme or Doctrine of It is Impotent unless It be Vitalized and Completed by the Present Personal Influence of God.

TABLE OF CONTENTS

CHAPTER VIII. THE BALANCE OF DOCTRINE 217

To View Religion as God's Personal Influence Gives Coherency to Conflicting Doctrines, to Contradictory Passages of Scripture, and to Opposing Elements in Human Nature.

CHAPTER IX. THE INCARNATION . . 237

The Personal Influence of God is Transforming the World as a Power of Social Evolution, not as a Rule of Social Segregation.

CHAPTER X. THE LEAVEN . . . 267

The Personal Influence of God is the Propagating Power of Christianity.

CHAPTER XI. HELL 293

The Bible was not Given to Reveal "Last Things" nor Future Events; not to Gratify Curiosity, but to Reveal the Laws of God's Personal Influence.

CHAPTER XII. LIFE IN THE HEAVENS . 331

God's Personal Influence upon His Eternal Sons.

APPENDIX 361

CREDO

"You would better," said a learned friend, who had examined the manuscript of this essay, "add a succinct statement of your creed, so that the reader may not be led by his own inferences to locate you theologically where you do not belong."

Hence:

I believe in the Trinity, in the Atonement, in Salvation through Faith, in Heaven, in Hell, in the Church, and in all the other doctrines of the historic creeds of Protestantism. But I believe that the common notions of these doctrines contain error. This error is an inheritance from the theology of the Roman Church, which substituted a complicated system of divine machinery to do what can only be done by the divine personality. The thought of this age is discovering the utter untenability of mediæval dogmatism, and is swinging back to that view which was held by the apostles and the Greek fathers. The theory, which applied to all our Christian tenets will most surely be a touchstone to separate the true from the false, the artificial

CREDO

from the real, is the theory which in these places is set forth; to wit, that Religion is the Personal Influence of God.

The views of this essay are such as can be held by a member of any of the principal evangelical denominations. The author is, and hopes to remain, a church member. He seeks not to destroy but to fulfill, to fill Christian concepts fuller of Christ's own meaning. This is no attempt to create a new-fangled Gospel. This volume pretends not to tell men something they do not know, but it seeks to give voice to what the common people do already think and believe. It aims to be an interpretation of present-day evangelical thought, not the heralding of a new cult.

CHAPTER I
THEME
Religion is the Personal Influence of God

"By the term 'religion,' I shall mean any theory of personal agency in the universe, belief in which is strong enough in any degree to influence conduct. No term has been used more loosely of late years, or in a greater variety of meanings. Of course anybody may use it in any sense he pleases, provided he defines exactly in what sense he does so. The above seems to be most in accordance with traditional usage."—GEORGE JOHN ROMANES, *Thoughts on Religion*, p. 113.

CHAPTER I

The proposition this book seeks to substantiate is that religion is the personal influence of God. At first glance that statement may not appear to mean very much; yet as we reflect upon it, as we apply it to all of our common stock of the doctrines of Christianity, it will be found to have a startling and far-reaching effect. As we bring this one idea to bear upon our thought about heaven, hell, salvation, the atonement, faith, and so on, we discover that it acts upon them very much as our knowledge of the law of gravitation acts upon our view of the many diverse and conflicting phenomena of matter. The movement of the planets, the differing weights of substances, and a hundred other facts of nature were but curious things, ascribed by some to magic and demons, and explained by others by ingenious shifts and contrivances, like the cycles and epicycles of the Ptolemaic system, until the all-regulating law of gravitation was announced; and then we perceived that those things which once we attributed to whim and mystery are all in harmony and all

THE RELIGION OF TO-MORROW

unified by one law. That religion is the personal influence of the immanent God, I conceive to be the central, all-ordering, and all-disposing idea that harmonizes, adjusts, and makes plain and reasonable the entire scheme of Christian thought, thus occupying in theology a position somewhat similar to the position occupied by the law of gravitation in physics.[1]

And religion is nothing but the personal influence of God. All of its operations, effects, and obligations are but phases of that influence. God's influence is of the same kind as that of man. It differs in degree. As one man affects another, so the person of God affects men. This is a simple, comprehensible thought.

---

[1] The exactness of this definition may be questioned; but I find it impossible to discover in the dictionaries or elsewhere a distinct and accurate meaning for the word "religion." It is used loosely, according to the view points of respective writers to mean (1) a recognition of and allegiance to a superhuman power, (2) a feeling of awe toward Deity, (3) a system of faith and worship, (4) the practice of sacred rites, and so on. Is it, then, a subjective human emotion, conviction, or practice; or is it an objective impulse working upon man from above? It seems to be a general term applied to various phases of man's relation to Deity, and is used subjectively or objectively, according to one's notion of divine things. When a positivist speaks of "the religion of humanity," he takes the extreme subjective point of view, regarding religion as a phase of mere human experience; while in this writing religion is conceived of objectively, as an influence constantly emanating from the immanent God. For one to say that this definition is incorrect, because religion is properly subjective wholly, will be equivalent to saying that I have not proved my proposition; and this, of course, he is free to maintain. But it will not be fair for him to assume for me a definition which I repudiate, and then to charge me with a wrong use of terms. Etymologically, it is certainly as correct to use the word "religion" to mean the energy of the divine personality, as it is to use it as is done in the phrases of the monastery: such as " to enter religion," "her name in religion is Mary Aloysia," "he is a religieux," and the like. (See Century Dictionary, under "Religion.")

THEME

This idea reconciles our theology to reason. It gives it intellectual beauty. It changes theology from a rude heap of unstable stones into a beautiful living temple. It takes away from our religion a great part of those objectionable tenets at which infidelity has leveled its bitterest shafts of ridicule.

Christianity has made wonderful progress. This is the more striking because at the same time the intellectual leaders of the age have become dissatisfied with its framework of creed. It is significant that salvation, regeneration, and the atonement, as facts, are to-day more potent than ever before in the history of men, while as theories, as explained by theologians, they are unsatisfactory to many of the most intelligent of our time. Over and over again have the common notions of almost every tenet of our faith been shown to be scientifically illogical; yet, strange to say, this faith remains full of an undeniable energy. How shall we explain this paradox? The irreligious may say it is merely the strength of superstition and primitive fear; but that will not do, for our religion is decidedly one of progress, it is vigorous with altruism, and certainly not inconsistent with intellectuality. The conservative may say it is because our theology is full of divine power, the foolishness of God being mightier than the wisdom of man. But it is a question whether the foolishness in question is of God or of ourselves.

The true explanation seems to be, that with all its covering of traditional absurdities, our quasi-mediæval theology yet contains the idea of God. It still brings God to men. Thus our religion succeeds in spite of its irrational forms, not because of them. Reducing all theology to conform to the one dominant idea of the personal influence of God takes away most of the elements that hinder its acceptance by the intelligence of mankind, and thus makes it a more perfect vehicle of God's influence.[1]

Those thoroughly imbued with mediæval dogma may be, and doubtless hosts of them are, truly and really godly. Even when men thought the stars were bright specks upon a blue cover, the sight of the heavens was inspiring. But as the knowledge that those glistening points are worlds floating in infinite distances only enhances our wonder and awe, so the removal of the irrational elements

---

[1] In insisting so strongly upon the divine immanence I do not wish to be understood as either denying, or in the least degree detracting from, the idea of the divine transcendence. But I consider the latter to be fully acknowledged and accepted by my readers: I take this for granted, and confine myself to the former, as being the thought which in these days it is necessary to emphasize. All the transcendency of God which is set forth by the Augustinian theologians I fully believe in; but, without abating our faith in this, it seems to me that it is God's immanence which is to be the note of the future.

THEME

from theology can only give new power to faith.

Conceiving religion to be God's personality influencing us, theology is changed immediately from a legal or a statutory science to be what may be called, in a way, a natural science. It can be then prosecuted with all the certainty and dignity we observe in studying sociology, geology, or biology. The apostles and prophets are our great teachers; but they are our Newtons and Keplers and Tyndalls, and not our Blackstones and Chittys. We are in a realm of fact, truth, and nature; not any more in the realm of dogma and opinion only. The Bible is seen to have worth because it "bears witness to the truth," not simply because it is the *ipse dixit* of the inspired men. Inspiration, then, becomes a question of whether Jesus and His apostles truly set forth the facts concerning God's person working among men, just as Linnæus's and Faraday's trustworthiness depends on whether they truly set forth the facts concerning the methods of God's working in matter. Too much importance has been given to the questions of the historical accuracy, to the secular proofs of the authenticity and genuineness of the Scriptures. These, indeed, are interesting and grave matters, but they do not to any degree affect the authority of the volume of sacred writings, which exists now, not primarily to inform us of historic happenings, nor to disclose to us the future of the world nor the future of the individual soul, but rather to bring us in touch with the divine personality by unfolding to us the character of God as evidenced in His laws, His workings, and His plans. The main reason, therefore, for believing the Bible to be inspired is not that the mass of evidence collected by Christian apologists is conclusive that the Book was actually written by certain supposed authors, but that, even as an anonymous volume, by whomsoever it was written, it reveals to the reverent and sincere reader the potent force of Deity, a force found in no other book. Thus our chosen theory relegates the question of inspiration to its true position, and puts it on its true basis.

Conceiving theology to be the science of God's personal influence transforms it in somewhat the same manner in which alchemy is changed to chemistry, or astrology to astronomy. There is a definite, undeniable, recognized force among mankind, just as electricity is in matter; this force is manifest in certain uniform phenomena, such as an individual conscience, in systems of religion, in individual, racial, and social ethical movements, in those moral sentiments which characterize

THEME

acteristic samples of modern cults. The student of the philosophy of religion must view all these as different evidences of a common force working in human ideas. What is that force? It is the growing idea of the immanence of God. Unitarianism was in the main a revolt against the artificiality of the Latin view of the atonement; Universalism against the artificiality of a scheme of future rewards and punishments as motives of conduct; Theosophy and Christian Science are bizarre expressions of the yearning of the common heart for a God usable, knowable, and present. The theory that religion is God's personal influence recognizes whatever is true in each of these tendencies, and, it would seem, satisfies the demand which they polemically express. Also, in what we call orthodox circles, or the more common body of Christians, we have seen a gradual dropping of the old methods of preaching. We are leaving off the "good old ways" of preachment. Didactic statements of the accepted theories of the atonement and vivid pictures of future woe and blessedness do not move men as they once did. Spurgeon was the last great preacher of that class which used this material, and he has left no successor. Mr. Moody, the most popular evangelist of this day, dwells principally upon God's universal love. The common phrases now are "a personal Saviour," "the life more abundant," "social salvation," and the like. We urge men to "accept Christ," rather than to "believe something."

Now, I know of no serious attempt deliberately to cast our present-day views into an intelligible system. It seems therefore necessary that theology should be readjusted, that it should repudiate distinctly its Roman basis, and set itself squarely and unmistakably upon a New Testament and ante-Nicene foundation. In other words, in our systematic doctrine, as well as in our practical preaching, we should get back to Jesus and to Paul. It is the purpose of this essay to suggest how this is to be done; the full details of the system I do not attempt to work out. I have confined myself merely to suggesting the true starting-point of a reformed theology, and to intimating a few of the more salient features of our creed that it harmonizes and makes lucid.

I have refrained from a historical form of treating this subject, or from a critical form, as my purpose is to speak to the common mind, to the laity as well as the clergy, to the general common sense of the people rather than to the critical experts. As much as possible I have also let the argument run upon its natural and original course without stop-

THEME

ping to quote, to refute, or to commend this and that author, for I have always thought that this method adds little weight to the value of one's own thought, and that it evidences a desire to exhibit the erudition of the author, rather than to assist him in making himself understood. And after all, common sense is little concerned as to who has said this and who that, except when we refer to the Scriptures; and, as Montaigne says: "There is more ado to interpret interpretations than to interpret things, and more books upon books than upon all other subjects; we do nothing but comment upon one another."

While I think the gist of this writing to be original, yet I am fully aware of the extent to which I am indebted to what others have written. If therefore some pick out this or the other thought herein which has been before and better said by another, I will enter now, in advance, a plea of guilty; only I do not believe that the whole matter has ever been set together and given the mutual interdependence that the reader will find in these pages. I think myself this essay to be a selection of thoughts and doctrines and views that are "in the air," so to speak, and if there be value in it, it is in the arrangement of the whole about the one central idea.

THE RELIGION OF TO-MORROW

In dealing with questions in any way pertaining to religion, one is upon sacred ground. The hopes we have formed concerning those we have "loved long since and lost awhile," to say nothing of our own moral surety, are so dear that whoever would shatter them for mere iconoclastic pleasure would be like a wanton boy destroying treasures of art. Whether they be true or not, no man should lay hands upon the dreams of a life to come unless he proposes to make those dreams brighter, better, and more conformable to reality; if he has only gone so far as to discover flaws in them, and has no word that shall give them strength, then he should keep silence. It is, therefore, not only because I think that our common ideas about religion, heaven, and salvation are mixed with error, but, also, it is because I think I may perhaps be of some help in setting them right, that this writing is undertaken. The design of this work is constructive, not destructive. The writer has not merely something to unsay; he has something to say, or thinks he has.

Much of the explaining that is done is to those who would rather not hear the explanation; for while beforehand they may have only imagined they knew, afterward they are sure they do not know. But my trust is that,

THEME

because certain things seem so lambent to me, I can illuminate them for others.

Practically, really, I believe the outline of theology here indicated is that which is in common use by most of the evangelical clergy of to-day. They have quietly and of necessity taken these views, and are working with them. But we still cling, in our text-books and seminaries, to the old formulas; we still theoretically defend the antiquated phrases of the Latin church, while actually we have left them and have made for ourselves new and better. Most of our preaching nowadays is of a personal, living, immanent God-Saviour, and not of a mechanical plan-salvation. The aim of this essay is to indicate a way in which our theoretic theology may be made to conform to our factual theology.

First of all, we are to consider the object and scope of God's personal influence; it is to change mankind from its sinful condition into a condition called "the kingdom of heaven"; not primarily to prepare us for another world, but to prepare us for right life here and hereafter, here or anywhere. (Chapter II.)

The agency by which this change is to be wrought in the race is not rewards and punishments, a motive explicitly superseded, but God's personal influence. (Chapter III.)

What is this change that is to take place in

us to make us fit citizens of God's kingdom? It is a change wrought by the presence of the immanent God upon our character. It is the same kind of a change, differing only in degree, that is effected in us when we come under the personal influence of a strong, noble man, for man is a spirit as well as God is, and he is a son of God. The Eternal Life, therefore, is God's life, which takes hold of us and assimilates us to itself according to the known laws of personal influence. (Chapter IV.)

God's living personality being the immediate and chief agency in our regeneration, it is not the Christ who died, but the Christ who died and rose again, that is the central figure of Christian theology. Any system of theology is deficient which represents salvation as consisting in the deliverance of man from the consequences of his sin by a dead Christ, rather than a deliverance of man from sinfulness itself by the risen and now immanent Christ. (Chapter V.)

The terms used by the new Testament writers in describing the operation of the new religion are only explainable by the theory of that religion being God's personal influence. Thus, grace is God's influence, faith our reception of it, the Gospel the news of it, and righteousness the consequence of it. (Chapter VI.)

THEME

The atonement, considered as a mere scheme, in and by itself, is of no avail to us, except as a sort of superstitious allaying of the fear of punishment. We are saved by God Himself; the death of Jesus Christ was the supreme revelation of the character of God; so vital is that conception of God which we only get by Christ's death that Jewish ritualism for centuries had been preparing the mind of the world to understand it; the Cross thus becomes the great sign and vehicle of the personal influence of God upon men. (Chapter VII.)

Christianity is built upon a personality, not upon dogma. Personality is the real edifice; dogma the scaffolding. Personality is the balance of doctrine. (Chapter VIII.)

The salvation of the world of spirits is coming as came the evolution of matter, by the assimilation of all things and all souls unto God. The personal influence theory explains the corruptions of Christianity. (Chapter IX.)

Personal influence is the force Christ carefully selected as the means by which the whole world is to be saved. It is shown how personal influence alone can do so great a work. (Chapter X.)

The sorrows of the wicked are explainable only upon the theory that the sole saving power is the personal influence of God. "Last things" are mainly speculative and not essential to the purpose of revelation. (Chapter XI.)

A form of thought, confessedly theoretical, is suggested concerning the future life; as the forms given by mediæval writers, equally theoretical, have lost their utility because of our increased knowledge of the universe. (Chapter XII.)

The whole is intended to prove that the theory that religion is the personal influence of God will be the recognized fundamental truth of the religion of to-morrow. For, based upon this theory, theology cannot decay but must grow and widen with the current of the world's intellectual and ethical progress.

SUGGESTIONS

The history of the world is its slow assimilation to God.

The proof of inspiration is the divine personality within the Book.

The personal influence theory does not explain all mysteries, but it brings us to see what are the true mysteries, God and Man, and what are the false, the machinery of ecclesiastical speculation and the paradoxes of mediævalism.

When theology is prosecuted as a study of the nature and effects of the personal influence of God it is transformed as if from the Ptolemaic to the Copernican theory, from Alchemy to Chemistry.

Religion itself has made wonderful progress while the science of religion has sunk into disrepute.

Theology should not be a science of dogma, as is the Law; but a science of fact, as are the natural sciences.

The apostles have been held as our Blackstones and Chittys; we are to consider them as our Newtons and Keplers.

There is something wrong with a theology that is saved from intellectual contempt only by respect for its subject matter.

The religion of to-morrow is the religion of the early Greek Christian fathers.

The heresies of an age best indicate its religious drift.

CHAPTER II

THE KINGDOM OF HEAVEN

The Purpose of God's Personal Influence is Transformation, not Transportation.

> "Ah, when shall all men's good
> Be each man's rule, and universal peace
> Lie like a shaft of light across the land,
> And like a lane of beams across the sea,
> Thro' all the circle of the golden year?"
> TENNYSON, *The Golden Year.*

"Christianity is making for this world a new heaven, and out of that a new earth. When we see new heavens, then we soon see new earth. We may say that the world has been made altogether new, and life wholly different, by the simple sight of God as the universal Father."—CLARKE, *Common Sense in Religion,* p. 166.

"The habit of adjourning our higher hopes from this world to the next has greatly interfered with their fulfillment. But this habit is manifestly giving way, partly from the growing interest in public life and philanthropic schemes, partly through a better understanding of the Old and New Testament. It seems clear that the object of the life disclosed in the Scriptures is not merely to save individuals, but to train first one nation and then mankind to become the city of God."—FREEMANTLE, *The World as the Subject of Redemption,"* p. 313.

"Whatever makes men good Christians makes them good citizens."—WEBSTER, *Speech at Plymouth,* December 22, 1820.

"The kingdom of God cometh not with outward shew; neither shall they say, Lo here! or, lo there! for, behold, the kingdom of God is within you."—JESUS, Luke xvii. 20-21.

CHAPTER II

God is and always has been immanent in the world. The best of men have always suspected His presence. Polytheism was close to the truth;[1] it failed because it missed the personality of God. Judaism grasped the idea of His personality, but was faulty in that it tended to limit Him and to make Him to be a local and national deity.[2] God has been in every age and race, brooding over His human children, slowly lifting them up by the influence of His personality, into a higher life. It is immaterial to this argument whether we say that man fell or that he developed out of the beast; in either case he has been a miserable, beastly character as far back as history and tradition shed their light. But there has been some force at work changing him gradually for the better. This force has operated slowly, with many reverses, often appearing to go backward, yet, as the student of history knows, steadily gaining ground. Wherever

[1] "Whom therefore ye ignorantly worship, Him declare I unto you."—Paul's Address to the Athenians, Acts xvii. 23.

[2] "The hour cometh when ye shall neither in this mountain, nor yet at Jerusalem, worship the Father. God is a Spirit."—Jesus to the Woman of Samaria, John iv. 21, 24.

there were men there was this power that makes for righteousness. In some cases, however, it worked more successfully than in others, for reasons unessential to our present discussion. It produced a wondrous civilization in Greece, a great religious conviction in the Orient, an exalted morality among the Jews. It is God. The same God is bringing all men everywhere up to the likeness of Himself by the influence of His personality. The Jews were nearer the truth than the others because they apprehended the most important fact concerning this force, its personality; therefore it is said: "Salvation is of the Jews."[1] But Jews and all failed because there was something lacking. That something was a clear, intelligible knowledge of Deity as a person interested in helping every son of man. In the course of time, when the social and intellectual progress of the world was sufficiently developed so that mankind could, in some accurate measure, understand Him, God embodied Himself in human flesh and spirit and came into humanity as the Christ.[2] Thus He for all time impressed the notion of His personality upon the race. But lest this person be localized, and thus the equally important thought of His immanence be lost sight of, Christ departed

---

[1] John iv. 22.   [2] Heb. i. 1–4.

THE KINGDOM OF HEAVEN

as a local figure and returned again as a Holy Ghost.[1] Thus we have the complete revelation of God as the Trinity; that is, as the Father He is the infinitely great Unknown and Unknowable Whom no man hath seen at any time; as the Christ He is knowable and definite and thus able to make a distinct impression upon men; and as the Holy Spirit He is personally present touching and molding all.

Now what is it that God wants to do among men? It is to alter their natures until they become like Himself. A humanity thus altered constitutes "the kingdom of heaven." To form this kingdom was the avowed intention of Jesus. One becomes a member of this realm not by any effort of his own except as that effort allows God's personality to influence him. When one enters upon a life of communion with God he is changed by the strong effect of God's character upon him to become like Christ. He is then set in an order of progress, his nature is then so reformed, that he is said to have a new life—eternal life.[2] "This is life eternal—to know God."[3]

And now we come into conflict with current popular theology. To most men what does

[1] "If I go not away the Comforter will not come."—John xvi. 7.
[2] "And I will give unto them eternal life."—John x. 28.
[3] John xvii. 3.

the word "Eternal Life" mean? It may not be an extreme statement to say that to very many it has no practical, present meaning except as something that we, before death, must prepare for. Although a few books and preachers of the more spiritual sort speak of it as a present possession, we usually look upon such talk as a kind of enthusiasm, while we think in reality eternal life actually begins at the close of this mortal life. It is reserved for true Christians as a happy reward after death. Eternity has its hither end at the grave; immortality begins where mortality ends. We urge sinners to repent and believe so they may "at last find a home in heaven." We sing:

> "O you must be a lover of the Lord
> Or you can't go to heaven when you die."

Popular theology is correct in identifying eternal life and heaven: they are one and the same thing. But neither of them depends upon place. The doctrine of heaven as a place set before us as a chief inducement is wholly unscriptural. The Bible does not teach that this sublunary existence is a "state of probation," the sole purpose of which is to determine into which of the two future cities, heaven or hell, we are to go, "according to the deeds done in the body." Christ

THE KINGDOM OF HEAVEN

used no such motive as dominant, nor sanctioned it. Heaven is something more than a city in which all the righteous are gathered, and at whose gates Saint Peter stands holding the keys. Eternal life is not a residence apportioned to those whose accounts balance with a credit upon the right side; the whole theory of balancing accounts is alien to the spirit of the Gospel. Heaven is not an everlasting pleasure-ground whither those go who have received a favorable verdict at a great court-room scene called "The Day of Judgment." It is not a land separated from earth by the "River Jordan," in whose dark waves all perish in attempting to cross unless they have been believers. There is indeed an element of poetic truth in all these figures, but as positive doctrines they are literalistic constructions of the scattered imagery of the Bible. To postulate as dogmatic fact what was revealed as mere prophetic coloring is to be overwise.[1]

[1] The idea of Jesus was to magnify this earthly life by showing how sublime and God-like it might be made; the tendency of mediæval theology has been to magnify this life the rather by emphasizing the *future consequences* dependent upon our use of it. While both seem to come to the same thing, it will be readily seen that the influence of the former idea as a central doctrine would be to make life large, full, and wholesome, and the influence of the latter as a central idea would tend (as we know it *has* tended) to make life despicable, empty, and morbid.
In a nutshell, the matter thus lies: Jesus' notion was for man to secure future bliss by concentrating his thought upon present godliness; the Latin system has been for man to secure present godliness by concentrating his thought upon future bliss. Although apparently the same, one process is the reverse of the other. One makes monks, the other makes men.

THE RELIGION OF TO-MORROW

The Bible contains no preachment about "getting to heaven" as the object of life. Not to get us into heaven, but to get heaven into us, is the theme of Jesus. Heaven, with Him, is a condition and not a place. The very first text of His ministry opposed the theory of a far-off heaven, for he came proclaiming: "Repent, for the kingdom of heaven is at hand."[1] Both He and His disciples urged men to accept eternal life right then and there, and never once took the tenor of advising or warning men so to act that they might enter into a blessed place after death only.

We do not wonder at the tenacity of this place idea, however. It is an old delusion of men to imagine that if they can but get into other surroundings, have different clothes, houses, means, and relatives, go to live in another city or country, or attain unto new skies, new soil, or new neighbors, then they shall be content. But even the heathen philosophers knew better than this; they knew that happiness comes from within and does not depend upon outward circumstances; and surely the Son of God knew more than they; He would not have made a mistake that even Epictetus and Socrates avoided.[2] So He con-

[1] Matt. iv. 17.
[2] "In a word, neither death, nor exile, nor pain, nor anything of this kind is the real cause of our doing or not doing any action,

THE KINGDOM OF HEAVEN

demned the teaching that one's character can be soiled by "that which entereth into him," and declared that it is "that which cometh out of man," from his heart, that alone can taint the soul.[1] A man without heaven in him would be wretched in the golden streets and smitten with ennui among the choiring angels; the water of life would not quench his thirst, neither would the fruit of the healing tree satisfy his desires, nor would the shining faces of the holy ones make him glad.[2] And a man having "Christ formed within" could walk around in the abode of the lost like the Hebrew children in the fiery furnace; the flame would not singe a hair of his head. Even if sent to perdition the joy of such a man would remain with him, for "what shall separate us from the love of God?"

> " While blest with a sense of His love
> A palace a toy would appear;
> And prisons would palaces prove
> If Jesus would dwell with me there."[3]

We may think that if we can get away from the hindrances of our present lot, from our

but our inward opinions and principles."—Epictetus, Discourses, ch. xi.
"One ought to seek out virtue for its own sake, without being influenced by fear or hope, or by any external influence. Moreover, in *that* does happiness consist." Zeno.
"He is happiest who wants the fewest things." Socrates.

[1] Matt. xv. 11.
[2] "Myself am hell." Milton (see line 73 et seq., Paradise Lost).
[3] Charles Wesley.

dull drudgery, our temptations, and our worriments, and fly to a land where all is delightful, we would be peaceful and perfect; but unfortunately we have left out of the enumeration of our enemies the greatest one of all—ourselves; and even in a land of angels we cannot escape ourselves. And, no matter what our condition, if we let the Holy Spirit into our heart we can rise to walk in heavenly life with Christ.[1]

This heaven-place error is inground into us. Almost all other reformers have hoped to better the world by altering man's environment. They have striven for improved systems of government, of taxation, of money, and of the distribution of property, and have fondly pictured the Utopias that would be attained could their respective schemes but be successful. But Jesus showed His divine wisdom by disdaining all such makeshifts. When He came to save men from their wretchedness He did not esteem it worth while to attack slavery, tyranny, malfeasance in office, false forms of government, or any such thing. He penetrated at once by the intuition of wisdom to the cause of all these wrongs; He was not led astray by symptoms, but went to the seat of the disease. He addressed Himself to the task of reforming men's hearts, aims, desires,

[1] Phil. iv. 11. "In whatsoever state . . . content."

THE KINGDOM OF HEAVEN

and views. It was a gigantic undertaking, one that none ever before had dared seriously attempt, and one which not all of His followers have thoroughly believed in since. But after all we are beginning to see that it is the only way substantial progress has ever been effected. No advance in human conditions has ever been permanent that has not been an advance of mankind itself. The only stable improvement in human affairs has been such as has followed naturally from improvement in humanity.

A great many Christians still do not believe in Christ's method. They regard the world as hopelessly lost. All God can do is to save a few elect souls from the wreck. They are appalled and blinded by the stupendous power of evil. They do not believe that the gentle, permeating force of the Holy Spirit will ever transform the world by His present methods, and their only hope is some miraculous interference of God to burn up the wicked and rescue the saints. The "second advent" theories are a discounting of the efficacy of the Holy Ghost to save the world; they go upon the assumption that the best He can do is to save a few, but to redeem a whole race is too much for Him. But patiently and quietly the Christ is lifting all mankind out of darkness into light. When He is through with His work it will be done, done right and not needing to be done over again.[1] God's plan is to make heaven for men, not by taking them away from the earth but by transforming them upon the earth.[2] He is to persevere until "all shall know Him from the least to the greatest,"[3] until "His people shall be all holy."[4] Then upon this globe we shall see the fulfilment of the promise, "Behold, I make all things new";[5] we shall indeed have "a new heaven and a new earth."[6] For there is nothing wrong with our planet but man, and other things only as they are affected by him. When this race has been changed, as it will be, earth itself will be as much a heaven as are those other places to which souls go after death. "For the earnest expectation of the creature (ktisis, the whole created world) waiteth for the manifestation of the sons of God,"[7] wrote Paul; that is to say, a transfigured humanity will transfigure its environment. Christ came not to condemn the world but to destroy the works of the devil in it, to

---

[1] Isa. liii. 11. "He shall see of the travail of His soul, and shall be satisfied."

[2] "I pray not that Thou shouldst take them out of the world, but that Thou shouldst keep them from the evil." John xvii. 15.

[3] Heb. viii. 11.

[4] "Thy people shall be all righteous." Isa. lx. 21.

[5] Rev. xxi. 5.

[6] Rev. xxi. 1.

[7] Rom. viii. 19.

THE KINGDOM OF HEAVEN

turn it into a paradise, to make the lion and the lamb lie down together, to stop war, to wipe away all tears, to abolish disease, so that "none shall any more say, I am sick";[1] and to do this, not by theatric interferences, but by the dispensation of the Spirit, by the transforming influence of His own personality upon the disposition of humanity. Paul grasped this thought when he exclaimed: "We know that the whole creation groaneth and travaileth in pain together until now,"[2] that is, that the appearance of the Gospel of the Son of God in the world is the beginning of the end of all evil. If there is anything hurtful upon earth it is because of man, as it is intimated in the story of Adam and Eve. If there are deserts, thorns, bleak moors, and destructive storms, they are merely the reflection of the moral state of man, doubtless designed by the Creator to show him in outward parable and parallel his inward soul, as all speech and ideas are formed upon the analogies of nature;[3] and when man shall have been made new, when the human stock shall have been regenerated, then there shall be nothing that may hurt or destroy in all the earth, and this planet shall be one of the "many mansions" swinging musically in "the

[1] Isa. xxxiii. 24. See also Isa. xxv., xxxv. and lv., Rev. xxi., etc.
[2] Rom. viii. 22.
[3] See Bushnell: "Moral Uses of Dark Things."

heavens."[1] The divine program is not transportation but transfiguration.

The complete salvation of man having been removed beyond the grave, it is necessary for common theology to make another wrong proposition, namely, that there is some sort of moral efficacy in death. We must expect, it is held, to spend our days here in worry and sin, but if we put our trust in God, in some way death will make us all right. Death is thus popularly held to have more power to renew the soul than has the Christ. The latter can only save us from hell, and write our names in the book of life so we can enter heaven, but to hold that He can make us heavenly creatures here—that is fanaticism. Although we are saved by Him, that only means we are assured of a home in glory, and we still must go on sinning and fretting and quarreling till "*death* shall set us free."[2] Jesus can only remit the *penalty* of our sins; it is all-potent death that shall break the *power* of sin in us. If Christ is said to cleanse us, that is only theoretically; for death is the

---

[1] John xiv. 2.

[2] "So when my latest breath
Shall rend the veil in twain,
By death I shall escape from death
And life eternal gain."—James Montgomery.

The hymns of the church, however, are remarkably free from ascribing any direct moral efficacy to death. The above instance is not a fair sample. The idea of death's moral value abides rather as a general impression among Christians, than as a specifically taught doctrine.

THE KINGDOM OF HEAVEN

real cleanser. We are born again theologically at conversion, but we do not become really new creatures until death does its work. In other words, *death*, not *Jesus*, is to gain heaven for us!

Now, where in the Bible, is any such theory? Are the redeemed in glory singing: "Glory to death which hath washed us?"[1] The fact is that in the New Testament death has *no moral force whatsoever*. Christ abolished death.[2] It is henceforth nothing. It is merely a milestone of life. It will change the *body*, but there is no reason to believe it will in any degree change the character. It will enable us to *put on* incorruption but not to *put in* incorruption. There is positively not one intimation in the Scriptures that one will arise from the grave with any better character or disposition than that which he had when he lay down in the grave. If heaven never gets into you here there is no ground to hope you will get into it hereafter.[3]

---

[1] Rev. i. 5. "Unto *Him*, etc., be glory."

[2] "Our Saviour hath abolished death." 2 Tim. i. 10. 1 Cor. xv. 54: "Death is swallowed up in victory." 1 Cor. xv. 26: "As a last enemy is death done away." Meyer's translation. Beet gives: "As a last enemy death is brought to naught." The verb at any rate is present, not future. "Not the God of the dead, but the God of the living." Mark xii. 27.

[3] "Christianity does not convince us of immortality by any process of argument—it makes us believe in immortal life by quickening all the immortal powers of the soul. It makes us live in the immortal part, and not the mortal part of our being; in the spirit, not in the flesh. This is the real argument of eternal life,—that we are alive now. The more of present life we have the more shall we believe in the future."—James Freeman Clarke, "Common Sense in Religion," p. 197.

The word "saved" has also been corrupted from its true signification. We make much of this term in revival meetings and current evangelical preaching. Some have the right apprehension of it, but with most of us it is mixed with a false quantity. "Saved," in the Bible, means rescued from sin, and is never narrowly confined to mean made sure of escaping punishment. But how often do we hear prayers that God will "finally save us in heaven," "at last save us," "forgive us now and in death save us," and the like?[1] Whereas, if there is saving to be done it is now or never, and we should pray to be saved day by day.[2] What is to happen at death is not in this day our concern; God will take care of us then; but the only salvation that should be our care is a present salvation from baseness and unto Christliness. It is not for us to worry about where we are going when we die, nor to be a Christian primarily to secure ourselves from woe after death. The life in Christ is to be preached and exemplified by Christians, as so full, so joyous, so complete, that the world shall turn to it as a thing to be desired. When Christians are no happier nor holier than good average non-Christians, it is useless to try to cozen men into the church by promises of

---

[1] The Lord's Prayer, the divine model, has only one reference to any salvation, that is, "and deliver us from evil."

[2] "Behold, *now* is the day of salvation." 2 Cor. vi. 2.

THE KINGDOM OF HEAVEN

future bliss, or to scare them into the church by bogies of future scenes of torment. Christ indicated the program of His church's victory; "And I, if I be lifted up, will draw all men unto me."[1] The Gospel's triumph waits for saved men and women to win the world; saved not so much from perdition as saved from sensuality, selfishness, hardness, greed, envy, jealousy, and all the weak and beggarly elements of common life; saved unto purity, thoughtfulness, courtesy, kindness, long-suffering, love, joy, peace, hope; in short, saved to become heaven-holders, not mere heaven-seekers.

The fear of death is nothing more than a superstition,[2] and Christ and His apostles never stooped to use such, although it has always been the policy of the mistaken church to deal tenderly with a superstition when it seems advantageous. Bacon says: "Men fear death as children fear to go into the dark, and as that natural fear of children is increased with tales, so is the other." It seems so right to induce one to come to Christ by revealing to him the terrors of the penal-

---

[1] John xii. 32.

[2] "For God hath not given us the spirit of fear; but of power, and of love, and of a *sound mind*." 2 Tim. i. 7. Not only is fear taken away from believers, but the energizing "spirit of the Gospel" is not a "spirit of fear." "Christ came to deliver them who through fear of death were all their lifetime subject to bondage." Heb. ii. 15.

ties beyond death, that we would hear a great outcry against any one who would condemn this policy. And yet by such preaching we have let down the whole tone of the Gospel, we have descended to the level of the heathen priests and medicine-men, and we have forfeited the respect of the sound sense and true culture of the world. The New Testament employs this motive sparingly. When Christ preached to the common folk did He begin or end by threats of perdition? No: His first sermon was "Blessed, blessed, blessed," a picture of the higher, better life He was to make possible for men. The young Messiah came preaching: "Repent, for the kingdom of heaven is at hand," and not "Repent, or the demons will get you by and by." When He called His disciples He said: "Follow Me!" and He did not first reveal to them the awful consequences of their sin. Now read carefully over all the places where He speaks of retribution, such as the parables of Dives, the Ten Virgins, the Last Judgment, and the like, and you will find that almost all these were directed against the scribes and Pharisees. He did not preach to "sinners," so-called, by appealing to fear, but thus to the self-righteous. And it is a question whether the scenes of retributive justice He portrayed in these illustrative stories are didactic state-

THE KINGDOM OF HEAVEN

ments of what is to take place after death, so much as they are visions of the ruin and contumely that invariably come to Pharisaic obstinacy and hypocrisy, whether in *this world* or in the next. It is an arbitrary assumption to hold that all these passages refer to the final Day of Judgment. Christ certainly did reveal the misery of the wicked, but this was not the tone nor the motive element in His Gospel.

Then examine the preaching of the apostles. Did they get their great power of conviction by heralding damnation after death to all who refused to hear? Fortunately the book of Acts gives us many samples of early sermons. Peter preached on one occasion, and many were pricked to the heart and repented and were saved. What was it he said that caused this? It was not any threat he made, but it was that he held up before them the Lord Jesus, the Man who went about doing good, whom they with impious hands had slain. It was *that* that smote them.[1] And so always true *conviction of sin* comes by preaching *Christ*, while it is only a desire to escape penalty that comes by preaching the wrath to come. Do you ever find in Paul's letters, or John's, or James's, or Peter's, any appeals to men to prepare for death, to make haste lest death

[1] Acts ii. 36, 37.

overtake, to come now lest to-night death may intervene, or such expostulation as we hear these days, such as, for instance, contorts the meaning of the text, "Prepare to meet thy God," making it to mean prepare to meet Him after death instead of prepare to meet Him now?[1] Truly there is a fateful tone both in Jesus and the apostles, a clear revelation of the eternal joy of them that accept the great salvation, and of the eternal sorrow of them that neglect it; but there is no such priestly and superstitious exploitation of death, the "King of Terrors," the awful mystery, to hurry ignorant men into perfunctory profession of a life they in no measure appreciate nor wish for, as we find in the latter history of the church. Saving with the gospelers, was a saving from *sin*, not primarily a saving from shadowy, dreadful torment in a future life.

The essential element in salvation is deliverance, not security; for the latter is merely a consequence of the former. Men are under the power of beastly impulses and evil habits and thoughts. Christ comes as a deliverer to break the dominion of sin and set men free that they may lead true lives. No one is ever saved in the sense of being insured against

---

[1] Amos iv. 12. "Therefore thus will I do unto thee, O Israel; and because I will do this unto thee, prepare to meet thy God, O Israel."

THE KINGDOM OF HEAVEN

falling again into sin, and hence into condemnation. Paul certainly was a saved man, and he declared that he had to keep his body under lest he himself should become a castaway.[1] Even the angels were not secure in this sense, for we read that some of them fell.[2] The whole insurance idea is pernicious. We are indeed secure in the sense of knowing that so long as we are in the love of God no harm can befall us, but the idea that, because of anything that we do or that God has done for us, we henceforth are removed from any possibility of sinning, is a dangerous tradition, inconsistent with free moral agency and unwarranted by Holy Writ.[3] Neither in this world nor in the world to come is any such artificial security guaranteed us. While we are living in Him, while He leads us, we are certain of peace and all good things and are safe from harm; but that there is any insurance policy issued to a soul in whom God does not abide as a saving presence, this teaching has done much damage in the world.

Progress, not security, is the object of religion. The history of the church illustrates

---

[1] 1 Cor. ix. 27.   [2] Jude 6.
[3] Paul's confidence was in *God*, not in any impeccable *state;* "I am persuaded nothing shall separate us from the love of God." Rom. viii. 38, 39: and, "I know *whom* I have believed (not *what* I have believed) and I am persuaded that He is able to keep." 2 Tim. i. 12.

this. God has been always calling a chosen few. But He called them to develop; they constantly misunderstood Him; thinking they were called to security. They were elected to progress; they thought themselves called to a fixed state of divine favor. So He has always been at last rejecting those whom He called and raising up others. Thus He selected the Jewish nation to develop the idea of God among men. When they persistently construed their privilege to be merely a selfish heritage because they were better than Gentiles, He cast them off. He raised up, then, the church, that through it the influence of His Spirit might develop men. The church made the same mistake, thinking it was segregated to be secure, not to progress. It conceived itself to be a colonization society to transport a few souls from a hopelessly lost world into heaven. Therefore in these times we see God doing great works outside of the church, through Christian, yet non-denominational agencies, such as the thousands of charities and humane institutions. While churchly dominancy as such is on the wane, the ideas the church stands for never had so much vitality. Thus He constantly chooses and lays aside His agencies, as they obey or disobey Him. He is continually saying, "Go on! Come up higher!" while the church

THE KINGDOM OF HEAVEN

continually misunderstands Him to say, "Here you may rest."

What does the New Testament mean by heaven, seeing it does not mean a place, nor mean a condition that begins at death? Heaven, in the New Testament, is used in two senses: first, the sky, as "clouds in heaven," "a voice from heaven," "looking up into heaven"; and second, the spiritual kingdom which Christ came to set up among men, as "the kingdom of heaven is among you." So that we have two ideas in the New Testament word heaven: first, the boundless universe, or skyey host, which always, since man first looked upward, has been the symbol of majesty and glory, and has been the inspirer of lofty thoughts; this is the symbol; second, the spiritual reality itself, the actuality typified by the symbol, that is, the realm of high and divine living, into which the Son of God came to lift men.

It is this last meaning that is constantly in the mind of Christ. He distinctly said: "The Kingdom of God cometh not with observation—neither shall ye say, Lo here! or, Lo there! for, behold, the Kingdom of God is among you."[1] The Kingdom of God is not up there in the sky, nor over there in the sweet by and by, but it is down here in

[1] Luke xvii. 21.

our breasts, over here among the pots and kettles.

Paul says the same thing in another way: "The Kingdom of God is not meat and drink," that is, it is not any materiality of time or place, "but righteousness and peace and joy in the Holy Ghost."[1] The Master would never have said to His disciples, "Go preach, the Kingdom of God is at hand,"[2] if He meant the abode of the blessed. Most of the parables were spoken to show what "the kingdom of heaven is like": but He must have had in mind the spiritual domain among living men and could not have intended to speak of the home beyond the grave, when He said that it was like a mustard seed, or a sower, or tares and wheat, or a draw net, or an unmerciful servant, and the like.[3]

There is an upper thought and a lower thought about any truth. The lower is earthy, tangible, narrow; the upper is spiritual, invisible, large; the lower is temporal, passing into the higher; the upper is eternal and abides. Paul says: "We look not at the things which are seen, for they are temporal; but we look at the things which are not seen, for they are eternal."[4] Heaven can never be

---

[1] Rom. xiv. 17. This, however, was not Paul's point in this passage.

[2] Matt. x. 7. See also Matt. iii. 2; iv. 17; Mark i. 15; Luke x. 9; xi. 20; etc.

[3] See Matt. xiii., etc.   [4] 2 Cor. iv. 18.

THE KINGDOM OF HEAVEN

seen with the eye, for the things of God are "spiritually discerned."[1] Speaking of the bliss of the redeemed, Paul declares that "eye hath not seen, nor ear heard, neither hath it entered into the heart of man to conceive the things that God hath prepared for them that love Him"—a text that is usually applied to the glories of the next world, which shows how tenacious a misconception can be, for the apostle, in the very next words following, adds, "but God *hath revealed* them to us by His spirit."[2] It is this upper thought that is always in the mind of Jesus. To it should be referred those sayings of His which allude to the heavenly kingdom.

Let us take some of these passages and see how much more sane and reasonable the upper thought renders them. When we are told to "lay up for ourselves treasures in heaven,"[3] is it not better to interpret it that we are to invest in men, to seek to be rich in what we produce of good to our fellows, rather than to put by good deeds to stand to our credit in the next life? The real wealth of the world is in healthy bodies, sound minds, and true souls, and we are to increase the supply of such treasures as this for ourselves; one is rich in proportion as he has developed manhood in others and himself, for this store

[1] 2 Cor. ii. 14. [2] 1 Cor. ii. 9, 10. [3] Matt. vi. 19-21.

"neither moth nor rust doth corrupt, nor thieves break through and steal."

"For great is your reward in heaven"[1] signifies the gain we secure in our inward stock of that "righteousness, peace, and joy" of which Paul says heaven is composed; and not that after death we will be recompensed for all the earthly pleasures we have missed here.

"Seek first the kingdom of God and His righteousness";[2] is it not more rational to construe this as an admonition to seek first the higher life than to seek first security after death?

Speaking to the Pharisees who had accused Him of casting out devils by the aid of Beelzebub, Jesus replied: "But if I cast out devils by the Spirit of God, then is the kingdom of God come unto you."[3] Is it that the holy city had come unto them?

"It is harder for a camel to pass through the eye of a needle than for a rich man to enter the kingdom of God"[4]—not for him to squeeze past Peter at the gate, but harder for him, with the multiform temptations to a sensual life that come with wealth to appreciate, to desire or to be willing to receive a life like that of Christ.

"'The publicans and harlots go into the

[1] Matt. v. 12.
[2] Matt. vi. 33.
[3] Luke xi. 20.
[4] Mark x.25.

THE KINGDOM OF HEAVEN

kingdom of God before you (chief priests)";[1] that is, their simple, open natures more quickly grasp my meaning and follow me, than your minds, so full of self-conceit.

"The kingdom of heaven suffereth violence, and the violent take it by force";[2] not that men storm the walls of the New Jerusalem, but that determined, intense souls easily win the higher life.

"Blessed are the poor in spirit, for theirs is the kingdom of heaven";[3] not that they are to be given rule over the future country, but that theirs is the disposition which is best disposed to assimilate with the life revealed by Christ.

"The same shall be called least—greatest in the kingdom of heaven";[4] not that there are ranks and degrees in the world to come (which may or may not be true; this passage has nothing to do with it), but that men apprehend the life of Christ in a greater or a less degree.

"It is given unto you to know the mysteries of the kingdom of heaven, but unto them it is not given"[5]—given to His disciples, not to the Pharisees. This is not to say the disciples were to understand the mysteries of the life beyond, for they did not, or if they

---

[1] Matt. xxi. 31. [3] Matt. v. 3. [5] Matt. xiii. 11.
[2] Matt. xi. 12. [4] Matt. xi. 11; xviii. 4.

did they never told them; but that they alone, receiving Christ, were to comprehend the wondrous powers and joys of the higher living; this mystery they did declare.

"And I will give unto thee (Peter) the keys of the kingdom of heaven."[1] What a world of churchly nonsense would have been saved if men had but grasped the upper thought here! The kingdom was the Christ-life, the key was the spirit that made it plain, unlocked it. The "power of the keys" is not lodged in any pope or church, but in the man who knows and trusts in Jesus, and thus acquires "the mind of Christ."

"Ye Pharisees shut up the kingdom of heaven";[2] they did not bar the doors of the city of the blest; that they could not do; but they, by their perversion of true religion, prevented men from seeing and entering upon the life of real godliness.

These illustrations might be increased from the New Testament, but perhaps enough have been set forth to show how much more wholesome and Christ-like our perception of the mind of the Spirit in the Book will be if we give constant preference to the upper thought.

Some may say, "But do you not destroy by this argument the hope of heaven, a sweet, inspiring, and healthful incentive?" By no

[1] Matt. xvi. 19.   [2] Matt. xxiii. 13.

THE KINGDOM OF HEAVEN

means. This hope is reasonable and well founded. We do not attempt to destroy it, but to rest it upon a sure and Scriptural basis. The true theory of a life of bliss beyond the grave is that it is the necessary, natural continuance of the divine life begun here. The point is, that heaven is not a reward, a different life or place bestowed on us after death as pay or wages for what we do here; but that if one now enters upon the Christ-life, he has entered upon an eternal career, upon which death has no effect. "Nor life nor death nor things present nor things to come" shall separate him from the divine inward power which raises him up to be God's true child.

We conclude, then, that the object of God's personality as revealed in Jesus, is to transform this race into His own image. How He is to do this with those who live upon earth, He has shown. What He is to do with those souls He has taken away, through death, to other spheres is not our concern. "What is that to thee? Follow thou Me!"[1]

[1] John xxi. 22.

SUGGESTIONS

The causal force in Evolution among animals and plants is the same as the causal force of Development among spirits—it is God.

The doctrine of the Trinity is the conservator of the idea of God's personality.

Broadly speaking, environment does not make man, man makes environment; in this sense heaven is a happy place.

There is no moral efficacy in death.

The whole insurance idea of salvation is pernicious.

Conviction of sin is wrought by God's personal influence; only desire to escape penalty is wrought by fear.

The essential element in salvation is deliverance, not security.

The true ground of our belief in a future life is that it is a necessary continuation of the kind of life we have here; thus Christ said merely: "If it were not so I would have told you."

CHAPTER III

DYNAMICS

The Power of Religion Consists not in Rewards and Punishments but in God's Personal Influence

"Thou hast heard that it hath been said by them of old time—but I say unto you."—JESUS, Matt. v. 21, 22.

"The first thing a boy has to do, is to learn implicit obedience to rules. The first thing in importance for a man to learn is to sever himself from maxims, rules, laws. Why? That he may become antinomian or latitudinarian? No. He is severed from submission to the *maxim*, because he has got allegiance to the *principle*. In every law there is a spirit, in every maxim a principle; and the law and the maxim are laid down for the sake of conserving the spirit and the principle which they inshrine."—ROBERTSON, *The Lawful and Unlawful Use of Law*.

"Our very religion itself has no surer foundation than the contempt of death."—MONTAIGNE, *Essays*, Vol. I., 74.

"The greatest, however, of all the obstacles to the habit of following truth, is the tendency to look in the first instance to the *expedient*. And this is the sin which most easily besets those who are engaged in the instruction of others, inasmuch as the consciousness of falsehood even if it exist at the outset, will very soon wear away. He who does not begin by preaching what he thoroughly believes, will speedily end by believing what he preaches."—WHATELY, *Difficulties in the Writings of St. Paul*, p. 49.

CHAPTER III

We have seen that the object of God is to redeem men by bringing them into communion with Himself. We next pass to the agency or means by which this conversion is to be effected. That agency is simply and only His personal influence. As men come to know Him, they will be "changed into the same image as by the Spirit of the Lord." The true, proper, and dominant motive, therefore, in spreading Christ's kingdom consists in manifesting Him in our lives and bearing witness to Him, so that through us others may be brought into touch with Him. This is the Gospel motive. It has completely superseded the temporary motive of rewards and punishments. We may safely say that rewards and punishments have been abolished by the programme of Jesus; provided, we keep in mind that it is only *as motives* they have thus been superseded by a better motive.

For as facts, as natural results inherently consequent upon all our actions, they, of course, must ever remain. Throughout eternity it must ever be that to do wrong brings pain, and to do right joy. But it is one thing to recognize this as a beneficent law of nature, and quite another thing to make it the dynamics of the Christian propaganda.[1]

The only system of rewards and punishments explicitly laid down in the Scriptures is in the Old Testament; and they were all temporal, they were not said to take effect beyond the grave. If the people were obedient, they were to be prospered in basket and store, to be healthy and numerous, to be victorious in battle and to be abundant in goods. The whole scheme was an earthly one. The Old Testament does not lift the veil of death to reveal the future. It is, therefore, the rewards and punishments *of this earth only* that are used in the Old Testament as incentives. When the New Testament preachers appeared, they dropped these incentives for a better one. The glories of heaven and the miseries of hell are never exhibited by them to induce men to become Christians.

Let us see how Paul especially laid stress on this. He says over and over that to Christians the law has ceased as a spring of con-

---

[1] Archbishop Whately has so lucidly covered this ground that a considerable portion of his essay "On the Abolition of the Law" is reprinted in the appendix. It is from his "Essays on Some of the Difficulties in the Writings of St. Paul," and as this volume, as well as many of Whately's other works, is hard to procure in this country (I had to get my own volume from England) perhaps the reprint in the appendix may be of use. It will well repay careful study; and all of the writings of this remarkably clear author are commended to the student. See appendix.

DYNAMICS

duct. But it has ceased not because the new dispensation is *against* it, but beyond it; just as a father has a set of rules with penalties attached for his little children, which rules and penalties, when the youths grow to manhood, are unused, not because they are no more true nor obeyed, but because the boys, if they are to form manly characters, must not any longer lean upon them, but learn to act upon their own spirit and intelligence.

"Not one jot or tittle of the law shall pass," said Jesus; that is, there will never come a time when those commandments are not just, when keeping them does bring reward and breaking them calamity. But there did come a time when the knowledge of reward and punishment became utterly insufficient to secure obedience to law, and another motive was needed. So Paul says the commandment became weak and unprofitable, and was disannulled, because it "made nothing perfect" (did not work well); "but," he adds, "the bringing in of a better hope did, by the which we draw nigh unto God."[1] He calls the law, the Old Testament rules, faulty, and says that it "decayeth and waxeth old and ready to vanish away," so that now in the Gospel we have "a better covenant, which is established on better promises." Rewards and punish-

[1] Heb. vii. 16-9; vii. 7-13.

ments will do for slaves, but Christ came "to redeem them that were under the law that we might receive the adoption of sons; wherefore we are no more slaves but sons; and having received this glorious gospel, how turn ye again to the weak and beggarly rudiments?"[1] The moving spirit of law is fear, and Christ takes away this spirit, for "we have not received the spirit of bondage again unto fear, but we have received the spirit of adoption, whereby we cry, Abba, Father."[2] What part of the law, then, was disannulled, and what part remains forever? The answer is, that forever the law, as a statement of what constitutes sin, and as a declaration of the evil results of sin, must abide; but that the part which has been removed is the motive by which men are induced to keep the law. For the fault with the law lay entirely in its lack of power to secure its enforcement. The preaching of its penalties and prizes was therefore abandoned, and in its stead came the preaching of "Christ, the power of God." For "what the law could not do, in that it was weak," God did by sending Christ to operate upon men by His personality.[3]

Why, then were rewards and punishments ever exploited? They are good for children— that is, they are of value for those who are

---

[1] Gal. i. 9.   [2] Rom. viii. 15.   [3] Rom. viii. 4.

irresponsible.[1] So young children are not responsible, but as the responsibility of their acts rests upon the parent, it is necessary for him to give them temporary and artificial props to hold them up in right conduct until they are sufficiently developed to walk for themselves. If we are forever under rules we can never grow, but must always remain babes. We must remember that God's object with us is not primarily to make us do right; there is something more important than this: it is that we have right characters. If all He desired were our proper conduct, He might have made us beasts ruled by instinct, or machines run by iron and steam. But His purpose is that we grow in grace and become like Himself. It is essential to growth that a man should train and use his own conscience. He must learn for himself to judge between right and wrong. He must continually be made to feel that he is the arbiter of his own destiny. Thus the law is called "a schoolmaster to bring us to Christ," but, now that the world has seen Him, "we are no longer under a schoolmaster."[2]

The whole law scheme is gone. Our position is not any more that of a king's subjects or a master's pupils, but that of a Father's

---

[1] Law may be defined as the conscience of one imposed upon another.

[2] Gal. iii. 24-25.

sons. But there is a timid and childish element in us that dreads responsibility. The tendency to go back to a set of rules is as powerful and obstinate to-day among modern Christians as it was in Paul's day among the Judaizing Christians. We tremble to trust our own conscience. Therefore we call the Bible our "rule of faith," when Jesus' words are not rules at all, but principles. We would regulate our conduct by chapter and verse. We drift to literalism, seeking there a shelter from the burden of personal accountability. We dare not cut loose from the schoolmaster and entrust ourselves to the Christ-Spirit.[1] Thus, also, we ask the church to make rules for us, to tell us what is permitted and what is forbidden in regard to amusements, dress, food, and drink, and such things. All such regulations are inimical to the manhood of its membership. The object of a church should be to strengthen and develop its people, and not to dwarf them. The net tendency of all ecclesiastical interference with private judgment is therefore to make a type of Christians that is zealous but narrow, inclined to pride and censoriousness. Rules make Pharisees.[2] Principles make Christians.

---

[1] See particularly on this point in the article from Whately in appendix.

[2] "Beware of the leaven of the Pharisees, which is hypocrisy." Luke xii. 1. Hypocrisy, literally, stage-playing, *acting* a part instead of *being* a character.

DYNAMICS

It is intrinsically impossible to encourage and foster nobility by rewards and punishments. One never does a noble deed because he expects pay for it, nor because he is afraid of some pain if he refuses to do it; he acts nobly only when he cares nothing for the consequences, when the deed so appeals to his heroism that he will do it though he suffer even disgrace and death thereby. Jesus appeals to this soldier instinct in men. "Follow me," He says, "and get persecuted and crucified"; and the divine soul of man rises to the call and follows Him, exclaiming, "I count all things loss for the excellency of the knowledge of Christ Jesus, my Lord. I esteem them but dung, if I may win Christ."[1]

It is equally out of the question to produce any sort of greatness in men by rules and penalties. The clerk in the counting-room who acts only by rules never rises to be anything else than a machine; while the proprietor is developed and made masterful by continually being forced to do and dare upon his

[1] Phil. iii. 8. Bravery, not fear, is the fundamental virtue of character. The first step toward God is not fear, it is the exaltation of the soul above fear of any consequences. Courage is the universal virtue. No race of men has been found that does not reverence it. The early men, apotheosized by heathen nations, were stained with other crimes, but none were cowards. If Christianity were grounded in dread it could but be pusillanimous. Bacon indicates the trend of this thought, how Jesus raised religion above cupidity and timidity, when he says: "Prosperity is the blessing of the Old Testament, adversity the blessing of the New."

own judgment. Christ came to make us kings, not good slaves; to train us to compare and observe and act as our own conscience gives the verdict. He simply supplies that conscience with a principle, properly orientates it, and then sends us out to stand or fall, and by falling to learn to stand. "Henceforth," said He, "I call you not servants, but friends."[1]

The making of vows, or the taking upon ourselves pledges, to follow a certain line of religious conduct is thus also hurtful to the character. For a vow operates as a sort of rule, and worst of all, a rule of our own poor making. Our motive henceforth is not to be principle, but our own decree. Anything is damaging that separates us from reliance upon our own character. Having taken a pledge, if we then fall, as we are liable to do, the fall is complicated by our sense of self-contempt for a broken word, which frequently acts to hinder our reformation. A fall from a mere resolution, as such, may be made of use to us by teaching us humility and reliance upon God; but when the matter is mixed up with a broken pledge we are simply making provision for despair. Christ alone in this life is intended to be our strength, and we supplement this divinely ordained safeguard at our

[1] John xv. 15.

peril.[1] "Swear not at all; let your yea be yea, and your nay be nay."

In reading what has been said above, it must be borne in mind that I here speak of rules *as motives*, and refer to the tendency to lean back upon some list or catalogue or church or priest or other external authority in order to satisfy conscience. The source and spring of right action should always be the *character;* that is, we should take care that we do right because we *are* right men, take care that we have right natures, that have become so assimilated to the nature of the indwelling Christ that it is *natural* for us to do right. Until that point in our development is reached we are not truly Christians. To do right because we ought, and yet to feel that it goes against the grain, is commendable; but while this may please us by showing us that we can overcome self, it should at the same time warn us that our natures are not yet up to the divine mark of what they *may be;* and it should encourage us not to stop until Christ has transformed our *tendencies* and *desires*, which indeed is possible.

Now, to accomplish this desired end rules may be useful—that is, rules are good as

---

[1] Jesus exacted no pledge from His disciples, nor they from their converts. The only disciple who did make a solemn promise to Him broke the promise and denied Him. "Peter answered and said unto Him, Though all men shall be offended in Thee, yet will I never be offended." The sequel we know.

temporary aids to bring us to right character; in fact, they are very helpful and necessary as *schoolmasters* to discipline us; but their value is just in proportion as they enable us to become so strong that we less and less need them, learning by nature and habit to do the things we begin to do by resolution; in other words, rules and their attendant penalties are good just as they gradually disappear, having led us to Christ. The law is a measure, a yardstick divinely given, so that we may test ourselves and see whether we be in Christ, for nothing is so easy as self-deception. It is a steam-gauge, to indicate how much moral force is in us; and if we *think* we be Christians and yet fail to measure up to the law we know we are *mistaken;* we have "tried the spirit," as John advises us, and found it faulty. But the law is *only* a gauge; it is *not* force. Therefore, if we do thus and so, only *because* it is the law, we will not grow.

Rules, therefore, are good only as they are used with sincere prayer for such inward spirit as shall make us want to do what the rule says. The object of every rule is to bring us into the best condition for receiving the influence of God. Our religious feelings are to be permanent, and therefore must have permanent channels of habit in which to run, for our emotions are also largely creatures of custom. What is begun in the will must end in the desires. Religious routine, stated times of prayer, the giving of the tenth, the keeping of the Sabbath, and so on, are so to accustom us to righteous practice that God's influence in us will be helped, not hindered. Now, to do these and similar observances because we think there is merit in *them*, and because we expect credit for them, is to make them ruin the character. We will find them growing more and more irksome, and as they are the more bitter, we will attach still the more value to them because of their growing unpleasantness; and thus we will discover in ourselves that *character* and *practice* are *running away* from each other instead of *coalescing*. But if we deliberately put on the "form of godliness" by sheer will, not because that form has any merit or will gain any external reward, but because by the assistance of the "*form*" we mean to give free course to "the power of godliness" in us, then shall we see the form by degrees swallowed up in the power.

As to what rules we shall adopt in order to assist us in coming more fully under the influence of God, the above principles make the matter clear. We are to use rules carefully, because they may be as dangerous to our spiritual life as they may be useful. The only rules or statutes that are of absolute use to every one are those given in the Scriptures. No church nor council has any right to add to, any more than it has to subtract from, the divine law as a universal rule. Thou shalt not lie, steal, and so on, are useful to *every* man; every man *must* use these practices if he would abide in Christ. Besides these, however, there are, for individual cases, or for certain places or times, other rules that are valuable. But what *these* are must be left to the individual conscience. The church may *advise* or *recommend* certain lines of conduct, but has no right whatever to *command* in this respect. For the church stands as Christ's vicegerent. When it expels a member, that is equivalent, as far as lies in its power, to the cutting off of the soul from Christ. Such weighty responsibility it certainly has no right to assume except for a direct violation of God's revealed law. The apostle Paul himself would not speak authoritatively concerning those who ate meat that had been offered to idols, a practice in those days of an exceedingly questionable and dangerous kind; but he led the Corinthian church back to the broad principles of Christian brotherliness, argued with them, advised them, quoted his own example and opinion, and—left it to their own consciences. "Let not your good be evil spoken of," he says. "Put a stumbling block in the way of none, neither of the Jews, nor of the Greeks, nor of the Church of God." This broad *principle* he leaves for their *own* application. If we, these days, consider it unsafe to let the individual apply a principle for himself, how is it the apostle was not governed by this fear? And if he chose the danger of allowing the individual to abuse his liberty, rather than the danger of laying down a rule, which he was undoubtedly importuned to do, and which it certainly seemed could have been only beneficial, yet which he saw to be the entering wedge of a new legalism, we may certainly profit by his example.

The case stands much the same with rewards and penalties. Men already know that a life of holiness and sublimity will bring joy incomparable, that it is better to do right than wrong, and that sin is misery. The Gospel comes not to magnify this fear and hope by unfolding the scenes of a future life; but it comes to utilize this abiding sense of hope and fear by the "good news" that it can give men a new *power* whereby they may live high lives. The Gospel is not an *extension* of the law; it is the *energizing* of the law. Therefore, preaching the consequences of sin or of righteousness is not preaching the Gospel, but the law; it is simply using the same old motives of selfish gain or ease that already actuate men in their struggle for profit and place and the gratification of appetite. But the Gospel is preached when we go beyond the matter of any reward or punishment for our deeds, and preach the possibility of a totally different kind of life; not in appeal to consequences, but "in the demonstration of the Spirit and of power." It is not declaring what will happen to us, but it is declaring Christ. Hope and fear are merely human emotions; to expect to rise by these into the new life is to think we may lift ourselves by our boot straps. God's person is a new force, not of ourselves, coming in upon us from above; it is another and higher power than ourselves, and by it alone can we be raised into the kingdom of heaven. Hope and fear are also schoolmasters; therefore, to make us sensible of the *need* of another kind of power.

The influence of God imparted to us by the Christ-Spirit is the potency by which we are changed.

To put it in a nutshell, the law consists of two parts: the rule and the penalty. The rule is of value to *show* us whether or not we have the right power of life, and also, by practicing the rule, we put ourselves in a proper condition for developing this power. As the power increases, the rule falls away in importance. The penalty serves to show us the emptiness and sorrow of life without this inward power. It should work, not to make us accept the Gospel from fear of the penalty, but to accept the Gospel to escape the *fear*. Fear is not the motive, but the motive is a desire to escape from that low slavery of a life that is ruled by fear. Becoming a Christian is not "escaping the penalty," so much as it is coming out from "the spirit of bondage unto fear" into "the spirit of sonship, whereby we cry, Abba, Father."

Even if hell be a punishment, heaven beyond cannot be a reward. You cannot pay for good work; it has no wage; it is its own wage. Virtue is so infinitely imponderable with vice that it is called its own reward. Nowhere in the Bible is bliss beyond alluded to as the pay of Christians. "Great is your reward *in* heaven"; but there is a vast difference between reward in heaven and heaven as a reward. The parable of the laborers in the vineyard was given purposely to show the fallacy of this wage-theory;[1] for the last received a penny even as the first; there is no distribution of prizes to doers of good deeds; "Man, who made Me a judge or a divider over you?" But while "the wages of sin is death, the *gift* of God is eternal life."[2]

[1] Read connectively Matt. xix. 27 to xx. 16.
[2] Rom. vi. 23. "The wages of unrighteousness." 2 Pet. ii. 15.

THE RELIGION OF TO-MORROW

When heaven and hell are made to be the Christian's reward and punishment, then we have left utterly the realm of the Gospel and descended again into the domain of the Mosaic law. But, it may be answered, we do not make these future states to be the reward and punishment of our *deeds* here, our moralities, but of our rejection or acceptance of *Christ*. If anything, this is worse. Making them the prizes of conduct might increase morality, which is a good thing; but making them the prizes of "accepting Christ" directly discourages morality and instigates hypocrisy. For if heavenly bliss in the next world is to be gained "not by works" but by something else, what is that something else? It is replied that it is conversion and a life of faith. Now, while this is true, in a way, yet the fact that we are to seek conversion and belief *for pay* inevitably debauches the conception of what conversion and belief are. The powerful commercial spirit is aroused to get this pay for the least work; to secure the reward for the least possible outlay of effort. Thus we set the theologians to work at *defining* the *essentials;* we want to know what is *absolutely essential* to salvation (*i. e.*, from future torment). Now, define the essentials as we may, we can never define them into life.[1] And

---
[1] "If there had been a law given which could have given life, verily righteousness should have been by the law." Gal. iii. 21

what is the actual, practical result? It is that very many professed Christians have substituted an *act* or *certain condition of feeling*, called conversion, and an intellectual acceptance of a certain credal formula, called belief, for the morality of the Mosaic law, and expect heaven for *this*, exactly as the Jews of old expected temporal prosperity for *that*. "Except ye be converted"—and did not we on a certain day of a certain year experience a change of heart at a revival? "He that believeth shall be saved"—and do we not nod the head and say Amen to all in the Bible and the pulpit? And all the while, thousands of us know nothing of the Christ-life as an elevating, transforming, eternal power within! Alas! we are still under the law, only we have put an artificial, theologic "essential act" in the place of Mosaic righteousness. Because that act has something about Christ in it, we think it is Christian. "This persuasion cometh not of Him that calleth you,"[1] it comes from the flesh. "Christ is become of no effect unto you, whosoever are saved by the law (by the legal effect of an *essential act*); yet are fallen from grace"[2]—fallen down from the high life, the life more abundant, into the pit of barter and sale, trading a pitiful

[1] Gal. v. 8.   [2] Gal. v. 4.

"gospel deed" for a "life to come."[1] If such there be who read this, "I bow my knees unto the Father that He would grant you His Spirit in the inner man; that Christ may dwell in your hearts by faith; that ye may be able to comprehend what is the breadth and length and depth and height, and to know the love of Christ, which passeth knowledge; that ye may be filled with all the fullness of God!"[2]

The keen world has not failed to detect a strain of baseness in such religion as most of us display and many ministers preach.

> " The fear o' hell's a hangman's whip
> To hold the wretch in order,"

sang Burns. Side by side with our church life, but outside of it, viewing it with a more or less good-natured contempt, there has grown up a class of people who are clean and honorable, with a high tone and chivalrous sentiment, a class that is composed of those whom Charles Kingsley would call "natural kingdom-of-heavenites." It is this class which has quietly assumed the moral leadership of civilization. It is their sentiments that are held up for admiration in current fiction. Mankind has turned to this refined and delicate hea-

---

[1] "For in Christianity there is no other essential than faith which worketh by love." Gal. v. 6, paraphrased.
[2] Eph. iii. 14-21.

DYNAMICS

thenism to pay there its choicest tribute of imitation. In fine, it is the Gentleman, not the Christian, the world respects most. Why is this subtle discounting of Christianity, why indeed, unless it be that the preaching of rewards and punishments has drawn into the profession of this faith a great swarm of people who are aliens from its sublime spirit? The mediæval church thought it was a fine thing to see numbers thronging into her courts as a result of her proclamation of heaven gained and hell avoided by "belief"; the leaders of the Reformation shook themselves partly free from the superstitious practices of the old church, but not quite free; they still retained many heathen doctrines and forms, and among them this legalizing preachment of rewards and punishments as motives, although for penance and absolution they substituted "justification by faith."

This brings us directly to the question: the preaching of heaven and hell as the motive force in religion, whence originated it? It did not arise among the apostles and Christ, as we have seen. When the disciples, stubbornly clinging to the "reward" idea, asked what they, who had left all and followed Him, should have, He did not dilate upon their bliss in the next world, but simply said, "And in the world to come eternal life,"[1] and immediately told the parable of the laborers in the vineyard, to which I have previously alluded. When Paul spake before Festus and Agrippa as when he preached at Athens, it was the resurrection that smote in upon his auditors. Follow his whole career through the Acts and Epistles,[2] and you will see his constant theme to be a living, risen, saving Christ, who puts in men *a new Spirit*, exalts them into a higher, diviner life. But when in after centuries the power of the Roman bishop began to predominate, and when the lust of members and temporal display and political power crept into the church, more and more concessions were made to heathenism, in order to induce the pagans to submit the more readily to the church.[3] Now almost every heathen religion luxuriates in descriptions of the future world. While the Bible speaks sparingly and only in

[1] Mark x. 30 and Luke xviii. 30 use this language, but Matt. xix. 29 has, "and shall inherit eternal life."

[2] Acts xxvi. 23-24. Those who wish to investigate this further are referred to Acts v. 42; viii. 35; x. 36; xiii. 38; xvii. 3; xviii. 5; also Acts ii. 32; iv. 1; iv. 10-33; v. 32; xiii. 33; xvii. 3, 18, 33; xxiii. 6; xxiv. 15-21; xxv. 19; xxvi. 6, 8, 23, etc., the former showing how the apostles preached *Christ*, the latter how they preached *Christ risen*. There were no exploitations of heaven and hell. Further instances will be given in chapter five.

[3] "The practical purpose for which the church had been established or for which Christianity existed, was not, to the Latin mind, primarily an ethical one; even * * * * the morality which the gospel enjoined was not an end in itself, but a means to a remoter end—the salvation of the soul from the consequences of sin in the future world. The doctrine of endless punishment for all who rejected the claims of Christ must have been from an early period the underlying belief which gave the strongest sanction to the church's authority." A. V. G. Allen, "Continuity of Christian Thought," p. 121.

hints and figures of the details of the life to come, the Koran has hells blazing with every refinement of cruelty, and heavens crowded with sensuous delights. Bear in mind that the rewards and punishments of the Old Testament were earthly, and that in the New Testament the future state is not exploited as a motive, and you will see that the custom of making hell's horrors and heaven's glory Gospel motives originated not in the Bible at all, but was borrowed from *paganism* by the monks at the darkest period of the church's history.[1]

And why was it borrowed? Simply because the church leaders must have *some* motive, and not having the real, Gospel motive—to wit, "the *power* of an endless life,"[2] they took the heathen motive, the *imaginations* of an endless life. The preaching of death's terrors and allurements will always be morbid, and makes a gloomy, unwholesome religious life. "*Memento mori*" is not a Christian motto. We are to remember life, not death.[3] We are not put here merely to prepare for eternity, but to begin a high life that stretches out into eternity. This life is not so much a

---

[1] "Christianity (under the papacy) approximated in its inmost principle to Islam." Ibid, p. 171.

[2] See Heb. vii. 16.

[3] "The more of present life we have, the more shall we believe in the future." James Freeman Clarke, "Common Sense in Religion," p. 197.

state of probation as of opportunity. The triumph of the Gospel waits for men who shall show forth its sublime possibilities. The world waits for the church to show it that glorious "life more abundant,"[1] full of hope, joy, peace, and "all the fullness of God." Civilization is hungry, lean, and empty; despair is in its literature, ennui is in its social life, fevered restlessness in its business. It craves "life, more life." It uses increasingly more alcoholic stimulants to whip the tired pulses into a semblance of enthusiasm. It refuses longer to be coaxed or scared by future visions; it would rather go to hell hilariously than go to heaven by humdrum and narrowness and drudgery. The present age resembles that Augustan period of which Matthew Arnold wrote:

> "On that hard pagan world disgust
> And secret loathing fell;
> Deep weariness and sated lust
> Made human life a hell."

This life is so paltry, so hemmed and balked by limitations, that it is not worth living, if we accept the pictures given by Eliot or Zola, Hall Caine or Nordau.[2] The time is ripe for

---

[1] "I am come that they might have life, and that they might have it more abundantly." John x. 10.

[2] "In novels—like those of Zola and Maupassant and the later works of Thomas Hardy, skepticism speaks with a harsh and menacing accent of the emptiness of all life and the futility of all endeavor. * * * Far apart as *Madame Bovary* and *Cosmopolis,*

DYNAMICS

a new manifestation of Christly life such as amazed and thrilled the apostolic age. Not hotter hells, nor more scintillating heavens, but lives, lives, lives, carrying about "an exceeding weight of glory," lives transfigured, inspired, filled with enthusiasm, displaying that "blessedness" of which the young Messiah spake in His first message. Such life is the real potency of our faith. Lacking this, it is useless for a feeble and doting church to turn to ghostly policemen to enforce what she cannot win.

The objection that may arise to this view is that it does not sufficiently emphasize the sinfulness of sin. It seems to be taken for granted by many persons that unless we positively assert endless punishment for sin and endless certain bliss for righteousness, we belittle the difference between the two. But such objectors forget that it is not the *penalty* that is to convince the world of sin, but it is the *Holy Spirit*, and He is to do it by showing Christ to the world.[1] These objectors are

---

Problema ische Naturen and *Middlemarch* and *Robert Elsmere*, may be in many of their features, do they not wear the same expression—the cureless melancholy of disillusion?" Henry Van Dyke, "The Gospel for an Age of Doubt," p. 17.

"One epoch of history is unmistakably in its decline, and another is announcing its approach. There is a sound of rending in every tradition, and it is as though the morrow would not link itself with to-day. Things as they are totter and plunge, and they are suffered to reel and fall, because man is weary, and there is no faith that it is worth an effort to uphold them." Max Nordau, "Degeneration," p. 5.

[1] John xvi. 8. Horace Bushnell ("Christ and His Salvation," p. 116) has a masterly sermon on "Conviction of Sin by the Cross."

quick to cry danger whenever such theory is advanced; they fear we are departing from the faith and removing the ancient landmarks. Upon this point I cannot do better than quote a clear putting of the case by Professor A. V. G. Allen: "It is suggestive to note how it [this objection] turns up in history when any teaching arises which contradicts the traditional methods of dealing with the problem of human evil. To the enemies of Christ it appeared as though the Saviour Himself were relaxing the bonds of moral order when He sat down to eat with publicans and sinners, or when he dismissed the woman who had sinned with no reproof, but with the gentle injunction, 'Go, and sin no more.' It seemed to the hostile Judaism tracking the footsteps of St. Paul as if his doctrine of justification by faith were not only deficient in its estimate of sin, but as if it put a premium upon sin—'Shall we continue in sin that grace may abound?' It seemed to the heathen mind, judging from Celsus' attack upon Christianity,

<small>Perhaps the gist of it may be embodied in this quotation: "In the days of the *law*, men had their visitations of remorse, respecting this or that wrong act; but I do not recollect, even under the prophets, those great preachers of the law, and sharpest and most terrible sifters of transgression, a single instance, where a soul is so broken or distressed by the conviction of its own bad state under sin, as to ask what it must do to be saved—the very thing which many thousands did, on the day of Pentecost, and in the weeks that followed, and have been doing even until now. So different a matter is it to have rules in a *book*, or rules in a conscience, from having them embodied into *power*, through a person, or personal character."</small>

that the doctrine of forgiveness was shallow and immoral, that in order to overcome evil it must be held that forgiveness was impossible, and that every sin must reap its penalty according to irrevocable law. It seemed to the excited mind of Latin Christendom as if the methods of Luther and Calvin, in dealing with sin, were of a nature to undo the sanctions of morality and to promote unbridled libertinism."[1]

We conclude, then, that the sole legitimate Gospel motive is the personality of God. We are to come under this influence ourselves, and through us others are to be likewise brought under the same developing, redeeming power.

[1] "Continuity of Christian Thought," p. 15.

SUGGESTIONS

The Gospel changed the system of rewards and punishments from statutory to natural law.

The chief difference between Judaism and Christianity is the motive.

God's object for us is higher than to make us do right; it is to make us be right.

There is no list of rules so onerous that men will not prefer it to personal responsibility.

The design of a church should be to develop, not to rule.

The final product of even the most perfect law was the Pharisee.

A pledge or vow is either to do a right or a wrong thing; none should vow to do wrong; whoever will not do right without a vow is not likely to keep a vow; therefore swear not at all, but let your yea be yea, and your nay be nay.

Not everything is Christian that alludes to Christ.

In proportion as we lose "the *power* of an endless life," we lean upon the *imaginations* of an endless life.

The Christianity of the past has successfully taught the world its lesson of the emptiness of this life; it is for the Christianity of the future to teach the world the fullness of this life.

Truth leads to expediency, but expediency never leads to truth.

True faith is faith in the truth.

CHAPTER IV
ETERNAL LIFE
Life Influenced by God's Personality Becomes Eternal in Quality

"This is Life Eternal, that they might know Thee, the only true God, and Jesus Christ, whom Thou hast sent."—JESUS, John xvii. 3.

"'La vie est vaine:
  Un peu d'amour
  Un peu de haine—
  Et puis—bon jour!

'La vie est brève:
  Un peu d'espoir,
  Un peu de rêve. . . .
  Et puis—bon soir!'

"The above is a terse and true criticism of this life without hope of a future one. Is it satisfactory?"—GEORGE JOHN ROMANES, *Thoughts on Religion*, p. 163.

"Each natural agent works but to this end—
To render that it works on like itself."
GEORGE CHAPMAN, *Bussy D'Ambois*, Act III., Sc. 1.

"To love her was a liberal education."
RICHARD STEELE, *Tatler*, No. 49.

"For God, who commanded the light to shine out of darkness, is He who hath shined in our hearts, to give the light of the knowledge of the glory of God in the face of Jesus Christ."—PAUL, 2 Cor. iv. 6.

CHAPTER IV

It would not be proper to pursue the trend of thought taken in this essay without endeavoring to comprehend clearly what eternal life is. It will not suffice merely to say that it begins this side of the grave. But we ask, What is it? how can we secure it? how may it be known? why is it called eternal life? It is, of course, impossible to define, or Christ Himself would have defined it. But it may be helpful to us to see *why* it cannot be defined, and how, although not *definable*, it is perfectly *comprehensible*.

It is impossible to define eternal life, simply because it is a condition of our personality, wrought in us by the personality of God. To define it would be therefore to define man and God, the two ever-impenetrable mysteries. A man begins eternal life when he begins to live the life which Christ led. Eternal life is the Christ-life. We obtain this by being brought into the personal influence of Jesus. It is illustrated by the familiar examples of personal influence known to us all. One cannot live with a strong, rich nature, such as that of Arnold of Rugby, or Mark Hopkins, or some good teacher or minister whom each of us recalls from his own past, without insensibly becoming like him, partaking of his views of things, entertaining his sentiments, repeating as though original his little ways and sayings—that is to say, he "follows him."

This throws some light upon what Jesus meant when He called men, saying, "Follow Me."[1] Now, this influence, better than anything else, explains the process of salvation. Of course, the effect of Christ's companionship upon us is as much greater than the effect of men's example and association as He is greater than they; but in kind it is identical. The reader will find this idea diffused through the whole New Testament. It is Christ's personality that saves, not anything apart from Himself, which He does for us, and because of which God imputes salvation to us. The whole Gospel is the gospel of a person, not of a plan. In searching the Scriptures relative to this point, let us see, first, what was said about Him; second, what He did; and third, what He said of Himself.

---

[1] Matt. iv. 19; viii. 22; ix. 9; xvi. 24: "If any man *serve* Me, let him *follow* Me." John xii. 26. "Serve," literally, to wait upon at table, hence to be of use to; "follow," to keep in company with, go about with; hence, "If any man would be of *service* to Me and help Me work, he can do it only by preparing himself for this by My *companionship*." Follow means more than imitate, the root idea in it is association and companionship more than copying an example.

ETERNAL LIFE

And first, what was said about Him and His work by the apostles? In the introduction to his gospel John says: "In Him was life, and the life was the light of men";[1] thus, under the similitude of light, describing the mode by which He was to save men, His character shining upon their characters. John the Baptist said of Him: "Of His fullness have we all received, and grace for grace";[2] we are saved by partaking of His nature. The angel said to Joseph concerning the child to be born of Mary: "And thou shalt call His name Jesus, for He shall save His people from their sins";[3] He Himself shall save them, not that they were to be saved on account of Him. To separate God from Christ in the atonement is vicious to correct thought; whatever our creed may be we must not make salvation an act of God with which Jesus had nothing to do but to supply a sin-offering; for "God was in Christ, reconciling the world unto Himself."[4] In saving

---

[1] John i. 4. Christ is called the Light also in John i. 9. ("Light that lighteth every man.") John viii. 12; ix. 5; xii. 46. ("I am the Light of the world") John iii. 19. ("This is, etc., that Light is come into the world and men loved darkness rather," etc.) So He was to be "a Light to lighten the Gentiles," Luke ii. 32. Remarkably in point is 2 Cor. iv. 6: "For God, who commanded the light to shine out of darkness, is He who *hath shined in our hearts*, to give the light of the knowledge of the glory of God *in the face* of Jesus Christ."

[2] John i. 16. Christ's work in us is pictured as a full vessel filling empty vessels, also in Eph. i. 23 ("the fullness of Him that filleth all"); iii. 19 ("filled with all the fullness of God"), etc.

[3] Matt. i. 21.   [4] 2 Cor. v. 19.

men "I and My Father are one";[1] one of the Gods did not die to appease the other God. The atonement was part of the mysterious way which God took to bring Himself to bear upon the characters of men.[2]

The phraseology of Paul is significant in this respect. No man made so much of the personality of Jesus as he. Using necessarily the Jewish phraseology of the sacrificial ceremony, he yet suffused it with the divine Person. Paul's passionate appeals to the world were not to win it to a wondrous scheme, a marvelous contrivance or syllogism, by which men could escape hell and get to heaven; but ever since he saw the face of that Man on the road to Damascus, who said to him, "I am Jesus whom thou persecutest," his one burning refrain was Christ. He did not preach about Him, but he preached Him. He did not preach the atonement made by Christ; he preached "Christ crucified."[3] The burden of his life was not any plan of salvation, but he declared, "I am determined not to know anything among you, save Jesus Christ."[4] So absorbed was he in his Master that he said, "For to me to live is Christ."[5] He intro-

---

[1] John x. 30.

[2] See explanation at more length in the chapter on the "Light of the Cross."

[3] 1 Cor. i. 23.   [4] 1 Cor. ii. 2.   [5] Phil. i. 21.

ETERNAL LIFE

duced the novel phrase, "in Christ,"[1] speaking of the saints as those in Christ; also its complement, "Christ in you";[2] nothing but the interplay of personalities explains such language. His assurance was not because he had accepted a divine plan, but "there is therefore now no condemnation to them that are *in Christ.*"[3] All else in life seemed of little worth, for he esteemed the world but dung that he might win Christ.[4] All the learning he had gathered at the feet of Gamaliel he threw contemptuously from him "that he might know Him and the power of His resurrection."[5] His theory of how the atonement takes away sin is not that it is by any substitutional process alone, not by any syllogistic reasoning, but because Christ has passed on through death, and now lives to raise all men up into a higher life. As he says to the Corinthians, "He died for all, that they which live should not henceforth live unto themselves, but unto Him that died for them, and rose again. Therefore, if any man be in Christ, he is a new creature; old things are passed away; behold, all things are become new."[6]

Notice, in the second place, what Jesus did,

---

[1] Rom. xvi. 2-7, 9, etc.
[2] Rom. viii. 10, etc.
[3] Rom. viii. 1.
[4] Phil. iii. 8.
[5] Phil. iii. 10.
[6] 2 Cor. v. 15-20.

and how He helped men while He was in the body. And observe particularly that it was not by imparting information to them, so much as it was by bringing them into contact with Himself. When He healed the sick it made no difference about their thought or feelings; all they needed was "faith," or that attitude of mind which made them willing to allow Him to work in them. *Their* state or opinions had nothing to do with His healing; *He* was all. It was not any process that cured, it was Himself. When a peculiarly stubborn case was told Him, He only said, "Bring him to *Me*."[1] It was His touch, His hand, His word that saved their miserable bodies. That is to say, His works of power were all works showing the efficacy of His *person*, and not of any art or knowledge He possessed. This is most clearly seen in the case of the woman who touched the hem of His garment.[2] To this day that instance remains as a type of His method. His triumph is to be only the spreading influence of His personality.

Note, again, what He said of Himself. He did not speak of Himself as forming a chief link in a plan to purge the world of sin. He did not regard Himself as one of the wheels in the divine mechanical scheme of redemp-

---

[1] Matt. xvii. 17. [2] Matt. ix. 20.

tion. The saving of the world was to be a personal matter performed directly by Himself. He, dying, was to save, not His death was to save.[1] "And I, if I be lifted up"—not My teachings nor My ideas and precepts—"shall draw all men unto Me"—not unto righteousness nor unto heaven, but "unto Me."[2] "I am the Way, the Truth, and the Life," He said. "There is no Way to be saved; I am the Way. I do not come to impart to men a system containing the truth about God; I am the Truth. I do not die to enable you to get life eternal after death; I am the Life. The true Way, the true knowledge of Truth, the joy of a full Life, are only in proportion as you come under My influence. Do you want to eat the fruit of the tree of life and live always? I am the bread of life; eat Me and you shall never die."[3] "I am the vine, ye are the branches." "Abide in Me, and I in you."[4] He did not tell them to do thus and so, and they should do great good; all their doing was to be useless except as under His influence; "without Me ye can do nothing."[5] A philosopher would have said, "Follow Truth"; but He said, "Follow Me; I am the Truth." When

---

[1] John xii. 32.   [2] John xiv. 6.
[3] John vi. 31-59 inclusive, discourse on bread of life.
[4] John xv. 1-8.   [5] John xv. 5.

the Holy Ghost shall come to you, "He shall testify of Me."[1] "The operation of the Holy Spirit will be but a continuation of the operation of My personal influence; it will be Myself, in a form suited for universal working among all men."[2] "It is expedient for you that I go away, for if I go away, *I will come again*, and receive you unto Myself";[3] but I will come as the Comforter, not the bodily, local Christ, but the spiritual, world-wide Christ, the immanent God, standing and knocking at the door of all men's hearts.

Such is the tone of Jesus' talk of Himself. That this should harmonize with any theory of Him that considered Him as merely an object to appease divine wrath, has only to be stated for us to see how absurd it is. His theory can only be that eternal life is the kind of life God leads; men can get this life because they are God's sons, they are akin to Him, their natures bear such resemblance to His that they can rise to share His concerns; they can get this life only by knowing God and coming under His influence; God was manifested in Jesus Christ purposely to enable men to thus come to know Him and to be exalted by Him.

[1] John xv. 26.
[2] "He shall not speak of Himself: He shall glorify Me: for He shall receive of Mine and show it unto you." John xvi. 13, 15.
[3] John xvi. 7 and xiv. 3.

ETERNAL LIFE

It may be answered that this gives no satisfactory theory of the atonement; it does not show *how* God pardons men for Christ's sake. It is just because this view of the case implies *no* theory of an automatic, self-operative atonement that it seems likely to be the *true* one. Perhaps nothing has done so much harm to the religion of Jesus as the attempts to systematize it. It is essentially non-systematic. It is the religion of a Person, and personality, while perfectly comprehensible, is evasive and undefinable. When you reduce Christianity to a series of propositions, it is no more Christianity, but something which differs from it as a marble bust, no matter how perfect, from the breathing form. When you pluck apart the lily you have gained some information, but the lily is gone; to obtain your knowledge you took its life; and God made the lily to lade the breeze with perfume and to bear seed, and not to gratify your speculative craving for knowledge. So it is with the life and work of Jesus. The moment you separate His life from His death, and assign to this one function and to that another, you have ruined the whole effect of Him. His death has absolutely no value to humanity apart from Himself. The saving power of Jesus abode not in anything He did or suffered, but in Him. All His words and deeds,

His death and His example, are dry, useless things apart from the real, living, present Christ-person Himself. The theology of Christianity forever abides in Christ's own person, and cannot be got out of Him. There are no "truths" of this religion; there is but the truth, that is Christ.

The doctrines of Christianity cannot be tabulated and arranged in books, because when you separate any doctrine from His personality it is not true any more; you have taken the image of the doctrine away, but you have left the truth with Him. That explains why so many doctrines seem sometimes true and sometimes false; they are only true when taken in connection with His personality. For instance, what is conviction of sin? It is seeing Christ. Men are not, as a rule, convicted of sin by looking at themselves, nor by being told how evil they are, nor by revealing the punishment for sin; but only by being brought into contact with His Spirit. So repentance is false when merely a reformation or a remorse for evil done; true repentance is caused by coming under the influence of Jesus. That was the genuine sorrow for sin which brought forth fruit unto life, when Peter caught that one look of His Master's face and straightway went out and wept bitterly; Judas's repentance was the wrong kind,

ETERNAL LIFE

the sorrow unto death; the one was true because it was repentance with Him, the other false because it was repentance without Him. Likewise conversion, if a change we note in ourselves alone, may be a passing emotion; but if it is the change brought about by beginning to know Him, it is true; false apart from Him, true with Him. Justification, as a legal condition before God because you have believed or done something or other, is false; it is true only as a conviction that now He abides in you, and he in whom He dwells must surely be accepted of God. Adoption is becoming His brother, His child. Sanctification is experiencing His work in your character. Regeneration is the new life and thoughts and hopes and longings He always brings with Him into the heart. Cleansing is the fleeing of all inward impurity from before His face. Without Him we can do nothing. So His Gospel is to be preached, not taught; we *preach* a *person*, and *teach* a *doctrine*. It is to be heralded, not explained. "Ye shall be witnesses of Me,"[1] He said, not that we should be propagandists of His doctrine.

Why, therefore, do we spend so much time in urging men to obtain all these various blessings? Why pray for a blessing? Were the apostles in the habit of doing so? Can

[1] Acts i. 8. "They overcame by the word of their testimony." Rev. xii. 11.

you point to one instance in the New Testament where the apostles, or Jesus Himself, led souls through all this programme of successive phases we have these days marked out—conviction, repentance, conversion, justification, etc.? No, you answer; but we have selected the scattered instances and tabulated and arranged them. But if they were to be so systematized, why did not the inspired writers do it? Simply because as systematized they are not any more true; we have turned from Christ to a system. Pray not for a blessing; pray for the Blesser. You do not want conversion; you need the Converter. Do not seek sanctification; seek the Sanctifier. There is but one true Gospel doctrine to preach to lost men, and that is "Come to Jesus." As I heard David, the Tamil evangelist, say: "Why do you search for gold nuggets, when you may have the gold mine? Why do you want bank checks, when you may own the bank?" Away with this petty logic-mongering, this mapping out of the soul! Many have been in despair because they could not recognize the successive states in themselves. They have been told to repent; they try to repent; then they examine themselves carefully to see if they have genuine repentance. When they think they have, then they are next told to have faith; this they also try, again scrutinizing themselves to see if the marks of faith are in them, being assured that unless they find faith in themselves they cannot be saved. And so on, through the whole "evangelical" process, they go, endeavoring to attain each state successively, looking carefully within to see if they have succeeded.

Many, in spite of the mistaken system, do obtain Christ, but many others obtain a mere mental satisfaction with themselves, a conviction that they are secure of being "at last saved in heaven," because they have done what they were bidden; but many others, alas! feel that they have been juggling with their emotions, and being unwilling to rest their hope upon syllogisms they turn away in despondency. And how very many professed Christians to-day have no real confidence and cloudless assurance toward God!

To avoid all this we must be determined to "know nothing save Jesus Christ." Repentance (turning about) is seeking to find Him. Conviction is wrought by getting a first touch of His influence; as Peter, when the divinity of his Master burst on him, cried out, "Depart from me, for I am an evil man, O Lord!"[1] Conversion: "If any man be *in Christ*, he is a new creature."[2] Justification: "There is

[1] Luke v. 8.
[2] 2 Cor. v. 17.

therefore now no condemnation to them which are *in Christ Jesus*."[1] Adoption: "Joint heirs *with Jesus Christ*."[2] Regeneration: "Quickened together *with Him*."[3] Forgiveness, pardon: "Blotting out the handwriting of ordinances that was against us, and took it out of the way, *nailing it to His cross*."[4] Consecration: "Your life is *hid with Christ* in God."[5] Peace: "For *He* is our peace."[6] Life: "*Christ, Who* is our life."[7] Sanctification: "Ye are *in Christ*, who of God *is made* unto us sanctification."[8] Love: "*Herein* is love; not that we loved God, but that *He* loved *us*."[9] Death: "Whosoever believeth *in Me* shall never die."[10] Resurrection: "*I am* the resurrection."[11] Judgment: "He that believeth on Him that sent *Me* shall not come into condemnation."[12] (This is the same word elsewhere used for judgment.)[13] The hereafter: "That *where I am* there ye may be also."[14] Waste no thought nor anxiety, therefore, concerning these different matters. Find Christ and you have found all. "He is

[1] Rom. viii. 1.
[2] Rom. viii. 17.
[3] Col. ii. 13; Eph. ii. 5.
[4] Col. ii. 14.
[5] Col. iii. 3.
[6] Eph. ii. 14.
[7] Col. iii. 4.
[8] 1 Cor. i. 30.
[9] 1 John iv. 10.
[10] John xi. 26.
[11] John xi. 25.
[12] John v. 24.
[13] As, "Reserve the unjust unto the day of judgment," 2 Pet. ii. 9: "Once to die, but after this the judgment," Heb. ix. 27. So that, whatever the "judgment" may be, those who are in Christ shall not come into it.
[14] John xiv. 3.

ETERNAL LIFE

all, and in all."[1] These blessings are but phases of His personal work in us.

Above all things look no more into your hearts. Cease morbid self-scrutiny. "Look up, not down; look out, not in." Look to Him, not to self. In me is food for despair only; in Him is hope. Whether I have passed through this list of orthodox prescribed states I never have been able to tell; neither does it concern me; but rather let me "win Christ, and be found in Him, not having mine own righteousness, but that which is through the faith of Christ, that I may know Him and the power of His resurrection!"[2] Self-scrutiny without Christ is ruinous; that way madness lies, and blackness and sin and suicide.

We see, then, that the sum of Christianity is the personal influence of Christ; the sum of religion is the personal influence of Deity. And personal influence was the only means Jesus used to make disciples.

If it be said that it is the Holy Ghost that is to be the agent of the Gospel's work among men, the answer is that the Holy Ghost is but the one God, the same who is Christ; the Holy Ghost is the universal God, and His influence is yet the personal influence of Christ, who was "the fullness of the Godhead bodily."[3] This Holy Spirit works only

[1] Col. iii. 11.   [2] Phil. iii. 9, 10.   [3] Col. ii. 9.

through men, not coming as an extraneous something down upon the isolated individual. Paul must be taken to Ananias before he can receive the Spirit. The apostles imparted Him by laying on of hands. Apart from humanity the Holy Spirit means nothing to us; apart from the Holy Spirit humanity means nothing, it is dead. Apart from Jesus' personality the Holy Spirit means nothing; He does not work at all except through the person of Christ. So apart from the Holy Spirit, Christ is nothing; that is, a mere Christ who lived and died two thousand years ago had as well never been, except He now lives again and works as the Holy Spirit among men. Not that the Spirit is only the influence of Christ; He *is* Christ and the Father; they are one, and being thus God, His work is the personal influence of God. The Spirit is not merely God's influence; but the Spirit's influence is God's influence.

Eternal life, then, is simply and only the kind of life Jesus led. It is to be obtained only by knowing Him, and by knowing and following Him, coming to be more and more like Him. That is the Scriptural process. "We are changed from glory to glory into the same image (the Lord's image)," says Paul, "even as by the Spirit of the Lord."[1] We

[1] 2 Cor. iii. 18

ETERNAL LIFE

are "predestined to be conformed to the image of His son."[1] "The new man is renewed in knowledge"—that is, progressively changed as we get more knowledge of Him—"after the image of Him that created him."[2] This is the power, the dynamic force that is changing the world; "Christ, the power of God, and the wisdom of God."[3] Jesus' personality is melting all the sin and sorrow out of humanity; being lifted up, He is drawing all men unto Him. This force is like the sun, the source of all earth's forces. It was working in Socrates and Plato and Buddha;[4] but now in Christ bodied forth and manifested unto us. It was in Abraham and the prophets, but they only "obtained a good report through faith, and received not the promise, God having provided some better thing for us,"[5] even Jesus' person. This is "the light that lighteth every man that cometh into the world."[6] So we perceive that the "immanence of God" and "the Holy Ghost" and "the personality of Jesus," these three are one. "This is life eternal—to know God."[7]

[1] Rom. viii. 29. [2] Col. iii. 10. [3] 1 Cor. i. 24.
[4] "Philosophy more especially was given to the Greeks, as a covenant peculiar to them—being, as it is, a stepping-stone to the philosophy which is according to Christ."—Clement of Alexandria, "Stromata," book vi., chapter 8.
[5] Heb. xi. 39, 40. [6] John i. 9.
[7] John xvii. 3. Note the kind of figures of speech used to represent the mode of Christ's operation upon men, and man's operation also upon his fellows, to save them; as, bread, water, light, salt, savor, quickening, love, and the like. Does any *reality* fit *all these figures* so well as personal influence?

SUGGESTIONS

Theological definitions cannot be fences enclosing truth, but spires pointing upward to the firmament of truth.

It is the commonest verbs of any language, that are irregular; and the commonest, best known things of life are the most mysterious; as love, life, and force.

The influence of one man upon another is of the same kind as the influence of God upon man, differing in degree only as God differs from man.

It is not what Christ has done, but what He is, that saves us.

"You in Christ" and "Christ in you" are explainable only by the interplay of personalities.

A philosopher would have said: "Follow truth"; but Jesus said: "Follow Me—I am the Truth."

Salvation by God's personal influence is possible because we are akin to Him.

The theology of Christianity forever abides in Christ's own person and cannot be got out of Him.

When you form a doctrine concerning Christ you have secured an image of truth, but left the truth itself in Him.

There is no other "plan of salvation" than this: "Come unto Me."

As Christ is "very God," so the Holy Ghost is "very Christ."

Eternal life is Christ's kind of life; we get it by walking with Him.

CHAPTER V

THE SHADOW OF THE CROSS

The Central Doctrine of Christianity is not Based upon the Cross, but upon the Resurrection, and Salvation is not the Legal Consequence of the Dead Christ's Deed, but the Present Effect of the Living Christ's Immanence, Made Possible by His Death

"I came from God, and I'm going back to God, and I won't have any gaps of death in the middle of my life."—GEORGE MACDONALD, *Mary Marston*, Ch. 57.

" Another morn
Ris'n on mid-noon."
JOHN MILTON, *Paradise Lost*, Book V., Line 310.

" Why thus longing, thus forever sighing
For the far-off, unattained, and dim,
While the beautiful, all around thee lying,
Offers up its low, perpetual hymn?"
HARRIET W. SEWALL, *Why Thus Longing*.

"I am the Resurrection."
JESUS, John xi. 25.

"But God, even when we were dead in sins, hath raised us up together, and made us sit together in the heavenlies with Christ Jesus."—PAUL, Eph. ii. 4.

"To build a new life on a ruined life,
To make the future fairer than the past,
And make the past appear a troubled dream."
LONGFELLOW, *The Masque of Pandora*, Pt. 8.

CHAPTER V

Most persons are under the same delusion that obscured the perception of Martha; they believe the lower, but cannot grasp the upper thought of the resurrection.

"Jesus saith unto her, Thy brother (Lazarus) shall rise again. Martha saith unto Him, I know that he shall rise again in the resurrection *at the last day.* Jesus said unto her, *I am* the resurrection and the life; he that believeth in Me, though he were dead, yet shall he live; and whosoever liveth and believeth in Me *shall never die.*"[1]

Just as heaven is popularly supposed to be situated the other side of death, so the resurrection is held to be that process by which we get out of this life and out of death into heaven. But Christ clearly meant something more than this. For just as He made the kingdom of heaven to be a present life, so He now speaks of the resurrection as an experience that waits not for physical death. He that accepts the Christ-life immediately passes though the death of the old worldly

[1] John xi. 23-26.

THE RELIGION OF TO-MORROW

life, is raised again, and here and now enters heaven. "*I am* the resurrection and the life." "He that heareth My word, and believeth on Him that sent Me, shall not come to the judgment, but *is passed* from death unto life."[1] This is an immeasurably loftier thought than the vulgar idea. The resurrection is not a shadowy thing of the next world only, but is a real, vital thing, that any man may know and prove and live.

As there are two forms of the heaven-thought, so there are two forms of the resurrection-thought—the resurrection of the body,[2] and of the soul or life. It is the first form, the bodily resurrection, that has chiefly engaged the attention of men, simply because it is a material thing, and human nature clings fondly to images, types, symbols, whatever it can handle as a tangible conception. The resurrection of the body substantially means to us all, the continued individuality and personality of the man; opinions differ as to whether the actual body that died shall rise again, be transmuted into a celestial substance, and once more be a vehicle through which the soul is to express itself, or, on the other

---

[1] John v. 24.

[2] "The resurrection of the body" is a credal, but not a Scriptural phrase. The Bible speaks of "The resurrection of the dead." Perhaps it would be more accurate to say that the two forms of thought upon this matter are (1) the rising of the dead at the last day, and (2) the rising of the dead now into the new, eternal life.

THE SHADOW OF THE CROSS

hand, the soul shall put on an entirely new body. While it cannot make a particle of difference one way or the other, while no one of good common sense cares in the least whether God will use the identical atoms of the old body or new atoms, yet about this point serious theological battles have been waged. Has it ever occurred to the reader that it is the trivialities, the appurtenances of religion that have been the storm centers of discussion? Whether a bishop shall wear a white or a black robe, whether we shall kneel or stand when we pray, whether in baptizing we shall use a pint or a tank of water, whether we shall rest on Saturday or Sunday as the Sabbath—that is, not *whether* we shall rest one day in seven or not, but *which* day of the seven it shall be!—and all such petty things have divided church organizations and furnished ground for vast sects to stand upon. Now, with the resurrection it is not of the slightest importance as to the form in which we enter upon the life beyond the grave. A sensible man knows nothing about it, knows that he knows nothing, and is perfectly content to know nothing, trusting God to give him "a body as it hath pleased Him."[1]

But the vital point for us to know and believe about the resurrection is not so much

[1] 1 Cor. xv. 38.

that it will take place for the body as that it may take place now and here for the soul. The upper thought of the resurrection is the rising of the life of a man out from the death-life into the glory of the Christ-life. It is the resurrection in this sense that is the most prominent thing in the preaching of the apostles.

In order to understand this it is necessary to look for a moment with clear eyes at the meaning of the word "death" in the New Testament. It also has two meanings—the grosser, that of the dissolution of the physical frame; and the more spiritual, that of a life of ungodliness. When we examine carefully into what substantially constitutes death we find that it is not the perishing of the animal organism, but the inability to see and appreciate things that are of true human concern. For instance, an insane person of sound body is more dead than one who, as was the case of Alexander Stephens, has a body almost useless because of disease, yet a mind bright and a heart warm. Bodily decay really has not so much to do with dying as spiritual and mental blindness. We can imagine one whose body has died and yet whose spirit is still active, as being more alive than one whose body is full of vitality, but whose spirit is imbruted. Going a little further into the

THE SHADOW OF THE CROSS

matter, we perceive that death, to use the phraseology of the scientists, is simply a lack of harmony and sympathy with our environment, and that thus one is more or less alive as he uses that environment.[1] A dyspeptic man is dead to pastry and sweetmeats, because he cannot assimilate them. A stupid lout is dead to the books as he walks through the library. One person may be dead to music; it bores him, he cannot absorb into himself the orchestral harmonies. Another may stroll through the art gallery and be dead to all the masterful human force there displayed, for it kindles nothing in him, does not digest in his soul to feed his aspirations and emotions. So one may be dead to cleanliness, another to fashion, another to sports, another to china, and another to flowers—things to which many persons are exceedingly responsive. Therefore, death, real death, is in proportion to our inability to apprehend and appropriate our surroundings. We call one who has passed out of his earthly life—we call such a one particularly dead, because, *as far as we know*, he has completely ceased to know or feel the world; and yet he may, after all, be simply made more alive instead of being dead. Now, Jesus and His apostles used death in the real and spiritual sense, and not

[1] Spencer, Drummond.

in its apparent and material sense. (The spiritual is always the true meaning of any word, the material is the symbolic meaning.) And as God, virtue, brotherliness, love, and the like are the most infinitely important things pertaining to men, therefore those who are irresponsive to these great things are more especially the dead. Not the collapse of the physical frame, but the debasement of the spirit is true death. Christ transferred the word "death" from bodily dissolution to spiritual decay, simply because He viewed the former as merely an incident, but the latter as a tremendous calamity. Body death is sad, mind death or insanity is far sadder and more dreadful, but a dead spirit wandering through an earth crowded with God and love and goodness, yet knowing nothing of them, is saddest, most pitiful, and most terrible of all.

Consider some of the Scriptures where death is so used. Of course, in many instances the common idea is attached to the word;[1] there is no straining nor mysticism in Christ's language, but common sense can easily discriminate and perceive where He talks of death in its ordinary acceptation and death as a spirit's paralysis. John, the gospeler with the keenest spiritual insight, gives

[1] Compare Luke xvi. 22 with John xi. 26.

THE SHADOW OF THE CROSS

us examples: "If a man keep My saying, he shall never see death";[1] "We have passed from death unto life"; "He that loveth not his brother abideth in death."[2] Paul, however, brings out the point more clearly: "To be carnally minded is death";[3] "When we were dead in sins,"[4] etc.

The upper thought, then, of life is to be awake to those interests, aims, and feelings that were in Christ, to see and live among the higher concerns of humanity. Of death the upper thought is to be oblivious to or untouched by these lofty matters. Of resurrection the upper and truer thought is to rise out of this deadness and to be quickened into this life. And these upper thoughts are not figurative and symbolic, but they are real, and correspond to actual facts, while the ordinary meanings, the lower thoughts, are only used of certain appearances and natural phenomena of whose real significance we can know nothing.[5] In the common usage of the words it is a veiled mystery what life, death,

---

[1] John viii. 51. Compare John v. 24; vi. 47, 50, 51, etc.

[2] 1 John iii. 14.

[3] Marginal reading: "The minding of the flesh," that is, thinking of, or being occupied with, things not spiritual; that is, a man is dead in the truest sense when his little world does not include the spiritualities. Rom. viii. 6.

[4] Eph. ii. 5.

[5] 2 Cor. iv. 18. "The things which are seen are temporal; but the things which are not seen are eternal." So the spirit of man is the reality, the body its passing expression; God is real, the universe a phase. Only from this point of view can we correctly interpret the Scriptures.

or the resurrection may actually be; but in the truer sense given these words by Christ, we can know and comprehend them.

It is the resurrection, and not the cross, that is the most frequent theme of apostolic preaching, for the latter was but the means, while the former was the end.[1] The cross stood for the cause of the pardon of sin, but the resurrection for the fact of the putting away of sin by the new life. The death of Christ was subordinated, in apostolic preaching, to His rising again. "It is Christ that died, *yea rather* that is risen again,"[2] exclaimed Paul. This was the motive of Peter's great Pentecostal sermon: "This Jesus hath God raised up, whereof we all are witnesses."[3] So much did Paul emphasize the resurrection that he declared: "If in this life only we have

---

[1] In the effort to give to the resurrection its full apostolic significance I have perhaps been led to discriminate overmuch between the respective values of the cross and the resurrection. The incarnation, the example, the teaching, the death, and the resurrection of Christ are one indivisible whole. They constitute the one great revelation of God through His Son. We may not say that one part is more necessary than another. But the point is, that, as mediæval theology exalted the legal aspect of the death of Christ to such a degree as to render the other factors almost dispensable, as far as our salvation is concerned, so now I strive to show that the resurrection, for the reasons set forth in this chapter, is the crowning culminating act of the Christ-revelation. It is the resurrection which the apostles brought most to the front, not, as is generally supposed, because of its evidential value only, but because of its spiritual significance and its theological importance. To give most emphasis to the example and teaching of Jesus is the characteristic of the humanitarians (unitarians, etc.); to emphasize unduly the cross is the characteristic of Augustinianism (the Latin theology); while to put in the most prominent place in the Gospel the resurrection and the "power" thereof was the apostles' custom, and such will be the theology of to-morrow.

[2] Rom. viii. 34.   [3] Acts ii. 32.

THE SHADOW OF THE CROSS

hope in Christ, we are of all men most miserable."[1] To the Ephesians he writes that the marvel of the ages is that God, "even when we were dead in sins, hath quickened us together with Christ Jesus; and hath raised us up together, and made us sit together in heaven-life with Christ Jesus."[2] He makes this to be the aim of God in creation: "For whom He did foreknow, He did also predestinate to be made like the image of His Son, that He might be the first-born among many brethren."[3] The greatest, most dynamic fact concerning Christ was not His death, but that He now liveth, for "if Christ be not raised, your faith is vain; ye are yet in your sins."[4] Not to multiply quotations, if we read carefully the epistles of the apostles we must be struck by the fact that it was the resurrection more than the cross, that is the great burden of their preaching. It was not until the corruption of Christianity by the Latin church that the cross was elevated above the resurrection, a mistake that lingers to this day, and one which is illustrative of a profound misconception of the Gospel, as we shall see later on.

Let us now ask *why* it is that the resurrection has this pregnant force. Why did the

[1] 1 Cor. xv. 19.
[2] Eph. ii. 5-6.
[3] Rom. viii. 29.
[4] 1 Cor. xv. 16-17.

immediate followers of Christ so emphasize it, why should it always now be a theme even more to be put to the front than the cross? It is simply because the resurrection means a living, present Saviour, a constant, daily Rescuer from sin, while the cross means a dying Saviour, a God participating in the woe consequent on sin that thus He may redeem us. The cross signifies the means by which is secured the cancellation of sins, the wiping away of the old writing on the heart's guilty tablet; the resurrection means the actual cancellation itself, the substitution of new for old writing. It is well to be given a medicine that will cure our disease; it is better to have the Physician who can administer that medicine; the dying Saviour is the medicine, the living Saviour is the Physician who applies His own blood. And that blood is of no avail unless He applies it. The cross means the preparation for forgiveness; the resurrection means actual forgiveness by the newness of life or the regeneration. As Paul puts it: "For if, when we were enemies, we were reconciled to God by the death of His Son, much more, being reconciled, we shall be saved by His life."[1]

It is not the blood alone that saves, but it is the resurrection—that is, the risen Jesus.

[1] Rom. v. 10.

THE SHADOW OF THE CROSS

This makes it all-important. The emphasis we put upon the phrase, "saved by the blood," is not Scriptural. We are not saved by the death alone of Jesus. It is not the cross, but the Man who hung there, that is our salvation. This misunderstanding has arisen from the old false notion of salvation, as though it were from a penalty instead of from a life of sin. The cross supplies the means by which the resurrection saves. "He was delivered for our offenses, and rose again for our justification."[1] Paul uses not the phrase, "the power of the cross," but he speaks of "the power of His resurrection."[2] We are not saved because Jesus appeased the overhanging wrath of Deity, but because He now lives for us, to help us and guide us by His Spirit out of our living death. Far be it from me to seem to belittle the transcendent majesty of the cross or the endless efficacy of the suffering Lamb of God; but what I say is that apart from the risen Saviour the atonement is of no avail; it simply has no efficacy at all because of our complete inability to *utilize it* to lead a new life withal. Because of the death of Christ we are *to be* purged, cleansed; but because of His reviving and living now we *are* thus purged and cleansed.[3]

[1] Rom. iv. 25. [2] Phil. iii. 10; 1 Cor. i. 18.
[3] "But if the Spirit of Him that raised up Jesus from the dead dwell in you, He that raised up Christ from the dead shall also

THE RELIGION OF TO-MORROW

To stop at the cross means a mere negative and impotent salvation;[1] to go on to the resurrection, a positive and triumphant salvation.

Now, this preëminence of the resurrection is not due to a theologic quibble; it is not all a question merely of which part of the "plan of salvation" is the most important, but the point is one arising from the nature of the case and is easily perceived by common sense. For the resurrection implies a living, operating Saviour personally saving men now by His own exertions, while salvation by the cross implies man saved by a device or sacrificial ceremony. The former makes the means of saving to be the influence of an ever-present, personal Deity: "Lo, I am with you alway, even to the end";[2] while the latter makes saving to be only a legal and formal cancellation of a penalty in the divine court records against men. Cross-salvation fits the notion of salvation as an act of securing a man's title to a future heaven; resurrection-salvation fits the idea, which in this essay is insisted upon as the true one, of salvation as

---

quicken your mortal bodies by His Spirit that dwelleth in you." Rom. viii. 11. The actual quickening is done "*by* His Spirit that dwelleth in you," and is done *because* " He raised up Christ from the dead."

[1] "And if Christ be not risen, then is our preaching vain, and your faith is also vain." 1 Cor. xv. 14.

[2] Matt. xxviii. 20.

THE SHADOW OF THE CROSS

a lifting of a man from a low life into a Christ-life, both now and forever. We are saved into eternal life because our Saviour has risen and works in us to destroy the works of the devil. In other words, it is not the death of Christ, but Christ Himself, by virtue of His death, that saves us. We pass from death unto life not as a legal or ceremonial consequence of what He did for us, but because of what He does in us now as a living Redeemer.

You will notice this view is strikingly conformable to all of Jesus' words about His mission. "Because I live, ye shall live also";[1] our life is dependent on His life, not His death. In His parable of the bread from heaven He said: "So he that eateth Me, even he shall live by Me,"[2] and "Except ye eat the flesh of the Son of man, and drink His blood, ye have no life in you";[3] and "He that eateth of this bread shall live forever";[4] all of which is about as plain as could be made that our eternal life is consequent upon His rising again and living on to impart His life to us. Again He said, "My sheep follow Me, and I give unto them eternal life, and they shall never perish, neither shall any man pluck them out of My hand";[5] in which passage He clearly represents salvation as a mat-

[1] John xiv. 19.
[2] John vi. 57.
[3] John vi. 53.
[4] John vi. 58.
[5] John x. 27-28.

ter personally attended to by Himself, He holding, guarding, and leading His sheep, and not merely by His death securing them an eternal title to bliss beyond the grave. And as if to clinch this meaning, He adds, in the next verse, "I and My Father are one,"[1] as if to say, "Deity does not give you salvation merely because I pay its price by My death, but I am Deity. My death and sufferings equip Me to keep and save you from sin." Again, in His great prayer, He said that God had given Him power to "give eternal life" to as many as the Father had given Him; adding, "And this is life eternal, that they might know Thee, the only true God, and Jesus Christ whom Thou hast sent";[2] that is, that eternal life is not merely an inheritance bought by the blood, but a higher career secured by knowing and living in communion with God in Christ. Paul also speaks of "Christ, who is our life,"[3] and, although often referring to Him as the source of our life, never once speaks of eternal life as given by Christ's death, that death being rather the groundwork of our redemption, atonement, reconciliation, bringing nigh, remission, and the like.[4]

[1] John x. 30.   [2] John xvii. 2-3.   [3] Col. iii. 4.
[4] In a rapid reading of the Acts of the Apostles I find the theme of apostolic preaching sixteen times to be the resurrection, while in not one instance is the atonement made the text of any address given. Paul does not say he is determined to know

THE SHADOW OF THE CROSS

So then we conclude that the doctrine of men's salvation by the atonement on the cross, meaning thereby that one who accepts it is made sure of bliss in the world to come,[1] is not a Scriptural teaching, but that the true Gospel is that our salvation, being made *possible* by Christ's death, is actually *accomplished* by the risen, living Saviour. The cross was the preliminary, the resurrection life of Christ is the real means of salvation. As the kingdom of heaven is not a place beyond death, so belief in the atonement does not secure entrance into that place; but as the kingdom of heaven is a new life for man, a "life more abundant" which death cannot touch, so the power of the risen Saviour gives us admission into and maintains us in that life. As salvation is not a theatric legal transaction of a God so bound by the letter of His own laws that He cannot pardon except a certain price

nothing but the crucifixion, that is, as is now commonly understood, the preaching of the atonement, but that his determination is to know naught but "Jesus Christ and Him crucified." In other words, he emphasizes the *personality*, not the act of Jesus. 1 Cor. ii. 2.

The reader will notice also, by finding in the concordance all the passages where the death of Christ is referred to in the epistles as a Gospel theme, that it is almost always coupled with His resurrection. For instance Rom. v. 1 with Rom. iv. 25; 2 Cor. v. 15; Gal. ii. 20; Heb. ix. 28; 1 Pet. ii. 24 and iii. 18; Rom. vi. 3 to 11 (this explicitly sets forth the true relation of His death to His resurrection); Rom. v. 6-11; Eph. ii. 12 13 with verses 5 and 6 (5, 6 explains *how* He does what is set forth in 12-13); Phil. iii. 10; Rom. viii. 34; Col. ii. 12-15; 2 Cor. xiii. 4; Gal. vi. 14 with 15; Col. ii. 20 with iii. 1, 3, 4; Gal. v. 24, 25; 2 Tim. ii. 11; Rev. i. 18; Rom. v. 10-21 (comparing Adam with Christ, Paul compares Adam's *death* with Christ's *life*), etc.

[1] It is not the acceptance of the Gospel that saves, but it is the reception of God that saves.

be paid, so the atonement does not, by satisfying divine resentment, admit us into a heavenly city the other side of death; but as salvation is a saving from sin and death-life and despair and animality, into righteousness and Christ-life and hope and the possibility of eternal progress, so the "power of His resurrection"—that is, the power of Him as a risen and now operating Saviour, accomplishes this.

It may be said that all this is immaterial, that it is only a fine and useless distinction without a real difference. But such is not the fact. There is a profound gap between the two theories. The one reduces salvation to a technicality, a court-room shift of a martinet Deity; the other makes salvation the working of an immanent Saviour-Deity constantly in men. The one lays the foundation for a superstructure of legalizing sophistries about what constitutes saving faith and essentials and the like; the other sweeps away all these confusing refinements and places the soul as a child in the immediate care of a present, loving Father-Saviour. The one made possible the vast perversions of the Latin Church; the other is the very spirit of the apostles. The one produces a contempt of God in unbelieving minds, as it shows Him to be an austere and exacting Judge; the other unfolds God as love and helpfulness, not as a

THE SHADOW OF THE CROSS

Judge letting a culprit go, but as a Shepherd going out after His sheep. To the one theory are traceable most of the bitter accusations of infidels against the church, while to the other very few have found objection. Most of the saints of the church have shone as holy examples just in proportion as they made no practical use of the theory that their salvation was a title to a future world by the death of Jesus, treating it as a mystery they believed but did not comprehend, and using as a *working theory* the idea of a risen Lord saving them daily from evil. The one theory has easily been perverted into the corrupt doctrine that a buccaneer and lecher could live in his sins, and yet by orthodox "belief in the atonement" make sure his "eternal life"; a corruption that would have been impossible had the church faithfully taught that eternal life hereafter is an impossibility except as a continuation of the eternal kind of life begun here, and that saving faith is not a mental consent to participation in the merits of Christ's death, but a reception of and communion with a risen, present Lord— a faith utterly absurd to claim unless it redeems us from sinfulness to a higher life. So therefore this is not a theologic hair-splitting; it pertains to a mistake that has disgraced and caricatured Christianity for ages, eating out the very heart of its purpose; it pertains to a truth which alone can make Christianity a real power and blessing upon earth.

The world has been slow to grasp "the mind that was in Christ." For ages we have lived under the shadow of the cross. For two long chiliads have men made the "wholesome words of our Lord Jesus Christ"[1] to be morbid, deathly, and benumbing sentences by which a wicked race was to thread its uncertain way to a better land. A far-off God was worshiped, while all the time He was near. A dead Christ was trusted, while all the time He was alive. A remote heaven was sung and sighed for, while all the time the kingdom of heaven was "at hand." Through the long night of mediævalism the world was saying, "Who shall ascend into heaven, to bring Christ down, or who shall descend into the deep to bring Christ again from the dead?" Yet all the time Paul's word thundered in vain against an iron system of theology, "The Word is nigh thee, even in thy mouth, and in thy heart."[2] We have lingered too long at the cross, chilled there by the despair of an Augustinian theology that seemed so true because it was as deeply wretched and black as the human heart itself. Let us be up and

---

[1] 1 Tim. vi. 3: "healthful words."   [2] Rom. x. 6-8.

THE SHADOW OF THE CROSS

go on to the open tomb, go on to meet a risen Lord, who ever liveth, whose presence abides with us, who is come again that our joy may be full. The cross has been degraded to be a superstitious sign, a talisman to ward off the devils of another world. By reducing salvation to a mere "plan" for obtaining security for the soul after death, there was made possible all the grotesque instances of vile lives going out clinging to the sign of the crucifix, assured by priests that "faith" would surely "save." Upon this theory was built the system of indulgences, of purgatory, of masses for the dead. Common sense protested, and was told to be quiet and adore. Reason refused to accept this death's-head theology and it was insulted and trampled into silence. It was held that man could not understand divine things, that it was natural that mere human intelligence should be unable to comprehend God's great "scheme." "It is certain because it is impossible," said a certain father.[1] But whereas salvation merely by a scheme to escape from future punishment thus insults all that natural reason tells us about God, on the contrary salvation from a sinful life and its consequences by the power of a living and immanent Saviour is most sweet and acceptable to what common sense

[1] Tertullian. Commonly misquoted: "I believe because it is impossible."

tells us ought to be the nature of God. Salvation by the resurrection, by a living, ever-present God, squares with Greek philosophy, with Oriental longings, and with all the highest expression of men everywhere, while salvation from future pangs by an atonement-scheme alone is artificial, unreasonable, and unscriptural. The latter was made, not by the apostles, but by Augustine and his fellows, who constructed their theology as special pleaders with the distinct object of bolstering the claims of the church; it was perpetuated by the church after the Reformation simply because it had acquired so much strength during its long growth through the Middle Ages, and had so struck its deadly roots through all theology that they were unable to get rid of it in their day. The time has now, however, surely come when we can begin to see "the truth as it is in Jesus"—to get back to Christ, back to Clement of Alexandria and the early Greek Church fathers.

We must bear in mind that the root and cause of all the morbidities of religion in the past has been the making of the "eternal life" of the Scriptures to mean only something beginning beyond the grave. This is the dead fly, which, if it be in the ointment of any conception of the Gospel, causeth it to stink. Given

THE SHADOW OF THE CROSS

eternal life after death only, and all the distortions naturally appear, such as salvation by God's machinery, instead of by God Himself, a low and legalizing fear of "the judgment seat," a false importance to deathbed scenes and repentances, a vast church professing to guarantee believers security, and the whole "insurance" idea of the Gospel. But when eternal life is a thing to be here and now imparted by a present Deity, when this life is called eternal not because it begins after time, but because it is so divine in its nature that death cannot affect it, then we perceive none of these evil effects. Eternal life as a future blessing lays emphasis upon our acceptance of an artificial divine scheme, and morality is of little consequence compared with a saving faith; but eternal life as an immediate condition to be entered upon by coming under the power of a risen Saviour is fruitful of good works, always abounding in the work of the Lord.[1] One quarrels with morality as a rival; the other shames morality by a righteousness which "exceeds that of the Scribes and Pharisees."[2] One is pessimistic, viewing the world as an evil to be escaped from; the other is optimistic, going

---

[1] It is worthy of note that it is as a conclusion and climax of his mighty argument for the *resurrection* that Paul exclaims: "*Therefore*, my beloved brethren," etc. 1 Cor. xv. 58.

[2] Matt. v. 20.

forth in supernal strength to overcome the world even as He overcame. One looks only on the earth as a vile planet to be burnt at last by an angry Maker disgusted with His failure; the other contemplates this globe as only waiting for the manifestation of the sons of God in order to be wholly redeemed and made glorious. The one gazes paralyzed on sin and the dead Christ it has slain; the other rises with streaming eyes from the open tomb to cry out in joyous hope, "My Lord and my God!"

The Reformation was at bottom this desertion of the dead for the living Christ. The crucifix was the symbol of the life of the church from the beginning of the predominancy of the Latin bishops until Luther. The reformers began the work of leading a despairing world away from its agonizing prostration before this awful figure out into the newness of a Christ-filled world. They themselves suspected not the extent of their work, and builded better than they knew. Luther, Calvin, Knox, Wesley, and the others clung more or less tenaciously to the old landmarks of human tradition, and were wise in so doing, as the transition was so immense that it could only be made gradually. But more and more in this age are the signs apparent of a longing for a return to the simplicity of

THE SHADOW OF THE CROSS

Christ. More and more is the idea of a risen and immanent Lord pervading the churches. The great revival of the eighteenth century, in its central themes of holiness and experimental religion, showed how the mighty heart of man was rising to the apprehension of a personally acting Saviour. The leaders of that revival, although unable to swing clear from the theological system that Rome had fastened upon all our conceptions of the work of Christ, still poured forth such a wealth of passionate feeling in their preachment and in their hymns, that the world was made to see that "the Lord is risen indeed." The old system cannot stand long against such singing as this of Charles Wesley:

> "My soul breaks out in strong desire
>   The perfect bliss to prove,
> My longing heart is all on fire
>   To be dissolved in love.
> Give me Thyself; from every boast,
>   From every wish set free;
> Let all I am in Thee be lost,
>   But give Thyself to me.
> *Thy gifts, alas! cannot suffice,*
>   *Unless Thyself be given;*
> *Thy presence makes my paradise,*
>   *And where Thou art is heaven.*"

The great revivals which characterize the life of modern evangelical churches have taken on more and more of the tone of the present, living Saviour, although much of the actual indoctrinating still keeps the old Augustinian formulas. The world is shaking off as a horrid dream the thoughts of a far-off God with a mechanical, legal plan of salvation, and of a salvation referring to the dim future only. We can never altogether cease to respect the Latin church, because it held for the world through the Dark Ages the body of Christ; but we are looking at it now as one who looked at the tomb of Jesus, saying, "Come, see the place where the Lord lay." We are realizing the second advent, the coming again of a risen Christ into men's thinking and practice, after for long ages He has been to us but a dead victim, a sacrificial lamb, a mere incident in the divine machinery of the atonement. The light of life is radiating throughout the world. Look no more into your plans and schemes you have marked out for Him. He is not there; He is risen. He is coming now into all civilization, government, philosophy, and dreams of men. "Even so come, Lord Jesus!"

It is Easter morning in theology. Throw away your crucifixes! Receive ye the Holy Ghost!

SUGGESTIONS

It is Easter morning in theology.

It is the trivialities of religion that have been the storm centers of discussion.

The spiritual is always the true meaning of any word—the material is the symbolic meaning.

The upper thought is the true one.

The keynote of apostolic preaching was the resurrection, rather than the cross.

The blood of the dying Christ is of no avail unless applied by the living Christ.

At bottom, the Reformation was a turning from the dead to the living Christ.

The immanence of God is the watchword of the future.

We respect the mediæval church for preserving for us the body of Christ; but we are coming to look on it as one looked at the tomb of Jesus and exclaimed: "Come, see the place where the Lord lay."

We are realizing the second advent.

Buddhism holds that desire is sin, existence is desire, hence to destroy sin, existence must cease; at this fundamental point it touches Christianity, only the latter teaches that existence may be transformed, it need not be destroyed.

CHAPTER VI

DEFINITIONS

Scripture Terms for the Operation of Religion are Explainable only by Assuming it to be God's Personal Influence

"Les jansénistes font la grâce un espèce de quatrième personne de la sainte Trinité. Saint Paul et Saint Augustin, trop étudiés, ou étudiés uniquement, ont tout perdu, si on ose le dire. Au lieu de grâce, dites aide, secours, influence divine, celeste rosée; on s'entend alors. Ce mot est comme un talisman. . . . Personnifier les mots est un mal funeste en théologie."—JOUBERT, *Pensées*, 35. (Quoted from Allen.)

"By grace are ye saved through faith."—PAUL, Eph. ii. 8.

"Men are apt to conclude that the 'righteousness of Christ' must denote something separate and distinct from the indwelling of the *Holy Spirit*, bringing forth fruit unto holiness, because they fear to confound together what they habitually, though unconsciously, consider two different agents."—WHATELY, *Difficulties in the Writings of St. Paul*, p. 191.

CHAPTER VI

Viewing religion as the personal influence of God in us, it will be perhaps helpful to restate the definitions of some of the principal terms, the phrases and words, in which the Scriptures and common theology describe its operation in us. These terms have been so much bandied to and fro in religious controversy that they have come to have artificial meanings. Or rather, we have become accustomed to use them as a kind of algebraic signs, standing for certain materials for debate or for unquestioning faith; as smooth coins passing current in our thought and speech, yet having the inscriptions thereon so blurred that we rarely ever look to see what exactly they are. Let us therefore take a few of the more important of them, and divesting ourselves as nearly as may be from all preconceived or traditional notions, try to find out what is actually meant by them. Let us take the point of view that religion is God's influence in us, and, assuming this as a working hypothesis, let us see what these common terms mean to common sense.

In the first place, it becomes plain, from

this view-point, that any gift or effect or merit or any such thing transferred to us from God means nothing at all unless we keep in mind that God's personality goes with it. There is no gift without the Giver, no blessing apart from the Blesser, no promise without the Promiser. All His benefits to and in us are but phases of His person as it bears to us and works by its influence in us. We get the most valuable things, not *because* He does or has done something, but we get such things from Him directly *as* doing or having done something.[1] This is a very important distinction,

---

[1] This is as true in material as in spiritual concerns. We do not get bread upon our table because God instituted certain laws of nature by which wheat grows, and so forth; He, after having set such laws in motion, going off somewhere and leaving them to run themselves. But God does personally and intelligently make the wheat grow, "God giveth the increase," God is in the oven changing the dough by heat into wholesome food. There is no slightest beat of the sparrow's wing, no deviation of the motion of a mote floating in the sunbeam, no alteration of the stream's eddy nor of the air's current, but is directly, intelligently and personally attended to by Him who thinks of and is conscious of all things at once even as we are conscious of and can think of but one thing at a time. This is the immanence of Deity in nature. It is not that God made gravitation, cohesion, and the like, but that these are phases of His utilization of matter. He did not make a universe and then retire to sit somewhere and *watch* it afar off. But the operation of force in matter is the *process of His making*. The one view is a *God-less* materiality; the other a *God-full* organism. The one view assumes matter as a fact, spirit as an explanation or phenomenon of that fact; the other takes the Spirit to be the reality, and matter its mode of expression.

A similar difference lies between the common (the Augustinian or Latin) theology and the New Testament (or Greek) theology. One conceives that the value of the Gospel lies in the perfection of the plan God has made, which is so complete that of itself it operates to save; the other, that the Gospel is merely a light shed upon the method God *is taking personally* to redeem men. By the Latin scheme God could very well have commissioned some angel to attend to the working out of the details of His redemption plan, to distribute the rewards and punishments, to bestow grace and balance the accounts; but by the apostolic scheme, more truly apprehended by the Greek fathers, God is the immanent, pervasive, omnipresent personality who Himself does all.

DEFINITIONS

and absolutely necessary to our getting a rational grasp of Christian doctrines. We must take the view here set forth if we wish intelligently to wed reason to faith, and not sadly to dismiss reason because of faith. We have so long been taught that Christianity is merely some sort of plan, out of which certain benefits accrue to us, that we need now to see it as a personal influence of Deity, working indeed by a plan, as all God's works are orderly and by law, but in itself of reality a Force or Power, not displayed *for* us, but *in* us.

Looking at our religion in this light, we observe, before taking up the terms in detail that it reveals it as a wondrously simple thing—not simple in the sense of small or definable, but simple in the sense of being coherent, a unity, and not confusing. "Martha, Martha," said the Master, "thou art careful and troubled about many things; but one thing is needful."[1] The Christian has not a thousand details to worry over; he has but one thing to do, to "keep himself in the love of God."[2] He is like the farmer, who takes no thought about the making of leaves and tassels and ears on the corn, but only tends faithfully the life of the seed and plant, knowing that so it will best make its own foliage

[1] Luke x. 41.   [2] Jude 21.

and grain. Or he is like the vineyard-keeper, whose sole task is to keep his vines healthy, leaving them to work out their own fruit. There are many fruits, but one life; many evidences, but one power; many forms, but one spirit. This was Jesus' meaning, it may be, when He admonished us to take no thought about what we eat and drink, "for is not the life more than meat, or the body than raiment?" and when He asked which of us by taking thought could add one cubit to his stature.[1] The personal influence of God being the essence of religion, all there is for us to attend to is to strive constantly to allow it fuller access into us.[2]

If this in truth is the essence of religion, we would naturally suppose the New Testament writers would have had some word for it, some term to express that influence viewed as a concept apart from the being of God Himself. Just such a term we find in the word "grace."[3] The apostolic signification of

---

[1] Matt. vi. 25.

[2] The gist of the incident of the rich young man, in Mark x. 21, it seems to me, is often overlooked; it is, that what he needed most of all was the Master's personal influence; "*One thing* thou lackest—follow *Me*."

[3] Grace, in Greek *Charis*, the root meaning of which is "that which gives joy or satisfaction." From this the meaning branched into 1, pleasantness of manner; 2, charm or elegance of person; 3, thanks, or an acknowledgment for a kindness done; 4, honor, fame, reward, etc., because these are pleasant; etc. In the plural, *Charites*, it came to mean "those goddesses through whose favor agreeable qualities and personal charms are bestowed on mortals"; their names are given in Pindar as Euphrosyne, Aglaia, and Thaleia, or Cheerfulness, Splendor, and Abundance.

DEFINITIONS

"grace" is that of the person of God radiating toward and into us. It is one of the new words of Christianity, or rather an old word transferred to be a vehicle of this new thought. Heretofore "grace" had meant favor or the attitude of kindness and benignancy in any one. And as God, when He was revealed in Christ, showed Himself so loving and forgiving, no better term than "loving favor" or "grace" was found to use as expressing His bearing toward us.

When God, as an immanent Spirit in His religion, was reasoned out of theology by the logic-mongers of the Latin church, leaving only the framework and scheme of salvation to operate among men, while Deity Himself was removed as a far-off Judge, then, of course, this term shared the fate of other terms. Being emptied of God, it was filled

These were mayhap in Paul's mind when he set forth the three Christian graces, Faith, Hope and Charity. The original color of the word may be discerned in the following examples from the classics, in each of which *charis* is the original word; Iliad 14, 235, I am *grateful* to thee; Aristoph. Av. 384, to *dispense* a *favor*; Polyb. 2, 5, to listen through *flattery*; "to talk charis" is used in Xenophon to mean "to speak with any one for the purpose of conciliating him"; also Xenophon uses "*dia chariton einai*," to be in a state of good-will or friendship with any one. Charis is of the same origin as, and a kindred word to, the verb *chairo*, to be joyful; the noun *charma* (Eng., *charm*) a joy, or a thing that produces joy; and the adjective *chartos*, pleasing.

The above examples are given that the reader may get the real flavor of the word *grace*, a flavor entirely different, it is to be feared, from that of our common notion. The consummate flower and force of Christian character by which it is to win the world, is its *grace*, that is, primarily, its agreeableness. The root-element of Christianity is that it brings *joy*. Morality is only the *means*. joy is the object. A morality or righteousness that does not work *loveliness* is not Christian. But we must remember that the joy and beauty of life come *only* through *rightness* of life.

with some sort of mystical, magic potency, miraculous and utterly incomprehensible by "mere reason." It was equally, of course (for the church never failed to claim for itself what it had robbed from God), held to be in the keeping of the church and ministry. It was transmitted by laying on of hands in baptism, confirmation, and ordination. It entered into men in the sacramental wafers and oils and in the sacred touch of priests. It passed over into the soul in absolution; *how* he never could know, he must simply believe it.[1] That it was artificial and smacked of superstition, was nothing against this view, for the more absurd a tenet was, the more merit was there in believing it. So dominant became this idea that all matters of religion were held to belong to "the kingdom of grace,"[2] in which was no law nor coherence except the decree of a God who was insulted when men tried to understand His ways. This kingdom differed from "the kingdom of nature" as much as the politics of the planet Mars would differ from ours. And although we have put by much of this kind of feeling about religious things, not a little of the magical, vague ele-

---

[1] "The Jansenists made grace to be a sort of Fourth Person of the Trinity."—Joubert. Allen says: "For the living presence in the soul of the spiritual Christ, the Latins substituted an inanimate thing which was designated in religion nomenclature as *grace*."

[2] First declared by Albertus Magnus, but adopted, systematized, and given popularity by Aquinas.

DEFINITIONS

ment of the thought about grace still lingers in the common understanding.

Now, if we will simply go back and place ourselves in the position of the sacred penmen, and endeavor to use the word with the same fresh meaning they gave to it, we cannot fail to be helped to saner thought. Suppose, for instance, we substitute the phrase "loving favor" for the word "grace" wherever it is found in the New Testament. This will assist us to see how the apostles regarded grace as simply the influence of God's reconciled, benignant face upon their hearts. The word, as thus expressing the influence of a loving and helpful Father, became a part of the oft-used apostolic salutation and benediction, "Grace be unto you," "The grace of our Lord Jesus Christ be with you all," etc.,[1] as if ever to remind the people that the central idea of the new religion was the revelation of a God who loves and is kindly disposed to us-ward. So, speaking of Jesus, John says that while the law came by Moses, "grace and truth came by Jesus Christ;"[2] for in Him the world first saw God as a benevolent Father. The law was the personality of God working in men to create the consciousness of sin; for the law was of course not confined to nor made by Moses, but was and is a conviction

[1] Rom. i. 7; xvi. 20, etc. [2] John i. 17.

of the hatefulness of sinfulness wherever man exists, revealing to him his vileness, making him condemn and loathe himself. Moses merely gave authoritative and definite shape to that universal law. So then law was one phase of God's influence, grace was the other, the new phase. By God's person working in men as a law, as an ideal of right and purity, men got the knowledge of sin as sin. By God's person working in men as grace, men got the knowledge of how to escape from sin. The embodiment of the one was the tables of stone; of the other, the man Christ Jesus.

Paul calls his being set apart to preach to the Gentiles the "dispensation of grace,"[1] because God's opening the kingdom of heaven to non-Jews was to the Jewish mind a marvelous act of liberality and amazing kindness. The primitive meaning of the word comes out in Paul's exhortation to the Colossians to sing with grace and to use grace in their speech, as if he tells them to use in song and sermon the same loving favor to men that God uses to them.[2] Peter calls the disciples "stewards of the manifold grace of God,"[3] for through them the world is to be made to see how kind and good is God—they have, as it were, God's kindness in their keeping, they are responsible for how they show it forth,

[1] Eph. iii. 2. [2] Col. iii. 16; iv. 6. [3] 1 Pet. iv. 10.

DEFINITIONS

and therefore they are to use "fervent charity" and "hospitality" one to another."[1] Again Peter says to us that we are to "grow in grace";[2] for as the flower grows in the sun's light, so are we to be developed by the beams of the divine love and goodness upon and in us.

As grace was the loving favor of God toward men, so "the Gospel," or the "good news," was the telling about that loving favor. Grace was the thing itself; the Gospel the relating of it. Grace was the fact; the Gospel the proclamation of the fact. The Gospel does not save, except by a sort of metonymy, or substituting one word for another which suggests it; as we say a man keeps a good table when we mean he keeps good food on his table. It is in this sense only the Gospel is called the power of God unto salvation; for certainly merely informing a man that God is loving and forgiving will do him no good unless he acts upon that information to make use of this love and forgiveness. Thus the *contents* of the Gospel is the personal influence of God; without that contents it would do us no more service than if a man should bring us a bag of gold and should give us the *bag* while he kept the *gold*.

As this loving favor of God shines upon all

[1] 1 Pet. iv. 8-9.   [2] 2 Pet. iii. 18.

men alike, bad and good, so the Gospel is to every creature without respect of persons. Will not all men therefore be saved? Certainly, as far as God is concerned they will. The same personal influence operates upon the wicked and the good, as the sun shines and the rain falls upon the just and the unjust. And now we come to see how this apprehension of religion as God's personal influence sheds a striking light upon a fact that no other theory has ever made reasonable—to wit, how, while God equally loves all His children, some of them wax worse and worse and may be ultimately lost. No theological system can possibly explain this, as a system. No mechanical scheme of salvation can make it seem right. If salvation is a plan for getting men to heaven, then, while God was making it, reason refuses to understand why He did not make it so it would take the whole world to heaven. If He excepts some men from His plan, it cannot be that He loves all alike. Driven by this absolutely irresistible logic, the church fathers took refuge in the old evasion of denying the rights of reason to meddle with the Almighty's machinery, and invented the doctrines of eternal foreordination and reprobation, that some men were made to be saved and some to be damned. When intelligence asked how

DEFINITIONS

a good God could do what no good man would do, it was met with the reply: "Be still. This is not an affair of intelligence. It belongs to the awful, mysterious kingdom of grace." Let us not judge these fathers too harshly. It was the premises from which they began their argument that misled them. Their conclusions were not the result of bad logic, but of a wrong starting-point. For religion is not, as they supposed, a plan, but it is the workings of an immanent, ever-present Deity; not a mere consequence of a dead Saviour's sacrifice, but the actual influence of a risen Lord.

And note how clearly this true theory lets the light in upon this dark problem. Being the influence of a personality, it follows the laws of personality, necessarily. Now, it is among the commonest facts known to us that one can open or close himself to another's influence. Going among bad men, we can resist the evil effects of their companionship, or we can submit, as we choose. Associating with a high-minded, large, and courteous character, we can rejoice in the influence of him upon us, and coöperate with it by our will, or we can set ourselves against it. And it is well known to all who have any powers of observation, that if we are brought in contact with a noble and generous nature, and if we do not yield to the play of his character upon us, if we do not assent to his influence in us, we are almost invariably *driven to the opposite extreme*, and become even more hateful and spiteful than we were before. Such was the effect of Jesus on the Pharisees; He actually made them worse; they became more firmly set in their bigotry and self conceit because of Him. It is as if a good man comes to us as a force the heart instinctively recognizes, a force which, if not surrendered to, arouses all the opposition in us and actually develops still further meanness in us.

One does not have to be a theologian, therefore, to understand this "mystery of iniquity." Just plain common sense is all that is needed. When we get the right point of view we can see very much further into the great problem of lost humanity. It is said, to give one illustration, when Pharaoh refused to let the Israelites go, after he had been frightened into a promise by the display of Moses' power, that "God hardened Pharaoh's heart." It was not the devil, nor Pharaoh himself, but God that hardened his heart. But how could a good God do this? After being hardened was he not then less to blame for the next lie? The plain explanation is in this law above referred to—that it is in the nature of human beings to harden when they resist softening

DEFINITIONS

influences. Nature is God; and nature drives further down those who struggle against going up. So Paul says that "even as they did not like to retain God in their knowledge, God gave them over to a reprobate mind."[1]

This brings us to the next term that figures so largely in Christian speech, "faith." Faith is merely the *attitude* of the man toward grace, the *influence* of God. Grace is God's personality acting upon us; faith is the way we receive that personality. Grace is the air around us, faith the opening of a window. Grace is the sunshine; faith is removing the shutter. Grace is food; faith, eating. Grace, water; faith, drinking. Now, a great many have stumbled over faith, as they have over grace. They have been unable to rid themselves of the notion that it is some sort of magic talent, a fifth sense, supplied miraculously to some peculiarly religious temperaments. There never was a greater mistake. Faith is "the gift of God,"[2] but it is given to every one. Nowhere in the Bible are we taught to pray for faith, and nowhere is it promised to give it if we ask. When some did pray for it we do not find the Master answered.[3] Some have the idea that faith is

[1] Rom. i. 28.
[2] It is a question, however, whether it is faith or grace which is called "the gift of God" in Eph. ii. 8.
[3] Luke xvii. 5-6. "The apostles said unto the Lord, Increase our faith. And the Lord said, *If ye had faith* as a grain of mus-

a kind of feeling or spiritual substance that God hands down to seekers. But while we are told to seek Him to find grace, we are never told to go to Him for faith. On the contrary we are distinctly commanded to have faith, as though any one could use it if he would. The reason of this is that faith is a faculty, just as sight and hearing. It would be absurd to close our eyes and pray for sight when God has already given us the power to see. If you want to hear, listen; do not go on clamoring for hearing, but keep still and hear. If you want to see, look; do not complain of lack of seeing, but see. If you wish to know God, to feel His grace, have faith; do not go on stultifying common sense by praying for a power which is inherent in your spirit, as sight and hearing are inherent in your body.

The matter is so serious that it behooves us to make it still plainer. Faith is the yielding of the man to the influence of God. It is not situated in the feelings or in the intellect, but principally in the will. Now, the will is the one most distinctly human part of a man. It is an imperial fragment of God, endowed, as God is endowed, with absolute self-mastery. It is the only thing in us that can

tard seed," etc. When the father of the boy afflicted with a dumb spirit prayed: "Lord, I believe; help Thou my unbelief," no attention was paid apparently to his *request*, but the Master acted upon his *declaration*.

DEFINITIONS

resist God; He may change our feelings or disorder our brain, but He will never lay finger of compulsion on the will. Looking at the wills of men we can echo the Psalmist, "I said, ye are gods." It is this that makes us precious in His sight above all His other creatures; for it is by virtue of this we are called "the sons of God." Without it we would be only God's machines acting like engines, or God's beasts acting from instinct. The appeal of the Father is not to our feelings, nor our understandings, but always to our will; "Whosoever will, let him come."[1] Therefore it is for acts of the will alone that we are responsible. We cannot control our feelings or opinions, except very indirectly, but we can do exactly as we please with our wills.

Thus it is that because faith is of the will, it is the fatal element. "Without faith it is impossible to please God."[2] We are told by the departing Jesus that those who have faith shall be saved, and those who have it not shall be damned.[3] "Through faith," says Paul, "we are saved,"[4] and we are "justified by faith."[5] So, by instances that the reader's memory can multiply by the score, faith is insisted upon as the one great essential saving

[1] Rev. xxii. 17.
[2] Heb. xi. 6.
[3] Mark xvi. 16.
[4] Eph. ii. 8.
[5] Rom. v. 1.

act of the human spirit. All things else God will give us; not this. Jesus Christ is called our peace, our justification, our sanctification, and all our other blessings; He is not called our faith. Faith is distinctly, purely ours. Why? Simply because it is the *willingness* of the man to receive the influence of God; it is man's *consent* to God's work in him; it is man's *coöperation* with the immanent Spirit's *operation* in him. To go back to our old terms, religion being the personal influence of God, faith is the man's allowing that influence to work in him.

When we come to examine the Scripture usages of faith we shall, however, find the word employed with a variety of shades of meaning; but they are all easily traceable by common sense and dignified laws of interpretation to the one meaning insisted upon above as the main signification. Every word, and especially a word of spiritual import, branches off into many secondary meanings according as the different parts of its significance are respectively to be emphasized.[1]

When it is said that faith is of the will alone

---

[1] Thus the word "see" means to behold with the eye; but, again, with the mind's eye, that is, to understand; and again, to follow with the attention, being thus used in Shakespeare; and again, to visit, as "to see a friend"; and again to experience, as "to see military service"; and again to accompany, as "to see one aboard the cars"; and again, to help, as "to see him through"; and again, to take care of, as in Chaucer, "God see you"; and again, when the word descends to colloquialisms, to find out, as "I will see if this has been done"; or, in gambling, to

DEFINITIONS

it is not meant there is no intellectual element in it; for man's being is not put up in separate sections, each distinct from the others, but will, intellect, and feeling are interwoven. Therefore we sometimes find the intellectual phase emphasized, and faith is used in the sense of accepting Christ and His Gospel as true. For certainly we cannot be influenced by any man or thing except we consider them to be realities; none is affected by an idle tale. Some there be who take evil advantage of this statement, saying: "I am not convinced of the historical verity of the account of Jesus in the gospels; hence I am excusable for having no faith." But this is making the intellectual side the only side of faith; whereas the most important side is the will side. Such a person, even doubtful of the Gospel's accuracy, certainly admits in himself a sense of right and wrong, a feeling of Ought; and this is the voice of God in all souls, though it is more or less covered with human imperfection. Now let him open his heart to as much of God as he *does* believe in, this conscience within him, and follow that; let him consecrate himself always to obey the highest, noblest impulses and to renounce

meet and accept a bet; and so forth. But all of these senses in which the word is used are easily traceable to the one original sense of being aware of an object by the eye. In like manner the diverging significations of faith are manifest offspring of the one parent signification, that is, the opening of the soul to the influence of God.

the wrong and base, and so doing he will surely be led to the perception of the grace and beauty of the perfect face of God in Christ Jesus; thus "the Father draws him to Christ."[1] The intellect is a slippery and easily confused thing, ethically; it acts truly only when clarified by a firm will obeying the noblest convictions. Thus Christ: "If any man do His will, he shall know the doctrine."[2] Some others unduly emphasize the sentimental side of faith, making it a matter of feeling; and as feelings come and go like the wind so they helplessly rejoice if they feel confidence and mourn if they feel it not. But it is wrong to put feeling, one of the maids of honor, upon the throne of will, the king; from such usurpation always results anarchy. Religion is not a matter of temperament, else certainly God would have made all men alike in this respect; and because He made all kinds of dispositions, grave and gay, quiet and energetic, visionary and pragmatic, credulous and skeptical, enthusiastic and conservative, it is shown that He intended one kind as well as another to have faith with ease. So among Christ's apostles were impulsive Peter and doubting Thomas, childlike Nathaniel and speculative Philip, sensitive John and practical James. It is *not* harder for

[1] John vi. 44. [2] John vii. 17.

DEFINITIONS

some dispositions to be Christian than for others; it is a reflection upon our Maker's justice to say so. It is not harder for one man to open his heart to God than it is for another; but it certainly seems to be when we conceive of religion as a set of *rules* or a mere *scheme of dogma*, to be obeyed in the one case, to be mentally assented to in the other. But religion being a divine influence of a Spirit immanent in us and around us, it mixes as well with one sort of constitution and frame of mind as with another.

Faith being the degree to which we open to God's influence, it is made the *measure* of His work in us. Thus Jesus in His miracles often said: "According to your faith be it unto you," or some such phrase.[1] Peter, with his whole being alive to Christ's influence, walked on the waves, but as doubt closed the door of his soul the power of God left him, and he sank.[2] Of the ruler, Jesus said He had not found so great faith as his in Israel, for that man was singularly frank and sincere in his taking as a matter of course the divine power of the Master.[3] Faith is the gauge of development, we proceed "from faith to faith,"[4] growing just as we admit Christ's influence fully into our lives.

[1] Matt. ix. 29, etc.
[2] Matt. xiv. 29.
[3] Matt. viii. 10.
[4] Rom. i. 17.

Take now a few passages of Scripture that bring out the varying shades of this one thought. "Justification by faith," the warcry of the Reformation, means not justification by mentally assenting to a scheme of salvation, but made to be just persons because we are willing to receive God's Spirit into ourselves and coöperate with Him. "The just shall live by faith"[1]—that is, not by trying to obey a list of rules in the law, but by receiving God. It is this that makes life in us; for we get eternal life not by our acts, but by taking into our souls the bread of life. So Jesus: "He that believeth on Me shall never thirst,"[2] and, "He that believeth on Me hath everlasting life."[3] He uses "believing on Him" and "eating the bread or drinking the water of life" interchangeably in the sixth chapter of John. Paul prays for the Ephesians "that Christ may dwell in their hearts by faith";[4] faith is that which admits and keeps Him there. Christ speaks of Himself as the world's light; it was the condemnation of men, not that they had sinned, but that, when light came, they chose rather darkness;[5] and speaking of men's receiving this light and walking in it, He uses faith (belief) as the term, thus, "I am come a light

[1] Rom. i. 17.
[2] John iv. 14.
[3] John vi. 47.
[4] Eph. iii. 17.
[5] John iii. 19.

DEFINITIONS

into the world, that whosoever believeth on Me should not abide in darkness."[1]

That faith is not our assent to a proclaimed "plan of salvation," but is the reception of the influence of a living, present, risen Lord, who as a Spirit is ever with us, is plain from the fact that faith is rarely linked to the death, but almost always to the resurrection of Christ, or to Christ Himself as an existing personage.[2] The apostles went not forth urging men to believe in the efficacy of Christ's death, so much as to believe in Christ "who is risen."[3] They exhort all to "believe on the Lord Jesus Christ,"[4] and speak of "faith toward our Lord,"[5] "faith in the Son of God,"[6] using the term in precisely the same phase of meaning that Christ Himself used it when He so often said, "Believe Me," "He that believeth on Me," etc.[7] Thus the Gospel *after* Jesus' death was the same Gospel He preached—to wit, faith in a living, present God in Christ. "If Christ be not risen," exclaimed Paul, "your faith is vain, our preaching is vain; ye are yet in your sins";[8] but according to the Latin theology, our salvation hinged upon the dead Christ;

---

[1] John xii. 46. Belief and faith are the same in the original.
[2] Acts xx. 21; xvi. 31; xix. 4; Rom. iv. 24; Heb. xi. 6, etc.
[3] Rom. iv. 24. Acts v. 30-31.　[6] Gal. ii. 20.
[4] Acts xvi. 31.　[7] John vi. 47, etc.
[5] Acts xx. 21.　[8] 1 Cor. xv. 17.

that it was that made us not "yet in sins."

The true meaning of faith further appears where the author of the Epistle to the Hebrews says that preaching did some persons no good, "not being mixed with faith,"[1] as though faith alone gave the ideas of the Gospel regenerative power. Sometimes we hear a phrase nowadays like "appropriating faith," and are told that we must not only believe in Christ, but appropriate Him. This is feeling after the truth; although, once we correctly apprehend what religion is, we see there is no other kind of faith, in a Scriptural sense, but the appropriating kind.

That faith is the receiving, as grace is the giving forth, of God's influence is perceived from frequent texts that compare and contrast the two. Paul beautifully and accurately defines the respective terms when he writes, "By grace ye are saved through faith";[2] God's influence saves us out of a life of sin, and our faith is that which admits this power. Again he states, "We have access by faith into this grace wherein we stand";[3] through faith we come into the play of God's regenerating force. He puts the true Christian theory when he says concisely, "Being justified freely by His grace, through the re-

---

[1] Heb. iv. 2.   [2] Eph. ii. 8.   [3] Rom. v 2.

DEFINITIONS

demption which is in Christ Jesus . . . through faith in His blood."[1] That is to say, grace or God's immanent power is what saves us; the atonement is the tangible symbol and condition of that power; and it all comes to us by our admission of its influence into us by faith.

We pass next to Righteousness, the effect of Grace shining into us through the door of Faith. It has been a standing wonder to many why Paul seemed so jealous of any morality that was not of faith. The vehemence of his argument against "the righteousness which is of the law" has swung many minds, insecurely anchored in the truth, loose from their moorings. Antinomianism, or that doctrine which holds that it makes no difference how we act, just so we have faith, has stained the history of the church in all ages with its inevitable filth. Even those who would not admit themselves partakers of this heresy have considered faith as somehow an equivalent for good works, a substitute for them in a measure. Now, we perceive the root of this misconception in the same old notion of salvation as a plan, a plan for saving men into another country called heaven. Having this false subsumption in our minds, when we read Paul's writings about the two

[1] Rom. iii. 24.

kinds of righteousness, of faith and of law, and about imputed righteousness and the like, we are kept from antinomianism *only* by the sound and ineradicable repugnance to sin in our instincts; we have to close the Book and say simply that it surely *seems* to put good deeds at a discount, but it cannot be that we understand it. Thus we lose the whole force of the beautiful and striking language of Paul and force ourselves to consider it a mystery. Let us now apply even also to this matter of imputed righteousness the touchstone of our conception of religion as God's influence. That influence is called grace, its acceptance is called faith. Let us, in this light, read Paul. There is but one who is good, even God; all good deeds must be His kind of deeds; anything not like Him is bad; therefore righteousness is simply doing as God's influence causes us to do. The natural order is: grace the sun, faith the tree assimilating the sun's light and heat, righteousness the fruit borne by the tree. In one sense righteousness is all-important, for the object of a tree is fruit. But there is something more important *to the tree*, if we may personify it, than fruit, and that is, that it be alive. Life is the best of all. And you may pin apples on a Christmas tree, but it is still dead. Life comes not by fruits; fruits come from life.

DEFINITIONS

The difficulty with the moralist is that he reverses the natural order. Good deeds are still good even in a bad man, but they never can make *him* good, never can impart to him that eternal life which naturally is prolific in good actions like the apple tree bears apples; he will with all his good deeds be but a Christmas tree, dazzling perhaps in his outward acts pinned on by much effort, but yet dead. God is a Grower, not an Artificer. His plan, as is manifest in nature, is to make things come by a natural development, not artificially. So He desires the human being to *grow* righteousness, not merely to do it. Thus Christ, "I am the vine, ye are the branches. Herein is My Father glorified, that ye bear much fruit."[1] Thus we see our Heavenly Father, not as an impatient schoolmaster or petulant captain, caring most of all that His rules be kept, and angry with us when they are not; but as a Father indeed whose rules are nothing in themselves but aids to growth, a Father whose chief care is that we develop in us that kind of life which is true joy and peace and liberty.

This is the key to Paul's reasoning. He will insist on apple-tree righteousness and warn us against Christmas-tree righteousness. He is talking to men who seek life by putting

[1] John xv. 5, 8.

on the effects of life to cover inward death. When he says, "A man is justified by faith without the deeds of the law,"[1] it is intellectual felony to say he means that a just man does not keep the law; but his point is that deeds of law have nothing to do with justifying him, making him just and good. *That* is accomplished by God's influence coming into him by faith. Unfortunately, doing good is the whole matter of religion in most people's minds, simply because by one's deeds his religion is tested; but in Paul's mind life was the whole matter, and doing good but the manifestation of that life; they see the shadow, Paul saw the substance. Paul was just as earnest as any one that Christians should do right. He execrates over and over again the works of evil and uncleanness, and exalts virtuous actions, but is careful to call the latter "fruit of the Spirit,"[2] lest any man be tempted to merely put them on and not grow them. As for absolute righteousness the Christian teaching is more severe and exacting than the old Mosaic law or any other system of morality ever known. In the Sermon on the Mount Christ unfolded the inner meaning of right doing and rolled back upon the conscience of the race even right thinking and desiring. He declared that "except

[1] Rom. iii. 28. [2] Gal. v. 22.

DEFINITIONS

your righteousness exceed that of the scribes and Pharisees ye shall in no case enter the kingdom of heaven."[1] Thus does the "imputed righteousness" exalt and not let down the standard of morality.

The righteousness of faith is higher and purer than the counterfeit kind made by rules, because it is "of God"—that is, it is the effect of God's working in us. As He is absolutely good, so a man can do good only as he is absorbed by the imitation and emulation of love into Him. "But now," says the great apostle, "the righteousness of God without the law is manifested"; a righteousness not formed by rules and statutes; "being witnessed by the law"; looking at those old commandments we see that the operation of the life of God in us results in true divine deeds; "even the righteousness of God"; not ours except as we do it having come under His influence; "which is by faith of Jesus Christ"; for it is as the Christ that God shows Himself to us, through Him God's influence reaches us; "unto all and upon all of them that believe";[2] for this supernal influence enters our life only as we allow it, agree with it, submit to its effect upon us, or, in other words, have faith.

Sometimes Paul calls this *imputed righteous-*

[1] Matt. v. 20.   [2] Rom. iii. 21, 22.

ness. With the old plan-salvation in their minds men supposed this meant that God by an odd sort of bookkeeping credited a man with all good deeds if he would assent to the truth of the scheme He had proposed. But the fact is that imputed righteousness comes to the same thing as the righteousness of God in us, when we conceive religion to be God's influence, not His artificial scheme. "Abraham believed God";[1] not merely had confidence that what God said was true, although this is of course a part of faith, but he was a God's-man; of all the world in those days he was the man who associated with God, walked with God, and consequently came under God's influence; "and it was counted unto him for righteousness"; this yielding to God's leadings was esteemed by God a righteousness just the same as if Abraham had been obeying a written law; "therefore it is of faith that it might be by grace"; showing that true righteousness was manifested by this man before ever Moses gave the law, a righteousness obtained by grace, the influence of God, received by him through faith. Thus was "Abraham the father of us all, *like unto* Him whom he believed, even God, who quickeneth the dead"; for as Abraham came to assim-

---

[1] What follows is an exposition of Rom. iii., taking these verses: 3, 16, 17, 22, 23, 24.

DEFINITIONS

ilate the character of God, so may we by the same faith receive this grace. And as Abraham had righteousness imputed to him, so may we all; "it is for us also, to whom it shall be imputed, if we believe on Him that raised up Jesus our Lord from the dead"; for we, by opening our hearts in faith to the influence of this living, risen Lord, also have God's righteousness shown in us. This is not *our* righteousness, is Paul's thought, but as it is produced *in us* by the *Spirit*, it is *called* ours, *imputed* to us, or reckoned as ours. Thus it is said to be imputed, not because it is Christ's righteousness *credited* to us in the divine accounts, but because it is a righteousness springing not from us properly, but from the *influence* of another, Christ, *in us*. It is properly our righteousness, and yet it is "the righteousness of God" imputed to us, or said to be ours, because if we had never been influenced by Him we would never have had it.

SUGGESTIONS

Unless we conceive religion to be the personal influence of God, the chief terms of religion are but algebraic signs or smooth coins.

No gift of God is of real value unless God goes with it.

Emptied of God a religious term fills with magic.

Grace is simply the shining of God's face into our hearts.

A good man is a force the heart intuitively recognizes; if we do not yield and become better we resist and become worse. In this sense Jesus made the Pharisees worse than they were before. In this sense the Gospel is the damnation of some, as well as the salvation of others.

Faith is principally a function of the will.

The intellectual and emotional sides of faith are secondary; the will side is primary.

Few errors have done more harm than the notion that religion is a matter of temperament.

Justification means not called just, but made just.

Grace is the sunshine, faith the open window.

The Gospel after Christ's death was the same as the Gospel before His death—the acceptance of His companionship.

Religion differs from morality as the apple tree differs from the Christmas tree; in one case the apples are grown, in the other they are stuck on.

CHAPTER VII

THE LIGHT FROM THE CROSS

The Crucifixion is not the Atonement; It is but a Part of the Atonement; and It, or any Scheme or Doctrine of It, is Impotent unless It be Vitalized and Completed by the Present Personal Influence of God

"God was in Christ, reconciling the world unto Himself."—PAUL, 2 Cor. v. 19.

"God is the perfect Poet,
Who, in His person, acts His own creations."
BROWNING, *Paracelsus.*

"I wiped away the weeds and foam,
I fetched my sea-born treasures home;
But the poor, unsightly, noisome things
Had left their beauty on the shore,
With the sun and the sand and the wild uproar."
EMERSON, *Each and All.*

"He folded his arms and began to cry—not aloud; he sobbed without making any sound. He could not pray; he had prayed day and night for so many months; and to-night he could not pray. If one might have gone up to him and touched him kindly; poor, ugly little thing! Perhaps his heart was almost broken. . . . There was a secret he had carried in his heart for a year. He had not dared to look at it; he had not whispered it to himself; but for a year he had carried it. 'I hate God!' he said. He had told it now!

"'I love Jesus Christ, but I hate God.'

"Then he got up and buttoned his old coat about him. He knew he was certainly lost now; he did not care. . . . But, oh! the loneliness, the agonized pain! for that night, and for nights and nights to come."—OLIVE SCHREINER, *Story of an African Farm*, p. 15.

CHAPTER VII

The question that may already have been intruding itself upon the mind of the reader who has followed thus far the development of this argument is, "What of the atonement? If the operation of religion be confined to the personal influence of the immanent Deity, how does the death of Christ take away our sins?"

At first thought, it would seem that one holding the view of religion here set forth would be committed to what is called "Bushnell's theory," or the "moral influence theory," of the atonement, which, as commonly understood, is that the sacrifice of Christ affects us only as it is a noble example. While the most of those who repudiate Bushnell's position, it would seem, fail to do justice to the depth of meaning he gives to the example of Christ, at the same time they should at least recognize a difference between a moral influence theory and a personal influence theory. The latter is the theory of this essay. It may not be too much to say that it is only when we conceive religion, in all its workings, to be the personal influence of the God-Spirit upon the man-spirit that we can get any rational and satisfactory view of the atonement at all.

In a proper conception of God's work among His sons to redeem them the cross of Christ has truly the central and chief place.

> "All the light of sacred history
> Gathers round its head sublime."

Jesus upon the tree of agony is the greatest vision mankind has ever seen. This is the point from which all Christianity radiates, the great fact about which all eternal hope clusters. When, therefore, we say that the resurrection and not the cross is the dominant doctrinal basis of a proper theology we do not mean to belittle the latter, but merely to say that the mind of the church through the Middle Ages and till now has held such a mechanical and artificial view of the atonement as negatives "the power of His resurrection." The rising of Jesus from the dead, His consequent immanence among men, His present work in purging away and bearing the sins of men by His own self, these true phases of atoning work have been sacrificed to the supposed logical necessities of the terms in which the death of Christ is spoken of in the Scriptures. Atonement is a larger term than

THE LIGHT FROM THE CROSS

the crucifixion; it is a continuous work being carried on now by the Christ-God; the scene upon Calvary was one of its great parts.

We may not say that the crucifixion has been unduly magnified by the Latin theology (for it cannot possibly be exalted too much), but it has been magnified in the wrong way. It has been hardened into a legal device, a statutory provision, which by its own force, aside from the present work of the Spirit, carries with it divine forgiveness, under certain stipulated conditions. As a mere logical syllogism the death of Jesus has never convinced the intelligence of mankind that it sufficed to take away sin. The church theologians themselves never professed that their theory was reasonable. It was a strange, magic, and unreasonable act of God, by which He strangely, magically, and unreasonably calls men non-sinners although they are sinners, and takes them to a heaven for which they are in no wise fit.

Actual forgiveness of sins because of the sacrifice of Christ, apart from His present resurrection power, maintained its hold on the mediæval mind for several reasons. First, because all the terms which refer to it in the Bible are drawn from Jewish ritualism, and thus are most easily fitted to a system of dogma whose main idea was to exalt and uphold the church. In its bald Judaistic phraseology, without attempting to bring forth the depths of its spiritual significance as is done by Paul, it best suited a Christian hierarchy. Again, because of the very inconclusiveness of the argument, that because the Son of God died once, therefore all believers on Him should escape punishment, because of the element of magic in this, it appealed to the superstitious debasement of reason and emphasis of credulity which characterized the Middle Ages. Again, as Christ's death was a bloody and fearful spectacle it attracted an age that was fierce, gloomy, and cruel, an age whose chief theologic excellence was the stress it laid upon the torture and woe consequent upon sin. It was a tragic age and a magic age, and took to a religion whose keynote was a magical tragedy.

Besides this, it may be that it was a part of the divine plan that under this gloomy view of the process of divine forgiveness mankind should lie while their spiritual powers were as yet feeble and while the public mind was still gross and materialistic. It was a part of the education of the race, which has always proceeded from symbol to reality, from form to truth, from husk to contents. Expecting a princely Messiah, sitting upon a golden

THE LIGHT FROM THE CROSS

throne, or leading the chosen people to a war of conquest over the Gentiles, the Jews kept alive the hope of His coming; yet when He came His real reign and methods seemed so weak and intangible that His people knew Him not. Even so, holding to the atonement in Christ as simply a legal setting aside of the verdict against men by a divine substitute paying the full blood price, the Latin church preserved the idea of atonement until men should become able to see through this figure and symbol the sublime reality, how the Christ-Spirit now does actually purge sins. And as the Jews in Jesus' day thought that the mild Galilean blasphemed when He pretended to be that glorious Messiah of whom the prophets had spoken, so now any one who attempts to abate one jot or tittle from the legalistic, artificial view of the atonement, and to show that the reality is a present and spiritual fact, instead of a past and ritualistic fact, must be prepared to incur the wrath of some of those who are zealous for the supposed "faith of our fathers."

The two views of the atonement commonly held by the church, and taught to-day, are what are called the substitutional and the governmental theories. It is not the purpose of this writing to examine these views in detail, nor to undertake to refute the arguments by which they are commonly supported. Indeed, they are both right as Judaistic or controversial views, but as commonly understood they are not Christian. We do not deny their reasonings, nor deny that those reasonings bring properly their conclusions; but we simply set aside their whole point of view, and insist that they have failed to rise above the level of Judaistic thought. As a substitute Christ does bear our sins upon His own body; as a dying Son He does vindicate the unbending morality of God, but not in the way usually held. We are not saved as the conclusion of a syllogism of which Christ's death and man's sin are the premises. We are not saved as a necessary entry on the divine court records made there, because we, by an act called belief, are credited with the full merits of Jesus' blood. These bare and lifeless statements leave out the very force that makes the atonement atone—namely, "the power of His resurrection." A present, spiritual Saviour alone can give these propositions life, a Saviour who bears with Him in His present work all the equipment of His great sacrifice.

When we come to put the knife of common sense and sane biblical interpretation into these theories, to divide the true from the false, we find precisely the same *kind* of a

THE LIGHT FROM THE CROSS

mistake here that we found in the common religious notions to which allusion has been made in former chapters. We discover a persistent taking of the lower instead of the upper thought, a perception of the material and a missing of the spiritual meaning. In fact, it is the old enemy of the higher life, materialism, that has wrought as evil effects upon theology as upon philosophy. Materialism, a lack of spiritual perception, slew Christ; it has never failed to destroy the quality of the painter's and of the sculptor's work; it corrupts literature; it debases politics; it prostitutes science to be the cover and concealment instead of the revelation of God; and we need not wonder that it has transformed the warm and breathing theology of Paul and the early Greek fathers into the symmetrical and dead statues of Augustine and Calvin. It is not strange that an automatic and spiritless atonement scheme is held by those who suppose salvation to be merely a saving of men from punishment, instead of a transformation of their characters from sinfulness to holiness; who conceive the object of the Saviour to be to get men into a heaven-place, instead of getting them into a heaven-condition; who imagine religion to be a plan instead of a power of growth. The crude types of Jewish ritualism were built into a logical system by the Latin mind; Oriental imagery became Latin dogma; the typical "shadows of things to come," were hardened into doctrinal stones.

Let us now proceed to examine how the hypothesis, that religion is the personal influence of God, gives clearness and beauty, coherency and reasonableness, to the atonement in Christ. The atoning death of Jesus is alluded to by the sacred writers in peculiar terms that do not at all, at first glance, seem to conform to the notion that its effect lies entirely within the channel of personal influence. These terms are drawn from the Jewish sacrificial rites, and have about them the very air of a contrivance. Are we to brush them aside as mere symbols, and are we to say, as many in revolting against the churchly teaching have said, that they are but figures of speech, and that our Saviour's death was merely a sublime example for us to imitate in its spirit? By no means. While these terms are figures, yet they are divine figures, ordained and set forth of God in order to prepare those forms of thought in which the death of Jesus was to be rightly considered.

That death was the fulfillment of all types. First there was the Lamb type; He was "the Lamb of God,"[1] "the propitiation for our

[1] John i. 29.

THE LIGHT FROM THE CROSS

sins,"[1] "delivered for our offenses,"[2] etc. Again, He fulfilled the Priest type; all the order of priestly service was to prepare men's minds for the character of His atoning work; after Him should be no more priests, even as no more slain lambs upon the altar; He is the "one mediator between God and man,"[3] "a priest forever,"[4] etc. Again, He is said to take away our sins; "the blood of Jesus Christ cleanseth us from all sin,"[5] etc. He also is said to bear our sins, as the slain altar victim typically bore away the Jews' sins; "bore our sins in His own body on the tree,"[6] etc. He is further said to have bought us, redeemed us, or paid a price for us, by His death; for Peter says we are not bought by silver and gold, but by the precious blood of Christ, as of a Lamb without blemish.[7] Into one or another of these five forms all that is anywhere said in the New Testament concerning Christ's atoning work will fall.

Before taking up each of these figures, let us be reminded of the relation which the fulfillment of a type must bear to the type itself. We should bear in mind that the reality will be quite as unlike as it will be like the type. If it resembles the type completely, it will not

[1] 1 John ii. 2.
[2] Rom. iv. 25.
[3] 1 Tim. ii. 5.
[4] Heb. vii. 3.
[5] 1 John i. 7.
[6] 1 Pet. ii. 24.
[7] 1 Pet. i. 19.

be a fulfillment at all, but merely another, although a higher type. The fact, indeed, should resemble the symbol in form, but will differ in contents.

Now, we all know how perfectly Christ's death and ministry conformed to the method and plan of Jewish sacrifices. Wherein did it differ? In contents—as a man from a statue, as a flower from a picture, as an idea from a word. The arrangement or covenant by which God is to forgive men by Jesus Christ is thus plainly stated by the apostles to be a *new* covenant, one entirely different from the Mosaic covenant. For the author of the Epistle to the Hebrews says that the sacrifices and altar ceremonies of the old régime were "the example and shadow of heavenly things; but now, hath Christ become the mediator of a *better* covenant."[1] How is the new better than the old? It is in that the Jews under the old sacrifices knew not why they were forgiven, except that it was the promise of God. The sole merits in Jewish sacrifice were obedience and faith. It was a locked mystery. But the new covenant is an unlocked mystery. Paul says he is commissioned to declare this secret openly to the Gentiles. In fact, the word "mystery," in the usage of the apostle's time, meant just the opposite from what it

[1] Heb. viii. 6.

THE LIGHT FROM THE CROSS

commonly means now; for to us it means something hidden, but in apostolic usage it signified something *hitherto concealed* but *now* disclosed and made plain. Thus Paul writes that he is a minister of God to declare "the mystery which hath been hid from ages, but *now is made manifest* to His saints."[1]

Taking a general view of the whole work of Christ's atonement, the main thought in it all is that of sacrifice. This is also the dominant idea in the Mosaic ceremonies. But the latter had to do with only the sacrifices of "bulls and goats, by which it is not possible to take away sins"[2]—that is to say, sacrifice, in itself, is of no avail. ("Go ye and learn what this meaneth," said Christ; "I will have mercy and not sacrifice."[3]) Thus any view of the atonement which makes God to forgive men because the sacrifice of Christ in

---

[1] Col. i. 26. The word mystery is carried bodily over from the Greek *musterion*, which in classical usage means those religious rites and knowledge, hidden to the outer world, but revealed to the initiated. Thus the Christian is as one joining a secret society; to the world all is sign and symbol, but to him all is, or ought to be, plain. Thus Paul: "I would *not* that ye be *ignorant* of this mystery," Rom. xi. 25; "Behold, I *shew* you a mystery," 1 Cor. xv. 51; "(God) having *made known* unto me the mystery," Eph. i. 9; "By revelation He *made known* unto me the mystery," Eph. iii. 3; "When ye read, *ye* may understand my knowledge of the mystery," Eph. iii. 4: "God .... would *make known*—the riches—of this mystery among the *Gentiles*, which is, Christ in (or among) you." Col. i. 27; "To the *full assurance of understanding*, to the acknowledgment (epignosis, accurate knowledge) of the mystery of God," Col. ii. 2; "Great is the mystery of godliness," in 1 Tim. iii 16 means, not that it is very deep and abstruse, but that it is glorious, and majestic, as the rest of the verse shows. Nowhere is mystery used to mean something not to be understood at all.

[2] Heb. x. 4. [3] Matt. ix. 13.

itself is sufficient as supplying a substitute for them, is merely a mended Judaistic scheme, with a better *sacrifice* but no better *covenant.* To hold that men are forgiven simply because Christ died, is to make the fulfillment exactly like the type, just as narrow and as imperfect. But the death of Jesus *differed in meaning* from the death of lambs, bulls, and goats in the old order quite as much as it *resembled them in form.* That difference was that His death was a *self-sacrifice.*

Sacrifice means nothing at all in itself, but only as a type; but self-sacrifice does mean something in itself. The slaying of innocent lambs was the symbol of the self-chosen death of the sinless, incarnate God. This is the precise argument of the author of the Epistle of the Hebrews:

"For it is not possible that the blood of the bulls and goats should take away sins.

"Wherefore when He cometh into this world, He saith, Sacrifice and offering Thou wouldst not, but a body Thou hast prepared Me:

"In burnt offerings and sacrifices for sins Thou hast had no pleasure.

"Then said I, Lo, *I come* to do Thy will, O God."[1]

Thus the main idea that will, almost by

[1] Heb. x. 4-7.

THE LIGHT FROM THE CROSS

itself alone, correct and make reasonable our notion of the atonement is this idea of self-sacrifice, found in Paul: "God was in Christ reconciling the world unto Himself."[1] As if by one stroke all the irreconcilable absurdities in the common view of the attitude of "the different actors" in the atonement disappear, when we remember that Christ's suffering was God's suffering. God and Christ are one, not two. It was "the fullness of the Godhead bodily"[2] that endured the agony of the crucifixion. This changes the scene at once from that of a merciless Justice expending its wrath upon an innocent victim, to one in which a dear and loving Father *Himself* comes to die for us. The aspect alters immediately from a Judge, driven by the limitations of His own statutes to extricate Himself from a dilemma by slaying His own Son, to a Creator who in the fullness of time and at the proper place in the development of mankind reveals Himself as redeeming men by participating in their struggles and sufferings.

The very innocence of the Christ-God gives His sufferings a redemptive force. There is nothing that redeems when the wicked suffer the effects of their deeds. It is only when the innocent are involved in the misery and destruction which sin brings, that sinners

[1] 2 Cor. v. 19.   [2] Col. ii. 9.

begin to see the "sinfulness of sin." Thus Jesus vindicates the morality of God; thus He maintains the righteousness of the divine government; not because God could not forgive until He had His "pound of flesh," not because some one must bear on himself all the tortures of hell which the divine statutes declare to be the prescribed penalty of sin, not because literally

> "At one deep draught of love
> He drank damnation dry,"

but because only by the self-sacrifice of the innocent and upright can there be brought home to the hearts of offenders the wretched and awful results of sin and rebellion. Instead, therefore, of holding that the death of Jesus "establishes the law"—that is, makes manifest the inflexible righteousness of the law—by supplying a victim who received all the penalty upon Himself, it is better to say that He "establishes the law" by revealing the evil results of sin upon One who was pure, harmless, and undefiled. As the law of Moses revealed sin by holding up the perfect code of morality before men, so the life and death of Jesus much more revealed sin by disclosing to mankind what sin will do to a holy Being. The Latin theology is ever concerned about penalties and punishment; the

THE LIGHT FROM THE CROSS

Pauline theology speaks constantly of sinfulness and the evil life.

It may be objected that this view obscures the personality of the Son as distinct from that of the Father; but the answer to this is, that whatever may have been the mysterious difference between those two persons, we are certainly warranted by Jesus' own words in thoroughly identifying them in the great work of redemption. In an effort to construct a logically operative atonement theory the two persons of the Godhead have been separated. The consequence has been a satisfaction to the reasoning processes of the mind, but a dissatisfaction to the heart. The moment we make two actors in the great atonement scene, in order to make it fit the precise terminology of Jewish ritualism, that moment we have sacrificed the reality to the type. The evasive tincture of Arianism is that which gives an unpleasant and unlovely hue to this great act. For God to visit our punishment upon another does not reveal Him as One "altogether lovely"; but for God incarnate in the Eternal Son to take our sin upon Himself—this has the pathetic touch of love. To suppose God to be compelled by a something called Justice to submit His Son to the death of the cross, does not give a very high idea of justice, but gives to justice a cruel and narrow meaning, and exalts it, as an attribute of God, above and beyond God Himself. But for God to be so full of the essential element of justice that He is not willing for His children to struggle on hopelessly in the losing battle against sin, but is moved to "take upon Himself the form of a servant" and come down to live, suffer, and die under the same load of sin's wretched consequences which weighs on men, this makes Christ's death to exemplify and exalt, not a stern Justice superior to God Himself, but a Just God in whom Justice, Love, and Mercy are as if different gleams from various facets of the same jewel.

The preparatory and symbolic truth, therefore, of the Mosaic ritualism was that salvation was to be by sacrifice; the "new and better covenant" of the real atonement was that salvation is by self-sacrifice. Thus is the reality like, yet unlike, the symbol. And, indeed, self-sacrifice is the law of any kind of salvation among sentient spirits. The enemies of Jesus told the truth when they taunted Him as He hung upon the cross, saying, "He saved others; Himself He cannot save." We see that of course He could not. It becomes apparent that as no man can save another, in any small degree, and save himself, too, so even the Almighty could not (the words are used reverentially and with a view only to

THE LIGHT FROM THE CROSS

their grammatical significance) save men and save Himself also. The deplorable state of mankind called for so priceless a ransom that humanity could not furnish it; sacrifice, the greatest men could offer, was too small to avail; nothing but a divine self-sacrifice could meet the requirements.

This spirit of self-sacrifice is to come also upon us; we are also to give ourselves for a lost world. This thought is frequently found in the New Testament. If the atonement be merely a device, such a thought would be presumption, if not blasphemy. But when we understand the death upon the cross to be a sublime revelation of God, and not merely a divine piece of machinery, we see how we can give ourselves for those about us, even as He, the All-Father, gave Himself for "the sins of the whole world." How can the old mechanical idea of Christ's atoning death fit such a passage as this? "As Thou hast sent Me into the world," said Jesus, "even so have I also sent them into the world."[1] Thus He spoke in His last great prayer. Again, after His resurrection, He met with His disciples and once more declared, "As the Father hath sent Me, *even so* send I you."[2] Paul also speaks of "the fellowship of His

[1] John xvii. 18. [2] John xx. 21.

sufferings"; [1] and in another place writes that he endures all afflictions "for the elect's sake." [2] He even uses this remarkable language: "I rejoice in my sufferings for you, and fill up that which is behind of the afflictions of Christ in my flesh for His body's sake, which is the church." [3] He goes in fact to the extreme length of saying that he could wish himself accursed from Christ for his fellow-countrymen's sake. [4] The atonement has, therefore, for its great underlying law of power, that through it God's influence, as a spirit of self-sacrifice, enters the world. This is the dynamics of Christ's death.

This, however, is not all of this atonement. It is not merely a display of divine love that is to influence us by its example to go and do likewise. It is not a mere theatric exhibition. It also contains within itself such a revelation of God as actually purges our sins when His Spirit comes in upon us. If it had been *only* an exhibition, it would not have needed the system of Judaism to prepare for it. But that system, by its types, supplies us with the proper full conception of the bearings of this great work.

Let us now take up these various Mosaic symbols, and see how they, when taken in

[1] Phil. iii. 10. See also 2 Cor. iv. 10.
[2] 2 Tim. ii. 10.   [3] Col. i. 24.   [4] Rom. ix. 3.

THE LIGHT FROM THE CROSS

connection with the fundamental idea that religion is the personal influence of God, make plain the atonement. And first, the Lamb type. The slaying of a lamb was a prominent feature of Jewish sacrifices, and Christ is called "the Lamb of God." It was the blood of this lamb that was the essential thing. "Without shedding of blood is no remission."[1] Blood was sacred. No man must eat it; even a stranger eating it must be put to death; it must be poured out unto the Lord.[2] Why was this? The Jew never knew. All that he could understand was that it was God's ordinance. God might have forgiven His people (perhaps he thought) some other way; but for some unknown reason He prescribed this way, and without sacrificing life none need expect pardon. Now, the death of Jesus, the Lamb of God, elevated the old sacrificial language into a wonderful luminous newness of meaning. He came to fulfill, to fill to the full, the law and the prophets. *Now* we see what the Jews never saw. The dying Lamb saves because without giving life there is no saving life. When Jesus by His death showed the reality, of which the altar was the symbol, He showed it as resembling and yet differing from the type. It resembled it because His sacrifice was a blood-shedding, a

[1] Heb. ix. 22. [2] Deut. xii. 23. Lev. xvii. 10 14.

life-giving; it differed from the type in that His sacrifice was a self-sacrifice. The forms of both the type and the reality were the same; the spiritual contents were not the same.

Thus we perceive how it is that the blood makes our peace with God. Christ atones, makes God and man "at one," not because He pays the fixed price for sin, but because in Him God enters sympathetically into the world's struggle. We must not put the hard, commercial aspect upon this matter. We cannot confine God's majestic workings down to our customs of bargain and sale, nor to the makeshift something we call justice in our courts. Who shall say that sins are charged upon the books and Christ's blood credited; or that, unless the statutory provision of death for sin be carried out, God refuses to be pacified? What pitiful logic-machinery this, from which to grind out salvation! The Jew saw the spilt blood on the altar, but he knew not why it "propitiated" God; he only knew it was God's command. But Christ made known this mystery that had been hidden in all altars through the ages, by showing that the shed blood was the sacrificed life of the noble, the high, the potent, and the pure to save the mean, low, weak, and degraded; even, indeed, God Himself suffers in Christ for the sake of the men who pierce Him.

THE LIGHT FROM THE CROSS

It is the law of life that sinners come to sorrow and the upright to peace. Now this naturally estranges the two classes. If they are to be "at oned," brought into unity again, it can only be either in the devil's way of giving peace to sinners that they may enjoy it with the righteous, or in God's way of the righteous stooping down to take upon themselves the sorrows of sin, thus in helpfulness lifting the sinners to a better life. God represents all that is holy and pure; mankind's story has been black; the natural tendency would therefore be for God and mankind steadily to drift apart; the atonement therefore is made when Christ, the God incarnate, stoops to take on His own shoulders our stripes, to pour out His own blood under sinful persecutors.

One great trouble with the church to-day is that it fails to seize this spirit of the atonement. Regarding it in the old, hard, commercial way as a stipulated price paid for sin, the church-member considers, that having accepted this agreement, and having by belief and repentance appropriated it, now therefore he is entitled to its benefits, a peaceful and happy life.

This separates him from sinners. They must suffer on; he is to live in peace. Thus there is a great gulf fixed between them.

Thus, in a way so subtle and profound that they knew it not, the hard, commercial view of Christ's atonement was the underlying cause of that spirit of segregation which in Romanism developed into monasticism and in Protestantism was manifested as Puritanism. This view of the atonement tended to estrange the church from the world; it did not "at one" in social life at all. It did not, and does not, break down the "middle wall of partition" between the elect and the unregenerated, but it strengthened that wall. But the atonement conceived of as a divine self-giving is permeating more and more in these days the mind of the church, and in Protestant missions to heathen lands, in social reforms, in so-called "applied Christianity," and in many kindred ways it is reconciling the world and the church.

In fine, we may say that the secret of "the blood" is that it signifies the bringing together the holy and the sinful by means of the former voluntarily participating in the sufferings of the latter. Thus the empty, ceremonial *formula* of sacrifice is crowded full of the glorious *contents* of self-sacrifice. For us to hold that Jesus' death in some way, by some strange law of the divine court-room, removes from us the necessity of suffering penalty of our sin, is to go back to Judaism; that is pre-

THE LIGHT FROM THE CROSS

cisely all they could see in the death of the sacrificial lamb. This is to "fall from grace,"[1] to retreat from the light of the Gospel to ceremonial darkness. But to apprehend that, above and beyond all question of penalty, Jesus' death reveals to us a God participating in our struggle with and suffering by sin; this gives us the inward power to overcome sin, to purge our lives of its hateful virus, and to rise by the assistance of the ever-present Atoner and Helper into newness of life. Such is the meaning of the Blood.

But God in Christ fulfilled the Priest type as well as the Lamb or Blood type. He was at once the revelation of the divine meaning of both priesthood and sacrifice. He is not our High Priest for the sole reason that He "ever liveth to make intercession" for us. Never should we allow the force of an illustration to carry us away from a fact. The fact is that He is very God, the embodied representative to us of God; that He is called a "priest forever" is therefore but a shade of meaning of His godly character, which He

---

[1] Gal. v. 4: "Christ is become of no effect unto you, whosoever are justified by the law; ye are fallen from grace." Thus we see that by "falling from grace," in Scriptural usage, is not meant "backsliding" from grace into the world, but "backsliding" from a *true* and *spiritual* conception of Christ's work to a *Jewish* and *legal* conception of it; which is exactly what is done by the Latin theology.

intends to reveal to us.[1] As Christ surprised the waiting world by disclosing that the shed blood which availed was His own blood, the lamb of God's choosing was God Himself incarnate, so He unfolds to us that God is His own priest. In other words, the office of the priesthood was made, just as the custom of shedding blood was instituted, to prepare our minds for a phase of God's character as it was to appear in Jesus. Above all things, let us think not of Christ as a priest in such a way as to make God's nature farther removed from us, approachable not directly, but only through a mediator, but think of His priestly function as drawing God's character closer to us, bringing God and man together.

The essential element of a priest's office is that he brings God and man together, and is thus called a daysman, mediator, go-between, and the like. The atonement gives us the priestly view of God's character in Christ in that it exhibits Him as thoroughly sharing our life. How the priest redeemed the people from sin by sprinkling them with blood, or by other rites, the Jew never knew; it was a locked symbol; he only knew it was God's command. If we say that we can only *guess* why God pardons us for His Son's prayers'

---

[1] Heb. vii. 17. In Heb. iii. 1, Christ is called "the Apostle and High Priest of our profession." He is not *literally* one, any more than He is literally the other.

THE LIGHT FROM THE CROSS

sake, we fall back to the old legal darkness. It is not Gospel intelligence to hold that God only forgives us "for Christ's sake" because that is His promise. Reason asks at once why God could not simply forgive us directly; why this device of a go-between? But when we remember that "God was in Christ," we see that the days-man is God Himself. It was this method He took of giving humanity courage to approach Him. And why this method? Again we take the idea of religion as God's personal influence to make this plain.

For, as to personal influence, you have noticed that association with a very pure, noble nature is not attractive to base men. By this their own vileness only stands out the clearer. The whiteness of the good man shows them their own blackness. So it was with Peter; when the divinity of our Lord burst in on his mind, he fell down, crying, "Depart from me, for I am an evil man, O Lord!"[1] Knowing one to be holy, evil persons shun him. And this is why, although all races have had the idea of God, none of them have ever dared conceive of Him as directly living within them.[2] Knowing themselves

[1] Luke v. 8.
[2] It was the glorious news of the Gospel, on the contrary, that "the kingdom of heaven is within you." Luke xvii. 21. The reader will note that the marginal reading, in his New Testament, of this passage is, "among you," instead of "within you." Meyer, the great exegete, translates the word *Entos humon* (within you), thus: "*Intra vos*, in your circle, in the midst of you." He adds,

corrupt, the farther off they could push God the better they would feel. Hence they made idols, selected priests and days-men, some sort of mediator being desired to propitiate this flawless Being it troubled them to think on. Into this kind of savagery Christianity sank in the dark ages, losing the thought of the spiritual immanence of God, and putting Him afar off, connecting themselves with Him by a procession of priests, saints, rites, and the Virgin. The ideal of purity and holiness and absolute right was in men all the while, but it only tormented them. It was as a law, terrifying them; as a God, awful in vengeance. Thus it is that God, *in any other form than as the Christ*, works by His influence only a consciousness of sin. Men fled their own exalted ideals, in despair of ever attaining them. And they knew nothing of God except as One willing for them to flee—in fact, probably intending Himself to damn them forever from Himself because they were so repugnant to His nature. And here comes in the priestly aspect of God in Christ. For as Christ He is just as spotlessly perfect, yet *not* willing for them to flee; on the contrary, coming to seek and save, sympathizing, anxious to help, will-

---

that there is no objection, on the score of grammar, to the translation "within you, within your souls"; but Jesus is talking to *Pharisees*, and the kingdom was certainly not in *their* souls. See Meyer's Commentary, in loc. cit.

THE LIGHT FROM THE CROSS

ing to pass by sins if they will but try to rise from them. Therefore Christ's priestliness consists in that He has suffused the idea of God's *holiness* with the idea of *sympathy*. We no longer dread this kind of God. "For we have not an High Priest which cannot be touched with the feeling of our infirmities; but was in all points tempted like as we are, yet without sin. Let us therefore come boldly to the throne of grace, that we may obtain mercy, and find grace to help in time of need."[1]

In Christ was shown that trait in the highest ideal of perfect character that men never dreamed of before, that by virtue of being the highest it stoops to aid the lowest. By participating in our agony God showed in Christ His approachableness, so that we that were *afar*, aliens and strangers, are made nigh by His blood.

We therefore see how it was necessary to the influence of God, if it was to lift the world, that He should show Himself to us as a Lamb—that is, the incarnation of the spirit of self-sacrifice—and also as a Priest—that is, disclosing to us the fact that absolute perfection of character (that is to say, God) is not a spirit of segregation nor of asceticism, but of thorough sympathy and helpfulness. With-

[1] Heb. iv. 15.

out these two notions of the divine character it could not influence us as it does.

We pass now to the third aspect which the Scriptures give the atonement—namely, that Christ by His death takes away our sins from us, His blood cleanses us from sin, we are washed in the blood, and the like, the substantial thought of all of which sayings is that somehow Jesus' death causes us who were sinful to be pure. The great difficulty in grasping this idea, the reason why many minds have refused to accept it, and have thought it to seem absurdly illogical and smacking of a mediæval piece of theologic machinery, is that the *penalty* of sin has been tacitly understood to be the main, if not the only thing removed by the atonement. This is a part of the old materialistic thought. The chief aim of redemption in that programme being to get man into a place called heaven after death, of course the principal requirement was to remove the obstacle which would prevent his entrance therein. By accepting Jesus as one's substitute all objection to one's citizenship in this New Jerusalem would be overcome. But, on the contrary, the penalty is a subsidiary matter, as also is the heaven-place after death; these are factors that follow as necessary consequences to the real, vital and actual work of redemption,

THE LIGHT FROM THE CROSS

which consists in transforming a man from a beastly creature into a son of God, renewing and sublimating his character. If therefore our main contention be correct, that the regeneration of the life, and not the removal of the penalty, is the end sought in salvation, it must follow that the death of Jesus must do more than pay the price that satisfies the divine statutes and counterbalances the debit of our transgressions; it must have in it some potency that shall actually transform man himself. How, then, is this done?

Sin's seat is in the consciousness. The genuine repentance for sin is not the fear of its penalty, but the grief for its degrading presence. The problem, therefore, is not to remove the penalty alone. If that be done without taking away sin's presence, it is more a curse than a blessing, for in the proper order of God present sin ought to feel an impending punishment; and a salvation which takes away the punishment without purifying the heart from that which deserves punishment would be an immoral salvation, a salvation indeed by the devil, not by Christ.

Jesus, therefore, died to remove sin from the consciousness of men. He was not manifested in order to show us how God manages affairs in the court-room of the heavenly assize, not to complete the body of divine legal lore, not to give coherency to some "system of theology"; but "ye know that He was manifested to take away our sins."[1] He came not to complete the logical syllogism by which sinners are to be reckoned non-sinners; He came that "He might destroy the works of the devil."[2] It is not alone the results of a low life He is to save us from; it is the low life itself He is to change into a higher; results are secondary. The glory of His work consists not in that those who believe on Him escape the penalty of sin; but, better than that, and broadly including that and swallowing it up, His glorious work is consummated in that "whosoever abideth in Him sinneth not."[3] "As many as received Him, to them gave He power to become the sons of God."[4]

To take away sins, therefore, in any true sense, Christ must needs operate upon our sinful past, not to minify it by giving us the idea that it is not so bad after all; not to evade it by assuring us that its punishment has been annulled; but by giving us a *new* consciousness unburdened with the past. One cannot escape from himself. He has been sinful. As long as he lives he must bear that record with him. Only death, or a cessation

---

[1] 1 John iii. 5.
[2] 1 John iii. 8.
[3] 1 John iii. 6.
[4] John i. 12.

THE LIGHT FROM THE CROSS

of consciousness can eliminate it. The only way to kill sin is to kill the man. It is bone of his bone. Consequently it is just this that the Saviour of man does for him. He destroys the old consciousness and gives a new one. This is the divine miracle in redemption.

To understand something of this, which is not after all so strange as it may seem, take a simple analogy. In common speech we often say, "I am a new man." Some important event happens in our life that seems to make the past slough off and to cause our life to emerge into a new sphere of experience, by which we enter into new sensations, views, hopes, and convictions, and by which our relation to all things seems changed. Crudely speaking, some such change occurs when after being long sick we regain health; thereafter our mind is so altered in its fundamental operations that we look back upon the morbid state in which we were of late as upon the state of another man.[1] So, also, it is with personal influence; when we come to know a good and noble man and to be with him, his feelings, views, and whole atmosphere are

---

[1] "Cleomenes, the son of Anaxandridas, being sick, his friends reproached him that he had humors and whimsies that were new and unaccustomed. 'I believe it,' said he, 'neither am I the same man now as when I am in health; being now another thing, my opinions and fancies are also other than they were before.'"—Plutarch's Apothegms of the Lacedæmonians.

subtly absorbed by us, and we are so changed into his likeness that we begin to recognize his attributes as our own; we look back upon our former life, before we knew him, as upon the life of another person. Particularly is this the case if we find out after a while some heroic and exalted deed our friend has done for us, the light of which irradiates over all his life and brings him nearer to us. Thus, in some such manner, does the personal influence of God operate upon us in the atoning death and present companionship of Christ.

Being brought to know God by receiving now His Spirit, we become changed; being aware that this Being, whom we know, has done so wondrous a deed for us as to suffer and die in order to reveal Himself to us, we are pricked to the heart and stirred up to new nobility. "Therefore," says Paul, "if any man be in Christ Jesus, he is a new creature; old things have passed away; behold, all things have become new."[1] Our former life, with its sins and all their future penalty of alienation from Him, is gone. The coming in of the divine Spirit has killed our old self; it has perished as a hateful memory, and "he that is dead [and only he] is freed from sin."[2] Henceforth "for me to live is Christ."[3]

This is the reality of which the purification

[1] 2 Cor. v. 17. [2] Rom. vi. 7. [3] Phil. i. 21.

THE LIGHT FROM THE CROSS

by blood at the Jewish altar was the symbol. The sprinkling of blood, or any other lustral rite, did not actually purge sins away; it only illustrated the way in which God would proceed in the actuality. The author of the Epistle to the Hebrews gives the law of real purification: "Worshipers once purged should have no more conscience of sins. But in those sacrifices, under the law, there was no purging, but a remembrance again made of sins every year. But we are sanctified through the offering of the body of Jesus Christ once for all."[1]

Now, when we imagine God merely reckons our sins to be no sins by a sort of legal fiction, and because of the satisfaction made to His sense of justice by the sacrifice of Christ, merely *calls* our sins removed and imputes unto us righteousness, we are setting aside the present work of the atoning Spirit, we are confining the whole matter to a mechanical performance, and we are but erecting a new system of Judaism, differing not one whit from the reasoning process of the old, although we put the Christ in the same place that the Jews put the lamb. Though we may name this system Christianity, it is no different from the Mosaic dispensation. It is the same arrangement and process, with a new sacri-

[1] Heb. x. 2, 3, 10.

fice; we simply substitute the divinely chosen victim on the altar. But we must remember that God did not say He would change merely the *sacrifice;* it was the whole old *covenant*, the whole arrangement and process, that He promised to *abolish* and to substitute a new one. "Behold, the days come, saith the Lord, when I will make a new covenant with the house of Israel; not according to the covenant that I made with their fathers; but this is the covenant I will make after those days, saith the Lord; *I will put My laws into their mind and write them in their hearts; and they shall all know Me, from the least to the greatest.*"[1] If this means anything at all, it means that the covenant in Christ signifies a taking away of sins not by any sort of ceremony, type, legal fiction, or logical process at all, but by a transformation of the human soul by the entrance in upon it of the divine soul, and the consequent alteration of the very consciousness of man so that God's laws should be ingrained in the mind and heart.

This important conclusion carries with it another and not less important discovery, and that is, that sin is taken away by the Lamb of God's sacrifice *only* as we become new creatures in Christ Jesus. To speak technically, regeneration and forgiveness are the same

[1] Heb. viii. 8-11.

THE LIGHT FROM THE CROSS

thing. We are forgiven only as we are regenerated. The act of forgiveness is not merely "an act of the divine mind," which we can know takes place only because God promises to forgive when we "repent and believe"; for that *kind* of an agreement or covenant between God and man—that is to say, the kind of covenant whereby God agrees to do a certain thing provided we do a certain other thing; God promises to forgive if we believe and repent—is done away with, being the temporary, typic, and formal kind of covenant He made with the Jews. We now have "a new and living way" of cleansing from sin, or forgiving; it is by the present immanent Christ-God entering the soul of man by His Spirit and actually removing the old consciousness with its sin stains and giving us a new life. *This* is the *Gospel;* the *other* is *Judaism.* This is Pauline; the other is Latin. This is the religion of the apostles and the religion of to-morrow; the other is the religion of the logic-mongers and the religion of yesterday.

Only as we are regenerated are our sins removed. The old ordinance with its fictions and forms is vanished; the reality is here. The difference is exhibited in the common misquoting of a certain text of Paul by the careless preacher; we have often heard it quoted that "we are justified freely by His grace through Jesus Christ, whom God hath set forth to be the propitiation through faith in His blood for the remission of sins that are past; that He might be just, and *the justifier of the ungodly.*"[1] A very crude mistake to be sure, for the passage ends thus, "the justifier of him that believeth in Jesus." And yet the very fact that the error is sometimes made, and the added fact that it seems, at first thought, to mean after all the same thing, show how subtly the Latin theology has corrupted the apostolic idea. For if the atonement is a mere plan, working without the present power of God's personal influence as a Spirit, there is nothing wrong with God's "justifying the ungodly"; but the real truth is that the ungodly are never justified except as they cease to be ungodly, and they are justified when they are in Christ simply because they do cease to be ungodly.

If any man presumes his sins to be gone, merely because he has accepted Jesus as his substitute, yet not having his nature changed by the personal influence of God, he is mistaken. His sins are not gone; their whole power and guilt remain upon him. The sacrifice of the Christ-Lamb is of no more virtue than that of the Mosaic lamb, when taken apart

[1] Rom. iii. 26.

from "the power of His resurrection"—that is, His present actual influence as a Spirit on the soul. Unless he be changed, or "converted," he is not forgiven; for "except ye be converted, ye cannot see the kingdom of God." To attempt to draw a distinction between the act of forgiveness on God's part, and of conversion on our part, is to put asunder what God hath joined together.

Notice how, in apostolic teaching, the washing away of sin is nearly always coupled with the creation of a new life. To the apostles' minds the new birth is itself the dropping away of the old sins, for our old sins only go with our old self. This is cleansing by the living Lamb who gave His life for us on Calvary that He might now daily give His life to us. Christ fills the old form to overflowing with life and power. Peter says Christ bare our sins on the tree "that we, being dead to sins, should live unto righteousness."[1] The passing of sin without the entrance of a new life is a purely intellectual fancy, and has no foundation in fact. "There is, therefore, now no condemnation to them which are in Christ Jesus," writes Paul, but straightway qualifies by adding "who walk not after the flesh, but after the Spirit."[2] We are freed "from sin and death," not by a fiction or the

[1] 1 Pet. ii. 24.   [2] Rom. viii. 1.

mere acceptance of a fact, but by "the *law of the spirit of life*"; and "if any man has not the *Spirit* of Christ, he is none of His."[1]

If all we have to do in order to get rid of sins is to accept and believe in the plan as it is formally declared, why not go on accepting and go on sinning? A great many doubtless so live. To them the Christ is but another Jewish lamb which merely "calls to remembrance" their sins and assures them of their escape from the penalty of them. With no life such as God's personal influence creates, they consider themselves "saved," because they accept the creed, acknowledge the syllogism, and make the oblatory prayer at due intervals. Paul had this very kind of people to contend with. Precisely the same dead Judaistic cast of thought about Christ faced him as now faces us. The sixth chapter of Romans is extremely timely and up to date. "What!" he exclaims, "shall we continue to sin because God promises to take them all away? God forbid! How shall we, who are *dead* to sin, live any longer therein?"[2] Thus he does not meet the argument of these mistaken persons, but he repudiates their *premises*, rejects their point of view, as much as to say that salvation is not so much making sinners secure of a future heaven as it is making sin-

---

[1] Rom. viii.   [2] Rom. vi. 1-2.

ners *cease* to be sinners. He uses another illustration: "What! then, shall we sin because we are not under the law, but under grace? God forbid! Know ye not that when ye were sinners ye were sin's servants and under sin's influence; but now, God be thanked! ye are under the righteous influence of God, freed from sin only as ye become servants of righteousness."[1] Still again he turns the subject to a third phase, comparing us to a woman formerly married to sin, but sin having died, now remarried to righteousness; and if she marry another man while the first husband lives, she is an adulteress, so that one claiming to be God's man and still living with sin is a spiritual adulteress.[2] Thus by these three examples, that of the dead come to life, that of a servant of one man transferred to another, and that of a woman set free by death from a husband, he makes clear to any one who will see, that the efficacy of Jesus' blood avails only those in whom His present Spirit works an utter severance of the new life from the former life.

The author of Hebrews says that "once purged from sin we should have no more conscience of sins"[3] in us. John echoes this, saying that we have confidence toward God because "our hearts condemn us not";[4] and

[1] Rom. vi. 15-22
[2] Rom. vii. 1-4.
[3] Heb. x. 2.
[4] 1 John iii. 21.

Paul, also, "The Spirit beareth witness with our spirit that we are the children of God."[1] Thus I do not merely blindly *believe* God *considers* me not a sinner, but I am *conscious* of not being a slave of sin. How this God's influence comes upon me and raises me up to be another man, transfiguring, as it were, my very self, Paul vividly thus sets forth: "I am dead to the law that I might live unto God. I am crucified with Christ, nevertheless I live; yet not I, but *Christ liveth in me;* and the life which I now live in the flesh I live by the faith of the Son of God, who loved me, and gave Himself for me."[2]

This may shed welcome light upon a certain dark passage of Scripture that has troubled many souls: "For if we sin willfully after that we have received the knowledge of the truth, there remaineth no more sacrifice for sins, but a certain fearful looking for of judgment and indignation."[3] For not a few have considered this to mean that if a truly converted man fall into sin he cannot again be forgiven, a meaning wholly repugnant to the general trend of all Christ's and the apostles' teaching. But the language of this text is significant of its true meaning. It is not said there remaineth no more *forgiveness*, but "no more *sacrifice* for sins." Now, we have

[1] Rom. viii. 16.   [2] Gal. ii. 19, 20.   [3] Heb. x. 26, 27.

THE LIGHT FROM THE CROSS

seen that one gets the benefit of Christ's sacrifice only by His changing of him into a new man; therefore one who goes on willfully sinning, yet claiming the merit of the atonement, is reminded that when he ceases to be a new creature, at that moment the sacrifice of Christ ceases to avail him. He is counting on the sacrifice covering his presumptuous sins, when "there remaineth no more sacrifice." For Jesus' sacrifice is of virtue to us, *not* merely as a part of a plan, but *only* as it changes our natures.

So, also, is it with the "sin against the Holy Ghost" that will never be forgiven in this world nor the next.[1] The Holy Spirit *is God, is Christ*, as immanent in the world and operative upon us. He alone can cleanse us from sin by enduing us with a new life. Hence, to sin against Him—that is, to close ourselves against His influence—is simply to reject the only thing in heaven or earth that can deliver us from sin. Thus this dictum about the unpardonable sin is reasonable when we accept the view of religion set forth in this essay. But if Christ atones for all sin by His death alone, without the added necessity of the personal influence of His Spirit on men's life, then it is unreasonable, artificial, and statutory. God's influence

[1] See Matt. xviii. 22, etc.

alone saves men. Of this influence the fact of His death in the incarnate Son is a necessary part, yet that historic death without His personal influence directly upon the life is valueless. It is only as a Spirit that He comes in contact with us to influence us personally. *Hence* it is that whosoever rejects that *personal* touch rejects the only thing that can save him. How *can* "the sin against the Holy Ghost" be forgiven when *forgiveness itself means* the entrance of that Spirit into the life?

And now we come to see *why* it is that the resurrection is the crowning theme of the Gospel, and why without the resurrection the atonement means nothing at all to us. For it is not the fact that Christ died, but the fact that *having died*, He now lives to *use* that death, that is our salvation. Unless He apply His blood, it is of no merit. We cannot get any benefit from His sacrifice except as receiving it at the hands of the living, risen, present Christ-Spirit. So, therefore, the apostles continually couple the death with the resurrection. As He died at the hands of sin, so let us crucify our old man with his lusts and lawlessness, put him to death as one of the survivors of the mob that slew our Lord, bury him by the similitude of baptism, and then let us rise in newness of life, even as the

THE LIGHT FROM THE CROSS

Saviour rose, viewing all our past career as an accursed thing; henceforth let us be filled with God, having eternal life, sitting in heaven. "Reckon yourselves dead to sin," cries Paul, "and alive unto God. They that are Christ's have crucified the flesh and its evil passions; let us now live and walk in a new atmosphere, even God. If the Spirit of the rising Jesus dwell in you, He shall also make quick and alive your mortal bodies."[1]

As our rising from the dead puts on us a celestial body, let us, also, risen from the death of our old selves, "put on the Lord Jesus."[2] He is to be our new garment; the old we have cast away. Now, one is not conscious of himself, he is conscious of his clothes; that is, he thinks of himself not as naked but as clothed. Even so we will no more consider our own weak personalities, but will present ourselves to ourselves as endued with God. The old appetencies may remain, evil tastes and habits may linger in the new creature; but I will not think of them as myself, "but sin that dwelleth in me,"[3] yet a sin impotent because of the Slayer of sin that rules me. It will take time and cultivation to be wholly absorbed into the Spirit's image; traces of sin's marks will

---

[1] Rom. vii. 2-13 and viii. 11.   [3] Rom. vii. 17.
[2] Gal. iii. 27 and Col. iii.

remain, evidences also of its power to tempt; but Christ is Master; day by day He will deliver me. John alludes to this dual consciousness: "If we say we have no sin, we deceive ourselves,"[1] he says in one place; and yet in another place: "Whosoever is born of God doth not commit sin; whoso commits sin is of the devil."[2] This is a contradiction, and we must remember that the Spirit that inspired the Scriptures inspired also its *contradictions*, and that in the form of two conflicting statements we often get a truer view of the real truth than could be presented in any other way. The point with John is that the overmastering consciousness is of myself as a sinless being like the God-Spirit I freely receive, but beneath ever remains the sub-consciousness of myself as a frail and erring man. The problem of life is more and more to lose the old in the fullness of the new: "*Now* are we the sons of God, and it doth not yet appear what we shall be, but we know that when He shall appear we shall be *like Him*."[3]

We pass now to consider the atonement as not only typified in the old forms as a cleansing, but as a transfer of our sins over upon God. "He bare our sins in His own body on the tree."[4] The scapegoat bore away into

---

[1] 1 John i. 8.
[2] 1 John iii. 9.
[3] 1 John iii. 2.
[4] 1 Pet. ii. 24.

THE LIGHT FROM THE CROSS

the wilderness the sins of the people.[1] But God in Christ does not bear our sins *just as* the scapegoat; that was a mere form. The goat did not really bear away the transgressions of the people, and they knew it to be only a shadow. But Christ bears our sins like the scapegoat in form, but *unlike* it because He *does really* take them on Himself. And only by keeping in mind that all Christ's life and death are explainable *only* by His still being present as an immanent Spirit can we understand the substance of which the old ceremony was a picture. We are not to understand Jesus' bearing our sins upon the cross as a fact, but as the introduction to a fact. We were not living then, and how could He bear our sins when as yet we were not born? Hence we see that this bearing of the evil consequences of the sins of those human beings in that age in which He lived in the body is to show us that He now and forever, "once for all," bears the sins of all men who will come to know Him as the immanent Spirit. What is it to bear sin? Evidently to take upon Himself the effect of sin. Now, that effect is its pernicious, ruinous influence upon our character, and He now as a helpful Spirit actually removes from us these effects. He does this by virtue of having suffered and

[1] Lev. xvi. 8-10.

died. As we see Him enduring all that sin can do to harm, we receive the idea of His sympathy and help in us. The struggles and temptations of sin, therefore, coming to us are met and swallowed up by the influence within us of this Man who "was tempted in all points like as we are."[1] Knowing Him, we walk daily with One who feels all our trials, equipped by His experience in the flesh to be the "Captain of our salvation."[2] Coming thus to Him in every hour of need, pouring all our woes into His ear, "casting all our cares upon Him who careth for us,"[3] fighting no more against sin, but simply passing the conflict over to Him, we know that He did not merely *once* bear the *penalty* of our evil, but that He does *now continually bear* all our present evils. "Surely He hath borne our griefs and carried our sorrows. He was wounded for our transgressions, He was bruised for our iniquities; the chastisement of our peace was upon Him, and with His stripes we are healed."[4]

Again, there is another phase of the atonement presented by the apostles. Jesus is said to be our Redeemer, by His blood to have bought us. Paul declares we are not our own but we are bought with a price;[5] Peter, that

---

[1] Heb. iv. 15.
[2] Heb. ii. 10.
[3] 1 Pet. v. 7.
[4] Isa. liii.
[5] 1 Cor. vi. 20.

THE LIGHT FROM THE CROSS

we were not purchased by silver and gold and such corruptible things, but by the priceless blood of Christ.[1] What is the meaning of this? Let us see. To buy a thing is to acquire ownership of it; thereafter we have a claim upon it as ours. Now, it is of course impossible to own a sentient spirit, endowed with a free will, as one would own a horse. How do you own your friend or lover or wife? Only in so far as you have claims upon them, claims of affection and loyalty. The Bible frequently uses the analogy of wife and husband to show the relation between God and His people.[2] Now, what sort of a price can a man pay for a true wife? There is but one price—love. This is the price God pays for us. It is said to be paid by Jesus' blood because God's pouring out His life in Christ's death was the profoundest and most moving spectacle and declaration of love; "greater love hath no man than this."[3] So great a love, manifested so feelingly, at once establishes an imperial claim upon us. Akin to Him by nature, we are proper subjects of His love; there is nothing contrary to nature in our union. Unworthy of Him by nature, we make His display of affection the more illustrious. That God, who as Christ commended His love to us by dying, yet lives not far from

[1] 1 Pet. i. 19.   [2] Jer. iii. 14, etc.   [3] John xv. 13.

any one of us, if haply we may feel for Him and find Him. His claim upon us is only a claim of love; He puts by His other claims. To the ownership of love there is but one crime, it is neglect and coldness; there is but one requital, it is to love in return. To grovel before Him as subjects before an Oriental monarch, to pay Him only outward, formal obeisance by church rites and reverence, to crucify ourselves in a desperate struggle to keep His laws, all without letting Him into our hearts, and to suppose that by these means we acknowledge His claim—this is to wound and pain Him. For what does love require but love again? And what does a yearning Father ask but affectionate trust? And of what value to such a Father are all moralities, reverences, and ceremonies except as indications of an inward joy in Him and a desire to please Him we love? Therefore, we conclude that Jesus did not buy us in the sense of one of the persons of the Trinity paying a blood price demanded by another person of the Trinity, but in this sense, that God was in Christ purchasing the love and confidence, the gratitude and trust of all humanity by revealing Himself as One altogether lovely, self-giving and beneficent.

We thus perceive that when we apprehend the atonement as the equipment of God's per-

THE LIGHT FROM THE CROSS

sonality so to present Himself to men as to save them, we have such a view of this great doctrine as reconciles all that is anywhere said of it in the Scriptures. Our God is no more a far-off, dreaded Deity. He is a self-sacrificing God, in Christ as the Lamb pouring out His blood and life for us; He is a priestly God, in Christ coming close to us that we may see His anxious face and feel His throbbing heart; He removes our sins, by the entrance of the Christ-Spirit into us, giving us a new consciousness of ourselves; He bears our sins, being as an immanent Christ-Spirit ever present to hear, to help, to uphold, and to strengthen, "with every temptation to provide a way of escape,"[1] with His grace to be all-sufficient for us in every trial; He is our Owner, not as one owns slaves and chattels, but our owner by the right and title of a matchless love that awakens a loyal response in every true man.

An objection that may be argued against this view of the atonement is that, after all, it makes Christ's death essentially theatrical; that is, it makes Him to die, not because He must pay the penalty of men's sins, but merely to show or to illustrate the character of God. But this objection probably arises from confusion of thought due to the strong

[1] 1 Cor. x. 13.

bias which the priestly terminology gives to the Lamb of God's sacrifice. Reduced to its simplest terms the objection amounts to this: if Christ's death did not satisfy divine justice, then He had no good reason to die. But it must not be forgotten that according to this personal influence theory, Jesus' death *did* exalt divine justice, and did it in the only way the inflexible law of sin's punishment can best be emphasized—that is, by the voluntary submission of the innocent to the consequences of sin. His death did pay our price, not the price needed to placate the resentment of Deity, to be sure, but the price of love which alone can purchase hearts. His death did provide us a substitute, not a substitute on Calvary alone, by which all sinners escape their penalty, but a continual, living substitute, also, for all men everywhere who will use Him. His death *was* absolutely necessary, not because Deity must be appeased, but because Deity *must*, in the fullness of time, thus disclose His true self to mankind.

Those terms which seem to imply the universal salvation of all men, good and bad, are simply inexplicable by the Latin theology. Christ is said to be "the propitiation not of our sins only, but also for the sins of the whole world."[1] Now, if all that was needed

[1] 1 John ii. 2.

THE LIGHT FROM THE CROSS

was to provide men a substitute in the divine court-room, why cannot all sinners as well as saints be saved? This sort of universalism was the legitimate offspring of the old theology. The only way to avoid it was to hold that God had foreordained certain elect souls for salvation and the rest for reprobation, or else to hold that while the merits of the atonement plan are indeed universal, yet it is so only to those persons who accept the stipulations that accompany it; both of which theories have powerfully dominated portions of the church. But how much more simple and Scriptural is the theory herein advanced— namely, that, *as a scheme*, Christ's death is of no avail at all to any one, but when the present, immanent Christ, as a Spirit, exercises His personal influence upon the life of any man, that influence saves him because of its character as shown forth in Christ's death. In other words, the crucifixion, as was said before, is but a part of the atonement; as a whole, the atonement includes Jesus' life, death, and *present personal influence*.

At last we see how it is "in Christ," or "for Christ's sake," that He forgives. To the Jew of old the sacrifice of the lamb stood for God's forgiveness only because the law of God so stated; he could only guess at the intent of the ordinance. Let us not, then, be mere ancient Jews, believing that God for some reason pardons us because of the perfect Lamb's death, but let us grasp the *purpose* of the death, the blessed argument it contains, as thus set forth by Paul: "He that spared not His own Son [spared not Himself], but delivered Him up for us all, how shall He not with Him also freely give us all things?"[1] Truly, in this act "God commendeth His love to us." We do not believe He forgives us simply because He promised to, and we are not simply "resting on the promises"; but because, if He is the kind of person who on the cross cried out, "Father, forgive them; they know not what they do," then that kind of a God would certainly receive and welcome a penitent sinner.

The value of the atonement, therefore, is the *revelation of the character* of God and of His disposition toward men. No longer must He be supposed a far-removed Conservator of the world, a distant Deity dwelling in unapproachable light; but He bends, He comes near, He enters into our affairs, incorporates His personality into our flesh and blood. Our great struggles with sin and circumstance, He is not indifferent to them. He makes them his own. Into the thick of men sighing for deliverance he plunges, and Himself

[1] Rom. viii. 32.

THE LIGHT FROM THE CROSS

assists them "with groanings that cannot be uttered." Their battle is His battle; their hope His hope. He will expose the blackness of sin as it was never seen before. The horrors of distorted human passions, He goes to meet. He is dragged from prison to court, smitten, beaten, spit upon. He gave His back to the smiter and His cheek to them that pluck out the beard. Smirched, begrimed with filthy hands, with welts on His back where the scourge fell, His face red and His eyes near blinded by the blood trickling from the mock crown, He stumbles on out of the gate, an accursed Being, at last to be raised in a triumph of all that is devilish and malignant upon a racking cross, to die with a shriek of utter torture wrung from His dry lips when burst His mighty heart. Well might Isaiah, as this scene passes before his prophetic eye, exclaim:

"And it shall be said in that day:
Lo, this is our God:
We have waited for Him, and He will save us.
For He said, Surely they are My people,
My children;
So He was their Saviour.
In all their affliction He was afflicted;
In His love and in His pity He redeemed them;
And He bare them, and carried them.
Doubtless Thou art our Father,
Though Abraham be ignorant of us and Israel acknowledge us not;
Thou, O Lord, art our Father, our Redeemer:
Thy name is from everlasting."[1]

[1] Isa. xxv. 9.

SUGGESTIONS

The atonement is not a *syllogism*, as the old theology made it; nor a *theatric example*, as the new theology makes it; but it is a *revelation*, as the future theology will make it.

The value of the atonement is that it characterizes God.

God gave His revelation in Oriental imagery, not in Latin dogma.

It is the subtle tincture of Arianism that has deformed the atonement.

The force in salvation is self-giving.

In Christ's sufferings the idea of God's holiness is suffused with sympathy.

God is His own sacrificial Lamb and His own Priest.

Men always believed in perfect holiness, but, until Christ, they never thought it could stoop to help the lowest.

God is not a spirit of segregation but of assimilation.

The passing of sin without the entrance of God is purely an intellectual fiction.

Forgiveness is also subjective.

The new consciousness is the basis of the new confidence.

The sin against the Holy Ghost is fatal, because it is the sin against the only form in which God touches us.

The law showed God's height; the cross, His depth; the resurrection, His breadth; these are the three dimensions.

CHAPTER VIII

THE BALANCE OF DOCTRINE

To View Religion as God's Personal Influence Gives Coherency to Conflicting Doctrines, to Contradictory Passages of Scripture, and to Opposing Elements in Human Nature

"Health is the vital principle of bliss."—THOMSON, *Castle of Indolence*, c. ii., s. 55.

"Morality, when vigorously alive, sees farther than intellect, and provides unconsciously for intellectual difficulties."—FROUDE, *Dirus Cæsar*.

"While adverse criticism has from age to age gone on destroying particular theological dogmas, it has not destroyed the fundamental conception underlying these dogmas. It leaves us without any solution of the striking circumstance, that when, from the absurdities and corruptions accumulated around them, national creeds have fallen into general discredit, ending in indifferentism or positive denial, there has always arisen by and by a reassertion of them; if not the same in form, still the same in essence. Thus the universality of religious ideas, their independent evolution among various primitive races, and their great vitality, unite in showing that their source must be deep-seated instead of superficial."—SPENCER, *First Principles*, p. 11.

CHAPTER VIII

There has been a tedious war waged over the matter of dogma. For a long time in the history of Christianity it was thought to be the chief, if not the essential, thing in religion, and the church exercised all her authority and arrayed all her learning and zeal to the end that the people might know what doctrines contained the truth and what were false. Then came the reaction. At present we are swinging to the other extreme, and it is the fashion to say that a right creed is not, after all, the most vital element in religion. The more accurate thinkers have perceived that, while correct dogma is not so all-availing as it was once held to be, yet the form of our belief has a certain necessary relation to our character and conduct. "As a man thinketh, so is he."

Many have been puzzled to understand how, if we admit right creed to be essential, we can escape going on to the full logical conclusion that dogma should be the prime concern of religious institutions charged with the propagation of Christ's teaching. The unloosing of this mystery is accomplished by the theory here presented, that religion is the personal influence of God. It is the dimly growing consciousness of this truth that has led us away from emphasizing dogmatic instruction. It is the conviction of this truth, now in the air of our modern spiritual life, that relieves the stern prominence of the credal tests of former times. We feel that while truth is absolutely necessary, yet somehow dogma is not all truth; but we have not yet formulated a statement of what *is* truth. There must be some qualification to the statement that belief is fatal; but we have failed to set forth distinctly what that qualification is. There must, then, be given some theorem concerning dogma, which shall limit its iron essentiality, at the same time conserving its utility. Such a theorem is this:

That doctrines of religion are true only in so far as they are indications of the character and work of the personality of God.

Doctrines are finite enclosures of thought. A personality is an abysmal thing. A doctrine, therefore, may be true, but can be but partly true; because no finite definition can include an infinite object. There abides in every true doctrine something that is not true at all. What that untrue part is, can be determined only by the test of the personality.

THE BALANCE OF DOCTRINE

A system of religion, consequently, that is based upon certain dogmatic statements must always contain much that is erroneous. It is only a faith that is founded upon a personality that can be forever true; for it will have within itself the touchstone by which the truth can ever be distinguished from error in any credal statement; it will have a constant power to modify and remodify, to alter and adapt its creed to its growing apprehension of the true nature of the personality upon which the faith hangs; and it will be able to do this without stultifying itself, it will be able confidently to repose in a statement of truth, even knowing that statement to be partly untrue, because it feels that, with a fuller knowledge of the divine Person, the untrue will be corrected and the true established.

Such is the real nature of the Christian religion. It is centered upon God's personality; and yet it is rich in helpful doctrines, those doctrines not being considered the ultimate deposits of truth, but as marks by which the intellect approaches toward and apprehends the main and actual truth, which is God's person alone.

If we now will apply the test of personality to some of the old theological controversies, we will find that it strangely and lucidly resolves the difficulties, and mightily comforts the intellect in its effort to grasp religious thought. "Truth," said a certain popular lecturer, "is clean cut." There never was a greater mistake. Lies and half-truths are clean cut; but in truth is always a fading point of mystery, a dim and shadowy perspective of infinitude. For there is but one absolute truth: God, who is infinite; and any clearly defined fragmental fact that seems true is only true when taken in connection with all the rest of the body of truth. In other words, there are no fragmental truths; there is but The Truth. The bearings and relations and interdependencies of each separate truth are as much a part of it as the stated and visible part. The little grain of sand you may hold on your finger-nail has threads of relation running out to the remotest star; it is bound by gravitation and other influences to all nature; and hence you cannot say you really know that sand grain until you know the vast All of the universe.

Let us, then, apply God's personality to a few mooted doctrinal contradictions, and we will see:

That the personality of God is the balance of doctrine.

For instance, God is just. That is true. Yet it is but a portion of truth. Carry it to

THE BALANCE OF DOCTRINE

the extreme length of the *abstract idea* of justice, leaving behind you the person of the One who is just, and you need not travel far till you find your truth a falsehood. For the *abstract quality* of justness has no room for mercy or forgiveness. It was this that forced the logic of Latin theology into the construction of the "substitutional" or "governmental" theories of redemption. The theological logicians could not see how absolute justice could forgive, and *it* cannot forgive; therefore they substituted Christ in the sinner's place and had that justice vent itself upon Him. Justice, having now fully exhausted itself upon Jesus, Mercy was free to come in and pardon the guilty. There is no trouble with the logic of this reasoning; the error is in the premises. For God is *not* Justice. He is just. The human, finite idea of justice is not broad enough to cover His person. There is a vast difference between our having to do with Justice on the one hand, or with a just Father on the other.

Take, on the contrary, the statement that God is merciful. Grasping this thought, and taking it away from God's personality, many have concluded that God will not punish any one, that the atonement is unnecessary, and that all, saint and sinner, repentant and repenting, alike, will be freely forgiven and made happy. Here is precisely the same *kind* of error, leading to a directly *opposite* result. Both are wrong. The justice of God is not entirely a truth by itself, neither is His mercy; both are true only where they shade into, coalesce with, and eventually modify each the other. In short, all antipodal doctrines about God must be balanced by His personality.

So of foreknowledge and free-will. Foreknowledge is certainly true, but unless it be always qualified by what we know of free-will it is not true. Led to its logical conclusion the fore-knowledge of God, as an abstract idea, plunges us inevitably into fatalism and irresponsibility, rendering us automata. In the same way abstract free-will of man unmodified will end in atheism. Therefore, we are ever to keep in mind that these are mere indications or *phenomena* of the two great infinite *persons*, God and man. The vanishing point of every dogma is personality. What *that* is we can never fully know, any more than the scientist can ever know *what* is life or force. The great fixed, unalterable fact of religion, absolutely indisputable, is that God's personality influences man's personality. All other dogmas concerning God or His works are tentative, to be held only as they harmonize with this dominant truth.

THE BALANCE OF DOCTRINE

If it be objected that this theory is indistinct and not "clean cut," it may be answered that *for that very reason* it is more liable to be true. For a theory that does not frankly recognize the abyss of unknowable truth about religion is *ipso facto* false. A theological system that reduces God's nature and work to a series of propositions, said to be true absolutely, and not only in connection with His personal mystery, is theologic materialism. And intellectually considered, the old theology was materialistic. The same fault lay in it that now lies in the modern scientific dogmatism. The old theology pinned its faith to certain authoritative statements of fact; it refused to assent to new facts, not because they were opposed to God as we see Him in nature and revelation, but because they were *prejudicial to their statements*. Some of our present-day scientists are making the same mistake; they have discovered certain facts in nature and educed from them certain laws; and, although they themselves do not pretend to have discovered *all* the facts and laws of nature, they reject religious facts, not because they are not fully substantiated, nor because they do not agree with established data of personal phenomena, but because they cannot reconcile them to *their set* of facts. How much better would both scientific dogmatist and theologic dogmatist recognize that "vast sea of *nescience* upon which all science floats as a mere superficial film!" How much better would we all cling to the deep truth of nature and of God, accepting as fragmentary whatever facts we can discover, and reverently modifying all our little store of truth as new truth comes down upon us!

The personality of God is also the *balance of Scripture*. It is the only safeguard against the abnormalities of literalism. The Bible is indeed inspired; but it is not a collection of Medo-Persian decrees, it is not a bundle of separate verses, each completely, wholly, and unqualifiedly true. The Bible is not the truth; the truth is in the Bible. We are to use the Scriptures as an aid to discover God and to learn His ways. The great Book is our instructor and adviser, but it is of no use to us whatever except as it brings us in touch with the Person whose revelation it is. Every part of it, therefore, is to be modified by every other part. No verse is *true out* of the Book. The whole Book itself is true.

It would seem that the authors of Holy Writ were careful to compose their writings so that literalism would be an impossibility, and that common sense would forever prohibit our magnifying a particle of Scripture into an essential thing. For their favorite method is

THE BALANCE OF DOCTRINE

paradox. They abound in contradictions. They continually throw the inquiring mind back upon the idea that *character*, before conduct, is the result they seek, that it is God, and not a set of regulations, they are unfolding. Take for instance that most important of all inquiries, "What shall I do to be saved?" Notice how Jesus answers this question as it comes to Him in various guises. He has no one essential deed for all. He does not tell each to go to Mecca, or to do this, or to do that one chief saving deed. He has a different word each time, and answers no two alike. To Nicodemus He says that one must be born again; to the rich young man He counsels selling all and giving the money to the poor; in the parable of the last judgment He lays all His stress on charitableness; to the disciples He enjoins watchfulness; speaking of prayer He makes our forgiveness to turn upon the forgiving of our own enemies; at another time He says that "he that believeth shall be saved"; and of the woman who anointed Him He apparently accepts the deed as sufficient merely because she "did what she could." One who is looking to see what may be the saving deed, it seems to me, must retire from this array of conflicting advice utterly baffled. But common sense rejoices in its reasonable conclusion that what is essential is not any one *deed* at all, but a *state* of the character from which all these various deeds naturally spring. Two things are in all of these cases cited: on the one hand is the "Me" of the Christ-God, and on the other hand is the "me" of the man's personality. Viewing Scripture, therefore, as the revelation of that personality of God which contains in itself the harmonizing and adjusting element of all contradictions, given to bring the influence of that divine personality to bear on us, we see the whole Book balanced and made comprehensible.

The personality of God is also the balance of character—that is, it is only when we conceive religion to be a looking away from self and toward the Christ, that our nature develops normally. When we take religion to be merely a rule of life, a collection of maxims, to which we are to conform ourselves, we invariably grow one-sided. The religion of a personality is wholesome, the religion of a creed is morbid. The one makes sound growth and health, the other sickness and extravagant vagaries. Introspection is dangerous. The habit of using the Bible as a model and striving to shape our lives to its teachings, without seeking therein the spirit of the Book, is inimical to Christian manhood. For it is God's personal influence, not

THE BALANCE OF DOCTRINE

certain facts and rules, that is to mold us into perfection. And the Scriptures are to be used to enable us to bring ourselves under the full play of this divine Spirit.

This statement of the matter is founded in the known law of growth. Growth is essentially unconscious. "Consider the lilies, how *they* grow; they toil not, neither do they spin." There is no effort on the part of a plant to increase; it has simply to present itself to the agencies of nature, to wave its branches in the air and let its roots into the soil, and "*God* giveth the increase." Even so the Christian is to use Holy Writ, and all other good words and advice, as helps to till the soil and clear away the weeds, remembering that it is the divine source of life that is to uplift and ennoble him.

So all virtue is, in its best form, unconscious. The charm of the child lies in the fact that it does not realize its charm; and as soon as a little one comes to feel its cunningness, it becomes affected and no longer agreeable. The evasive touch of perfect beauty upon a lovely face is the unconsciousness of beauty. Egotism defiles the splendor of intellectual power. Ostentation spoils benevolence. "Let not thy left hand know what thy right hand doeth." Pride is merely self-respect degraded by self-consciousness.

The grace of manners is self-forgetfulness; without this quality courtesy is affectation. Prudery is self-opinionated chastity. Therefore, the fly in the ointment of any virtue is self. Now, understanding that it is only as we look away from self to God, only as we think of Him, only as we lift our hearts to Him in love, only as we receive upon ourselves the reflexive increment of holiness by turning to Him, we are saved from this bane of morbidness.

The mediæval monk prayed to God, but he studied himself. The anchorite watched his soul to see it grow, and chastened it with bodily mortification, dying at last in despair. The Puritan gloried in austerity, and the more his self-scrutiny grew, the darker became his heart and the more rigid his practices. The modern sanctificationist speaks ever of his own soul-states. And in all these we recognize something sickly and unnatural. The cause of it is, that God's Book, God's precepts, or our own experiences, when they become the object of supreme attention, narrow and dwarf the soul, for they were never meant to *hide Him from* us, but to *reveal Him to* us. But God Himself, in Christ, the more He is sought after, rejoiced in, and walked with, forgetting self, changes us from lower ever to higher righteousness.

THE BALANCE OF DOCTRINE

misconceptions and falsehood. Among people in Christian lands it is effectual as it is clearly apprehended and yielded to in a greater or less degree. In the true, full preaching of the Gospel of Jesus Christ it is brought to bear in the fullest, truest way, and therefore this Gospel is "the power of God unto salvation." What we call natural goodness is the more or less feeble radiation of that influence upon men, the penumbra of Jesus Christ. Hence, when the full Gospel of Christ is addressed to men, it is the continuation of the same power that has already been working within them as what they called "natural goodness." There are, therefore, not two kinds of goodness, natural and supernatural; it is all one, and all of God. He is "the Light that lighteth every man that cometh into the world," but in Jesus Christ He is the very "Sun of righteousness."

A religion that is the revelation of the All-Father's personality and His influence is equipped to be a missionary power. It goes to heathen peoples, not as another cult, but as the true solution of all they have had that is best. It recognizes their longings and religious systems as so many indications of the divine person's influence among them, obscured, degraded, and confused by error. It comes to them, using as a text their own ancient faiths, saying that "God who at sundry times and in divers manners spake in times past" to them, "hath in these last days spoken by His Son," "the brightness of His glory, and the express image of His person." It comes to them, as did Paul to the Athenians, proclaiming, "Whom, therefore, ye ignorantly worship, Him declare I unto you."

Hence, we conclude that if the power of the Gospel abides only in the *doctrines* of the Bible, then all the "outside saints" of ante-Christian ages and of present extra-Christian faiths have no connection at all with salvation; Job and Abraham, as well as the pious, sincere Brahman or Mahometan of this day, are equally aliens from the kingdom; but if the Gospel is the complete unfolding of God's personal influence, which in a measure always and everywhere has been at work among men, then the ancient patriarch was also under the power of the Redeemer of men, and to the earnest heathen we can say, in encouragement and joy, as a Gospel which is a "good news" indeed, "One thing thou lackest — follow Christ; receive ye the Holy Spirit, and He shall lead you into all truth."

It thus would seem that the doctrine here defended gives an intellectual coherency and symmetry to the entire Gospel plan.

SUGGESTIONS

Every dogmatic truth contains a falsehood.

There is no religious truth but personal truth.

All science is to be modified by nescience.

Religious doctrines are true as revelations, but not as definitions.

No finite definition can include an infinite object; it must be indicatory, not exhaustive.

A system of religion founded upon a Person can grow; if founded upon doctrine it will die.

Christian doctrines are milestones of Christian progress.

No dogma is true without perspective; it must recognize the unknowable.

The relations of a fact are as much a part of it as is the stated and visible part.

The personality of God is the balance of doctrine.

There is a vast difference between Justice and a just God.

Every thesis has its antithesis; each is true only where it overlaps the other.

A religion of dogma, intellectually speaking, is materialistic.

No text of the Bible is true out of the Bible

The contradictions of Scripture are the safeguards of common sense.

All growth is unconscious in its operation.

The world is in the penumbra of Christ.

The personal influence of God is the strength of missions.

CHAPTER IX
THE INCARNATION

The Personal Influence of God is Transforming the World as a Power of Social Evolution, not as a Rule of Social Segregation

"Conceived by the Holy Ghost, born of the Virgin Mary."—*The Apostles' Creed.*

"Divine Wisdom, to establish the salvation of mankind, and to conduct His glorious victory over death and sin, would do it no other way, but at the mercy of our ordinary forms of justice, subjecting the progress and issue of so high and so salutiferous effect to the blindness and injustice of our customs and observances; sacrificing the innocent blood of so many of His elect, and so long a loss of so many years, to the maturing of this inestimable fruit."—MONTAIGNE, *Essays*, Vol. I., p. 109.

> "For still the new transcends the old
> In signs and tokens manifold;
> Slaves rise up men; the olive waves
> With roots deep set in battle graves."
> JOHN G. WHITTIER, *The Chapel of the Hermits.*

"And ye shall hear of wars and rumors of wars: see that ye be not troubled; for all these things must come to pass, but the end is not yet."

"Fear not, little flock; for it is your Father's good pleasure to give you the kingdom."—JESUS, Matt. xxiv. 6; Luke xii. 32.

CHAPTER IX

There are many persons who may hesitate to believe that Christianity is the personal influence of God, because it appears to them that if it were so religion would have been always pure, while as a matter of fact it has been and is now very faulty. And not only so, but so-called Christianity has been directly responsible for some of the greatest crimes of history. Not alone imperfect has it shown itself, but positively devilish at times. Now, the way to meet this statement is not to deny it, for it is true. Some time ago the writer listened to a brilliant infidel lecturer as he brought against the church, in a series of telling climaxes, a railing accusation, charging it with impeding progress and with injuring humanity in a hundred ways. What he charged was every whit true; its falsity lay not in his misstatement of facts, but in his wrong point of view. And that point of view unfortunately was not his own, but was furnished him by the theologians, and is shared by most of those who profess Christianity. He was proceeding upon the assumption that it was the design of this religion to establish a church, saving a certain elect number out of the world. This is another phase of the old misconception of salvation as a scheme instead of a power; it shows how the wrong notion, which this essay combats, supplies for infidelity its chief if not its only ground upon which to stand.

But Christianity is not a contrivance; it is God's influence through Christ among men. Its design is not to rescue a certain chosen number from a perishing world, but to change the world. "God so loved the world."[1] "I am the light of the world"[2] Jesus said, He was "to save the world."[3] John said, "He is the propitiation, not for our sins only, but for the sins of the whole world."[4] The intent of God in Christ was not to organize a club or lodge of "perfect" people, which by additions to its membership was finally to enroll every human being on its books. His method was not to *make* a church, as one would make a house or a box, or make an association or society, but to *grow* a church. For the kingdom of heaven is like a grain of mustard seed, a lump of leaven, seed growing secretly.[5] His purpose was a development of a spirit among men, a renovation of their

---

[1] John iii. 16.
[2] John viii. 12, etc.
[3] John iii. 17.
[4] 1 John ii. 2.
[5] Matt. xiii.

THE INCARNATION

character and quality, and not an outward separation of some men from all others. This being true, it follows that the church, or that body of men representing the work of God, will not be ideal and relatively complete until the development is very far advanced. In its early stages it will, of course, be very incomplete; it will be a prey to wrong ideas; it will show monstrous mistakes; it will be full of perversions and errors. It is no sign it is not divine, that it has these flaws; it is truly divine if it shows it has inner vitality enough to live through them, to cast them aside, as the seed bursts its husk, pushes through the soil, and proceeds to make first the blade, then the ear, then the full corn in the ear. Therefore, as a holy institution the church is a failure, and the arguments of the infidel are correct. Grant him his premise, and you cannot escape his conclusion. But as the body containing a Holy Spirit it has evidenced constantly its divine origin by just that growth one would expect.

Christianity is not separate from humanity, but is incorporated within it. Christianity is human just as much as it is divine. If it was wholly divine, it would be useless, for we could never be touched by it; and it would be just as useless if wholly human, for then there would be nothing in it to lift us. It must be both if it is to help us. It must be a part of us, and in consequence it must grow with our growth, partake of our imperfections, and be subject to all the vicissitudes necessary to the development of creatures out of beastliness and narrowness into godliness and grandeur. The influence of God is always utterly pure and elevating, but men's apprehension and practice of that influence will be a thing of progressive stages. All life is an unfolding; Christianity is a life; therefore Christianity among men must be a gradual widening and enlarging of them.

It is because we do not appreciate this that we stumble over those instances in the Old Testament that, while represented to be a part of God's religion, were foreign to God's nature. The cruelties and inhumanities there related were simply illustrations of how a half-savage community worked out the influence of God within it. Many of the commands and permissions given by Moses and the prophets seem to be wrong, but were relatively right;[1] though they now appear faulty to us who know God in Christ, yet they were ever in advance of the people. If they had been always and absolutely right, they would never have influ-

---

[1] As Ex. xxi. 21; xxii. 18, etc., and others countenancing slavery, polygamy, slaughter, the killing of witches and the like. "And Jesus answered and said, For the hardness of your heart he [Moses] wrote you this precept." Mark x. 5.

THE INCARNATION

enced the Jews at all, but would have simply driven them to despair, because it would have been impossible for them to obey. God is *leading* His people in the Old Testament; and the shepherd cannot lead his flock unless he goes on just before them. For Him to have stood in the far-off gates of absolute right and from thence called His people, would have been for them not to have heard His voice at all, or, hearing it, not in the remotest degree to have understood it. So in law and psalm and prophecy we behold the influence of Jehovah working as leaven among a primitive and barbarous people. Contemplating the Old Scriptures in this light, they become luminous with divinity, and we are furnished the principle by which to discriminate between the divine and the human in the Book. Particularly in David do we see a rugged, half-civilized, kingly man, full of gross errors, fleshly and impetuous, yet permeated by a divine spirit that lifts him, struggling, weeping, and warring, up to some of the loftiest conceptions of Deity the mind of man has ever conceived. As an angelic being, David is a caricature; as a man of God, as an example of God moving upon and raising up a most human man, he is a splendid example.

Let us, therefore, freely admit all the faults

which an accusing infidelity lays at our door. Let us not boast that the church has never acted more like a wild beast than a child of God, but let us boast that it has had within it a divine power to shake off these errors and sins, to weep for them, and to have the courage to try to do better. The proof of the church's claim to be of God is not its impeccability, but its progress.

Let us glance over the history of the church. Rather, let us see how the influence of God has fared since coming upon earth in the Christ. Conceiving Christianity as a something that came into the world some two thousand years ago, that persisted through the dark ages, that reappeared in the modern era with unfaded strength, and that to-day is the most virile influence in civilization, we must admit that it is not only a divine, but also a most human thing. No better key to our correct apprehension of its career could be found than the account of the birth of its Founder. Many have taken offense at the alleged parentage of Jesus. Some have allowed its mystery to thrust them into doubt, some have treated the story as an absurdity, and still others have made it an occasion for blasphemy. But that His Father was the Holy Spirit and His mother was the woman Mary is in the most philosophical and reason-

THE INCARNATION

able accord not only with the events recorded in His earthly life, but also with the vacillating history of His church. That hypothesis is the most reasonable and scientific which accounts most nearly for all the phenomena. And what theory of the origin of this church is so satisfactory and agreeable to what we know of its fortunes as to suppose that it is half human and half divine? If you were to compose a story in which the hero is the child of a fairy father and a wolf mother, you would, if you were a skillful artist, depict one in whom the brutal and the ethereal traits are deftly intermingled. Sometimes his face would shine with an evanescent beauty and his step would be too light to crush a cowslip, and again he would be fierce, bloody, and repulsive, and not infrequently his manner would strangely combine suggestions of both the fairy and the beast. Does not the story of the church in some such way demonstrate its dual origin?

It is not meant that Jesus personally evidenced His human blood by imperfections, for none of us "accuseth Him of sin." In this first product of God and man the strong personality of God so completely suffused the grosser nature of His mother that, though He was in all points like as we are, yet was He faultless. He was "the First-born of many brethren," and as such the perfect type of what we are to become when we have been changed from glory to glory by the Spirit until we shall be like Him. In His person He represents humanity as it shall be when it is one with God "even as He is one with the Father"; that combination that seems so impossible, yet which dwells as a radiant ideal ever before men; thoroughly human, yet holy, harmless, undefiled. In Him God illustrated what His personal influence can do for humanity.

But Christianity, as a germ planted in mankind, did not leap at once to the perfection of this God-man, but has grown painfully and slowly, exhibiting at once the power of its Father and the frailty of its mother. Let us consider that growth in its infancy, in its youth, and in its manhood.

And first, its birth. The curse pronounced upon Eve was that in sorrow she should bring forth her children. And not only do men enter life through the gates of anguish, but all great ideas are born in travail. The great creators of literature were men who drank deep of the cup of agony: blind Homer, exiled Dante, imprisoned Bunyan, lonely Milton. Political ideas come forth in revolution and struggle; democracy has been baptized in blood. The advent of any great world

THE INCARNATION

epoch has been attended with fierce convulsions, mighty pains. And thus, also, this religion, destined to be prolific in letters, to revolutionize theories of government, to work gigantic reforms, to stimulate the human brain by the sublimest ideas it has ever entertained, was ushered into being amid the throes of a distracted world. The birth of Jesus was attended by the slaughter of all the babes of Bethlehem; His death was a crucifixion. And what giant passions were called forth by the efforts of the young religion, after its Author's death, to establish itself in the hearts of men! For three centuries the common people raged in riot against the disciples of Christ; the emperors smote them again and again with their mailed hand; fire, sword, and wild beast were turned loose upon them; and in no period of history have blacker, more hideous cruelties and more terrible sufferings been displayed than during this time, the days of the entrance of Christianity into mankind.

Thus did Earth bring forth her Son, thus found this Son a place among her other sons. For she has other children. Confucianism, strange, silent, respectful, with a stolid face of helpless misery and a mind full of inventions, looking ever longingly to the past; Egypt, her dead boy, once strong and glorious, now buried beneath the débris of history. Her Roman son was stern and vaunting, seeking to rule all his brethren with a rod of iron. Islam was her child Ishmael, fierce, fiery, iconoclastic. To each in turn has the mother looked for succor, but each left her in despair, unable to heal her deep misery. It is this child, Christianity, this child at whose birth among her sheep and oxen the angels rained down their hallelujahs; this child toward whose coming the prophets strained their eager eyes; this child which she called Immanuel, God with us—it is this child to whom she stretches out her arms for help.

Passing from the birth to the infancy of the new religion which embodied the influence of God, we see that in its babyhood it was like its Father. Infants are always pure and sweet. Early Christianity was almost idyllic. Even Gibbon pays respect to the spotless character of the early church. It is only when children grow up and *begin to absorb their environment* that they lose their artless loveliness. Although Christianity was a child of God, it was left in the hands of its mother, Earth.[1] It soon grew like her, and as she impressed herself upon it the infantine beauty gave way to the lines of excess. Christianity, the son

---

[1] The reader is to bear always in mind that the mother means here *humanity* rather than the Virgin Mary personally.

THE INCARNATION

of the world, has been long sowing its wild oats. It is not without significant connection with our present thought that the dominant church exalted Mary, the *mother*, during the period of the church's worst deeds; while since the standard of morality has risen, since the Reformation, it has been exalting more and more the personality and work of the Holy Spirit, the *Father*. Had Christianity not been corrupt, it would not have been the child of man; had it not ever striven against that corruption, it would not have been the child of God.

The traces of its human parentage are all too well known. It became cruel, and slew more men in wars against heretics than Jew and Roman had slain in their persecutions. Wars were prosecuted, and armies were led by popes, the vicars of the Prince of Peace. Christianity originated the Holy Inquisition, the most consummate engine for torture ever devised by man or devil. It became ambitious, grasping after the prizes of earthly position, greedy to reign. Its ministry were vowed to celibacy that they might have no family ties to divide their loyalty to the church, and thus interfere with the immense design of sweeping all thrones and kingdoms into its hand. It became greedy. In every land where it set up its banner it accompanied the preaching of individual self-denial with corporate rapacity, seizing the fattest revenues and choicest lands for itself. At one time the church owned two-thirds of the land of western Europe. Watching by the bedside of the dying, it mingled in its ghostly influence the pardon of sins and the securing of legacies. It trafficked in purgatory and indulgences. It became impure. Prelates were noted for their licentiousness. Condemning the marriage of priests, it winked at concubinage. It was its mother Earth's own child—drunken, lecherous, idle, earthy.

It became proud. Among populations of starving paupers it raised glittering cathedrals, imposing piles of masonry and art, blessing God by gold and marble and by weird chantings among forests of stately pillars, while it was cursing men by rack and thumb-screw. The court must obey the cowl; kings must receive their crowns from the head of the church. While Jesus rebuked him who called Him master, bishops and archbishops proudly resented the abatement of one jot or tittle of their numerous titles and honors. The successor of Peter the fisherman shone in gems, wrapped his delicate limbs in purple and fine linen, and excelled the pomp of Oriental monarchs.

All this, and more, it is idle to deny. It is

THE INCARNATION

deeply, shamefully true. When the infidel rehearses these things he is but telling what we frankly and fully admit. But there is more he does not say. He fails to note that it was not the skeptic nor the worldling that rebuked the shamelessness of the church, that protested against its abuses, that sealed his testimony against its evil doings by his own martyrdom. It was not the philosopher nor critic nor scientific gentleman; it was the Christian, prayerful, devout, believing God even more than the church believed Him, that worked its reformation. It was Savonarola, Huss, Farel, Zwingli, Luther, Wicklif, and Wesley, and not Galileo, Kepler, Kant, Spinoza, and Spencer, who roused the church to wash its bloody hands and clean its filthy garments before the Lord. In other words, the church emerged from its low estate by a power within itself—evil as its ways had become—not by any external power.

And bad as this mother's child was in the long night of mediævalism, it was *never as bad as she*. With all its colossal faults, it was never so faulty as the world in which it lay. Its errors stand out so conspicuously *because we know its Father*. It was cruel in an age of utter cruelty, barbarous in an age of lowest barbarism, unclean in an age of absolute filth, ignorant in an age of blindness. The clergy even in those days were as a whole a little better than the men of the world, although they should have been much better. And the church was never at any time during those dark days without evidences of its divine Sire. Did not indications of Him flash out in S. Bernard and Ambrose of Milan and Thomas à Kempis? And were they not to be seen in the spirit that erected hospitals and universities, in the real charity and self-denial that marked the early days of the brotherhoods of S. Francis and S. Dominic? Considered relatively, the Christianity of even those gloomy times must be credited with an element of mercy, hope, democracy, brotherhood, and morality, which the unprejudiced student cannot find in the very best that heathenism has ever done; it is only when we consider the church absolutely, or compare it with what it ought to have been, that its history seems so iniquitous.

Blood will tell. Christianity is a divine influence, but its work is to develop human beings. Earth is its mother. If it had always been holy, it would not be *our* child, but a foundling, a divine waif, which would have wandered awhile upon earth and died of homesickness.[1] Its ideals stamp it as heav-

---

[1] See Bushnell's "Salvation by Man," in "Christ and His Salvation," p. 271.

THE INCARNATION

enly; the corruptions incident to its development stamp it as earthly. If the inspirations it infuses in us show that it was conceived by the Holy Ghost, the flaws in its practice show that it is born of the Virgin Mary. Thus the birth at Bethlehem is at once a fact and a symbol. Our religion is child of sky and cloud; son of God and son of Mary; very God and very man.

It was not, perhaps, without divine purpose that, after Christianity had been engrafted in the race and its literature embodied in the perfect and delicate language of the Greeks, the waves of barbarism should roll over Europe and reduce mankind almost to a state of primitive barbarism, in order that this new influence should grow up through the successive periods of progress and make a civilization of its own, a civilization grounded upon its own ideas, and not upon those of the Greeks or Romans. All the luxuriant vegetation of Greece and Rome was plowed under by the barbaric hordes, and lay long in the soil wherein this new "branch of God's planting" was to grow, that it might spring from its own earth and unfold with the unfolding of men's minds.

Passing now from the youth we come to the manhood of this child, Christianity. The pessimistic opinions about our day are unfounded. Our alarm is based upon the observance of the decay of old institutions, the passing of old forms of thought, the wearing away of old vestments of belief; we do not always remember that new wine cannot be put in old wineskins. The world to-day has a truer conception of Christ than it ever had before; this new conception must make new institutions as garments for itself. Why should we care if venerable forms decay, if so be that Christ be magnified? "Thou fool! that which thou sowest is not quickened except it die." Out of the rotting bulb springs the lily, out of the decomposed acorn shoots the new oak, and out of the ferment of these times the personal influence of God is creating in us still truer ideas of what His religion means. The nature of the stronger parent will eventually dominate in the child. Slowly but surely the divine Spirit is imprinting His nature upon all our religious ideas. To be sure, the church is still stupid, dull, irresponsive to its high calling, but more and more the signs of its Father are showing. The trend of modern Christian thought, sentiment, and practice is more and more toward the character of God. Christ, as the very Face and Word of God, is moving upon men, even as He has been moving to raise them up from savagery to intelligence.

THE INCARNATION

He told us that, as there is but one God, so there is but one brotherhood. All men are of one blood. We are still a long way off from realizing the meaning and implication of this fact to the full, but how much already has it softened our asperities and broken down the divisions among us!

We owned slaves. Men of another color we bought and sold as cattle. And we verily thought we did right. But He kept whispering in our ears, "They are brothers, brothers, brothers!" We grew uneasy. We had no rest because He would not let us forget the black men were brothers. By and by we burst forth, "If they be brothers, let them rise and stand up equal with us!" War followed. The nation was like to be rent and ruined. War passed. The clouds blew off on the winds of peace. He smiled and said, "You did clumsily, but well; you have set free your brothers."

Little children worked in mines and factories until their ghosts peeped out through their gaunt bodies. He showed us them, and put His hand on them, and said, "Why have you cursed them when I have blessed them?" So we set the children free from stunting labor. We built schoolhouses for them. We took the millions of money before spent in war and gave it to train and teach the little ones.

Woman was but a more excellent beast. He gave us no rest until we released her from the harem and unyoked her from among the oxen and took her hand and raised her to the throne of love. We were shamed from our lives of license and uncleanliness, because He said to us, "They twain shall be one flesh." So we built woman a temple and called it "Home." We rescued love from beastliness and linked it with loyalty. And all because He would have it so.

We had a system of political economy which said, "Labor is also a commodity; it is to be bought cheap and sold dear, even as corn; it also is under the law of demand and supply."

But this displeased Him. "How can the laborer be a brother and a thing at the same time?" He asked. Then we awoke, we are now awakening, to protest that labor is not a tool of capital, but the partner of capital and its co-worker. The old system of competition and individualism, that worked measurably well when the laborer owned his own tools, we endeavored to carry over into a social state where capital owned all the tools and the laborer had nothing to bring to market but his hands. Then there was great evil; for the workman was again reduced to a slave, and his price was his wage. So He gave us no rest until we cut the laborer's hours from

THE INCARNATION

twelve to eleven, from eleven to ten, from ten to eight, so that he should have some time to make manhood as well as wages.

We gloried in war. Militarism like a deathly pest infected our literature, our imagination, our legislation, our whole life. Then He said again, "Brothers! brothers!" And we could but think, "If brothers, why warriors?" So He took the spear and showed us how to make it a pruning-hook, and the sword how to make it a plowshare. Gradually, gently, He led us on. At first private wars gave way to courts; then came partial spots of peace called "the king's peace," and "God's peace"; at length, when He had got the ear of the two foremost nations of earth, He said, "If two men go to court, why not two nations?" So began international arbitration. Whereat we prospered, for He was pleased with us.

He chose the lowly among us, and we were amazed, for we thought some men better than others. We had aristocracies and plutocracies, we had bespangled courts and nobilities. But He kept saying, "Brothers, brothers!" And because He gave us no respite we put aside monarchies and titles, and we sentenced the idea of privileged classes to death. We put the ballot in the hand of even the hod-carriers, because He insisted that we are brothers.

THE RELIGION OF TO-MORROW

Then there was much confusion and corruption, and some wise men said democracy is a failure. But He bids us wait patiently until it works out a nobler manhood.

Criminals we had. We punished them. We killed them. We called them enemies of the social order. But He still would say, "Brothers! brothers!" So we ceased first to mutilate and torture them. Then we left off to a great extent murdering them. We are now beginning to question if it is right to punish them. It is God's business to punish. So, therefore, we are trying to help even the criminals, because He calls them our brothers. We build reformatories, establish indeterminate sentences, and seek in many ways to cure and not exterminate the criminal. Ever because He says to us, "Cure, heal, help; do not avenge, punish, destroy."

In view of all this why should we clutch at the decaying forms while the life is so full about us? Let the dead past go. The future is full of hope. The light of life is breaking upon the earth.

> "Ring out, wild bells, to the wild sky!
> Ring out the old, ring in the new;
> Ring, happy bells, across the snow;
> Ring in the Christ that is to be!"

There is much uneasiness in religion just now. It seems to be an age of theological

THE INCARNATION

unsettling. But while some may view all this with alarm, it would seem that the true view is not to consider progress as doing away with religion, but religion as doing away by its progress, with forms no longer suited to its growth. The present pangs are merely "growing pains." The religion of Jesus is not a set form; it is a principle of human development. As it masters one age it forms a certain body or shell for itself out of the current notions of that age. Perfectly true and pure in itself, yet it must get such imperfect shape as the imperfectly formed ideas of that age may furnish, having, as Paul says, "this treasure in an earthen vessel." By and by, when it has grown and lifted men up into another plane of thought, coming into a larger age, the old shell becomes too narrow, it cramps its contents, the form that formerly protected its growth now hinders its growth. Then, like the chick in its shell, it picks and picks until it comes out into the fuller life for which it is prepared. That picking is what we call doubt. All advance in thought-life begins in skepticism. Not the irreverent sort which revolts at religion because it forbids sin, but the reverent sort that longs for a deeper, truer word for the growing idea. This is what Tennyson meant when he wrote:

THE RELIGION OF TO-MORROW

"There lives more faith in honest doubt,
Believe me, than in half the creeds."

The revelation of God must be reasonable, fitting the instincts of natural religion, supplementing by its full light that "light which lighteth every man that cometh into the world." And it is reasonable; the harsh and repugnant, the mechanical and absurd appurtenances to theology were not at all in the early Christianity of the days of the Greek theologians, but were grafted upon our religion during the dark ages of scholasticism.[1] In our days we are simply shaking off the incubus of Latin thought and getting back to the simplicity of Christ and the earlier fathers of the church.

Christianity is now apparently torn and divided in its theology simply because we are living in an age of liberty. But in all this diversity and conflict we are vastly nearer the truth than in the days of apparent uniformity. For our religion is peculiarly adapted to grow in an atmosphere of freest discussion and untrammeled doubt and unhindered opposition. It dwindles and pines under the shadow of any sort of authority or human protection.

---

[1] "For a thousand years those who came after him [Augustine] did little more than reaffirm his teaching, and so deep is the hold which his long supremacy has left upon the church, that *his opinions* have become identified with divine revelation, and are all that the majority of the Christian world yet know of the religion of Christ."—"Continuity of Christian Thought," p. 270.

THE INCARNATION

The widest variety of opinion is necessary. For all warring opinions must prove their truth each by striving to help men most, by excelling in benevolence and good-will and all the tender humanities Christ gave as the test of real truth. There is more of the spirit of Jesus among men now than in any era in history. Men may hiss the church, and it hurts; but what of it, if they reverence still the Christ, and scorn the church only because it is not like Him? More and more all men are turning to the Master for the solution of the problems of life and death. Sociology and politics and every reform are quoting Him more and more, each party shaming the other because it fails to measure up to His ideals. We cannot gauge the influence of Jesus by arithmetic. In public opinion, in the trend of reforms, in the undertone of literature, in the quietly accepted rules of social life, I find more of our Master.

> "God's in His heaven;
> All's right with the world!"

There is not the wide gap between the church and the world there was in apostolic days. The church is not as pure now as then; this is often charged. But we are apt to forget that while the church as such may not be so near His ideal, the outlying world is much nearer, and Christ came to save the *world*. No man with good judgment can deny that with all its evil, the present age is much nearer the ideas of Jesus than the age of Augustus. Therefore, facing Him, let the church say, "He must increase, but I must decrease." It may be that the church is to be cast aside for its refusal to go on according to God's plan; we cannot tell. Or it may rather be, and this is our prayer and hope, that it will rise renewed, grasping the full meaning of its opportunity, and in the century to come still make good its claim to be the body of Christ.

Certain it is that unless we rise to a higher conception of God's work, to truer ideas of what salvation and eternal life and the resurrection mean, we cannot long linger in this age. We cannot continue as an anachronism. We must shake off the bands and swaddling clothes of Latin theology and return to the simplicity of Christ. And there are many signs that the church is doing this. In the wide liberty of discussion we are developing an orthodoxy of spirit. In the extreme diversity of sects we are laying the foundation of the true oneness of Christ, which is not uniformity of opinion or ritual, but "the unity of the Spirit in the bond of peace," while unity of organization is a bond of contention.

THE INCARNATION

There is no true unity which is not made up of variety, else the parts will not fit together.

It may be but a fond and foolish dream, but the vision will rise before his eyes who sees in every church some measure of the Spirit, varying according to the different dispositions of men, the vision of the one universal church of Christ on earth, formed not by law nor by authority, but by the common consent and desire of the common sense of a race fully emancipated into the liberty of Christ Jesus, in which church all churches shall have a share, each shall lay a stone or frame a soft-shining window; in which church there shall be a ritual of service according to the Roman form, preserving the Latin tongue for its sonorous beauty (it being no more an "unknown tongue" when all know or may know what it means), and the Anglican public prayers, and the Methodist enthusiasm, and the glow and spirituality of all the quietistic sects, and the sterling principle of the Presbyterians, and the democratic government of the Congregational bodies, and the boldness to descend into the slums that is the glory of the Salvation Army, and if there be any others who name the name of our Master, even their portion also: "Jesus Christ Himself being the chief corner-stone, in whom all the building fitly framed together groweth unto an holy

THE RELIGION OF TO-MORROW

temple in the Lord; the whole, *according to the effectual working in the measure of every part*, making increase and building itself up in love."

In those days, soon to come, shall the sun as he runs his rim of light around a wakening world upon the Lord's day, touch the harp of praise in all temples, and the air shall fill with the Te Deum, the universal hymn, sung by all nations and by the islands of the sea, by "all men everywhere lifting up holy hands without wrath or doubting":

> "We praise Thee, O God:
> We acknowledge Thee to be the Lord:
> All the earth doth worship Thee,
> The Father everlasting.
> To Thee all angels cry aloud;
> The heavens and all the powers therein
> To Thee cherubim and seraphim
> Continually do cry:
> Holy! holy! holy!
> Lord God of Sabaoth:
> *Heaven and* EARTH ARE FULL
> Of the majesty of Thy glory."

SUGGESTIONS

Christianity is human as much as it is divine.

It is only when we conceive God's purpose to be the development of mankind that we can understand the Old Testament.

The proof of the church's claim to be of God is not its impeccability but its progress.

Christianity, conceived by Deity and born of humanity, has exhibited both the power of its Father and the frailty of its mother.

Infants are always pure and sweet; it is only when they grow up and begin to absorb their environment that they become corrupt; early Christianity was idyllic; then for a chiliad or so it has been sowing its wild oats; some day it will be a man.

Religion has had many reformations, but none of them were ever made by irreligious men; Christianity is reformed only by Christians.

Bad as the church has been, there has never been a time when it was quite so bad as the world in which it lay.

All advance in thought-life begins in skepticism; not the irreverent sort which revolts at religion because it forbids sin, but the reverent sort which longs for a wider word for a widening idea.

If the church is not so near Christ as it was in apostolic days, the outlying world is a good deal nearer; and Christ came to save the world.

CHAPTER X

THE LEAVEN

The Personal Influence of God is the Propagating Power of Christianity

"The kingdom of heaven is like unto leaven, which a woman took and hid in three measures of meal, till the whole was leavened."—JESUS, Matt. xiii. 33.

"The most essential feature of Man is his improvableness."—JOHN FISKE, *Destiny of Man*, p. 71.

"Christianity, then, has a power to prepare a godly seed. It not only takes hold of the world by its converting efficacy, but it has a silent force that is much stronger and more reliable; it moves, by a kind of destiny, in causes back of all the eccentric and casual operations of mere individual choice, preparing, by a gradual growing in of grace, to become the great populating motherhood of the world." — HORACE BUSHNELL, *The Out-Populating Power of the Christian Stock*.

"The desire of power in excess caused angels to fall; the desire of knowledge in excess caused Man to fall; but in charity there is no excess; neither Angel nor Man come in danger by it."—BACON, *Essays. Of Goodness and Goodness in Nature*.

CHAPTER X

Religion being merely the personality of God, Christianity the personality of Christ, how is it to be propagated? Can a personality be taught? What is the divine method of the spread of the kingdom of heaven?

Jesus had before Him as models three forms by which vast systems had been spread among men, each of them having had great success. The Greek method was by reasoning. By argument and the skill of dialectic the philosophy of Greece had dominated the master minds of the world. The Roman method was organization. By force and display of material grandeur Rome had assumed the control of the earth. The Oriental method was by the imagination. By playing upon the vague, unknown mysteries of life and death the powerful faiths of the East had risen to wide dominion. But Jesus chose none of these three. Because His religion was not a philosophy it could not be advanced by logic; because it was not an institution nor an organization it could not be aided, but only hindered, by authority and force; because it was not a superstition, it could in nowise be assisted by shadowy fears. His religion was none of these; it was a Life. As such it could only be spread by contact. As life goes from man to man so the eternal life was to follow the same channel. The disciples were called the salt of the earth and the light of the world;[1] and the personal influence of God was to go from individual to individual even as the flavor of salt is diffused from particle to particle, or as light is passed along a signal line from torch to torch, each lighting the next.

But the manner of the Gospel's growth is best seen in the parable of the leaven.[2] The illustration there given is so vivid and the analogy has such perfect truth throughout that it may perhaps repay us to pursue it.

In the very nature of fermentation we may see a profound illustration of the way in which the personality of Jesus affects the personality of the man. For the ferment does not produce the change in the mass by entering into chemical union with it, and thus producing a new substance different from both; which is the way that chemical changes are made, oxygen, for instance, uniting with hydrogen to produce water, or uniting with nitrogen to produce common air; but the alteration is

---

[1] Matt. v. 13, 14.   [2] Matt. xiii. 33.

strictly in the wort itself, on account of the presence of the leaven. This, in a peculiarly beautiful way, illustrates the "conversion" of the natural man into the new man in Christ Jesus, from the godless to the Christian man. For it makes clear the two points about conversion which seem so strange. First, the change is not spontaneous; no man of himself, without the presence of God in him, can develop into a Christian. Yet, secondly, the change after all is simply a change in the man; although different in his character, yet he is the same, with the same passions and will as before. Take the fermentation of milk, the souring of sweet milk, a process by which the milk sugar of the milk, by a mere re-arrangement of its particles, passes into lactic acid. Professor Dittmar cites this case of milk, and after comparing it with instances of mere chemical change, concludes that "fermentations, as a class of chemical reactions, are characteristically non-spontaneous, and consequently must be caused by reagents, although these reagents have no place in the mere balance-sheet of the reaction. In fact," he continues, "experience shows that no fermentable chemical species will ferment . . . unless it be kept in direct contact with some specific 'ferment,' which, although it contributes nothing to the substance of the products which figure in the equation, nevertheless induces the reaction 'by its presence,' as the phrase goes."[1] Although this does not *explain* the rationale of God's action on the soul (for that is as inexplicable to us as the reason why fermentation takes place only in the presence of leaven, yet leaving the leaven unchanged, is inexplicable to the scientists), yet it *illustrates* how it is that after conversion no part of the individuality of the soul has been lost, the soul and God still each retain their respective personalities, yet the soul is utterly different from what it was before, "by a rearrangement of its particles," as it were.

In the acts of Jesus, as narrated in the gospels, we see how He made use of this leaven method alone, to the exclusion of all other methods—that is, He made followers by His personal influence only, never by argument, by force, nor by any sort of working upon superstitions. The Pharisees challenged Him to show them a "sign," to awe them by supernal displays into following Him, but He replied that "a wicked and adulterous generation seeketh after a sign."[2] Again, they proposed to argue the case with Him, but He refused to fence at logic and confined

---

[1] Encyclopedia Britannica, article "Fermentation."
[2] Matt. xii. 39.

THE LEAVEN

Himself to illustrations, for "without a parable spake He not unto them."[1] Peter seized the sword and smote off the ear of the high priest's servant, but Jesus rebuked the attempt to use force in His kingdom;[2] and on another occasion, when the disciples wished to call down fire from heaven upon their opponents, He declared, "Ye know not what manner of spirit ye are of."[3]

One is struck with the calmness and, it almost seems, the apparent indifference of Jesus in making converts, as compared with the zeal of His followers in after ages. There was no enthusiasm in Him for recruiting and organizing His army of believers. Often He openly discouraged them that would have come after Him, because their motives were bad. To some He said they followed Him merely for the loaves and fishes;[4] another time He insisted that men should count the cost before entering upon such a life;[5] He reminded others that the foxes had holes and the birds had nests, but the Son of man had not where to lay His head.[6] None of His disciples took up with Him as a result of the issue of a course of reasoning. We do not read that one of His true followers became such because of His miracles, at least none of

[1] Mark iv. 34.
[2] Matt. xxvi. 51.
[3] Luke ix. 55.
[4] John vi. 26.
[5] Luke xiv. 28.
[6] Luke ix. 58.

THE RELIGION OF TO-MORROW

His more noted and intimate followers. But how were His disciples made? Only by His personal influence. "Follow Me," and straightway some forsook their nets, and another his seat as a tax-collector, and followed Him. Mary and Martha were devoted to Him before ever He raised Lazarus; 'twas not His ghostly power, but His own self that won them. And after His death the disciples went everywhere witnessing for Him. They reasoned and they performed miracles, to be sure, but it was as witnesses they conquered, it was through "testimony" they won others to that Christ who had won them. Thus the touch of Jesus brought His immediate followers, their touch in turn brought others, and so on, even as the leaven leaveneth the whole lump.

The wisdom of Jesus in choosing this form of power, to which to commit His Gospel, is apparent in that personal influence is the most *powerful* force known to this day among men. All other modes of commanding men are superficial and leave the inner man untouched. Jesus penetrated beneath all these and seized the real force that moves and molds mankind. By force and arms you may change one's actions—the conduct, but not the man. By argument you can change his opinions, but not his emotions and his will.

THE LEAVEN

By marvelous displays of grandeur and glory you can change his feelings, arousing awe, admiration, or fear; the sentiments, not the reason. By wealth you may bribe him, excite his cupidity, and thus again change his conduct, but not his reason nor his will.

But when you attach a man to you as a friend, and he comes under the spell of your personality, the whole man is subtly changed to become like you. He begins to imitate your ways—that is, you are altering his conduct; he begins to talk as you do—that is, your opinions are becoming his; his taste and feelings copy yours; even his will is conforming to your will. And all this transformation is going on in him with his entire approval; he delights in it; and, not as in the case of the other agencies, where he resists all other forms of power brought to bear on him as repulsive to his self-respect, now he boasts of and coöperates with the influence of his friend in himself.

Many phases of life show the potency of personality. This power is increased by the numbers of those partaking of it. By addition it acquires dynamic force in geometric ratio. So in the unquestioning obedience to fashion's decrees, wherein we all quietly submit, we are simply yielding to the pressure of the persons about us. No one adopts a style of dress because it is reasonable, for these styles are often most unreasonable, but we meekly yield to the most absurd of them rather than resist this force and be called eccentric. So what we call public opinion is the most mighty power to-day known. The two greatest nations of earth are confessedly governed by it, and in a less degree are all the other civilized countries. Thrones are but as reeds before it. It makes armies victorious or defeats them. It enforces law and without it any law is a dead letter. And public opinion is nothing but opinion which has gained resistless energy by acquiring the power of many strong personalities; it is potent or weak in proportion to the numbers of men, and the personal force of the men, who hold it. Did Jesus foresee that in the ages to come this force of personality, to which He boldly intrusted the propagation and defense of His kingdom, would thus be the acknowledged chief power in human government and all human concerns? Did He not know that, once His Gospel became the personal conviction of a sufficient number and quality of men, it would then become an irresistible tide, needing no law nor army nor organization behind it, but sweeping on to overwhelm the earth, "as the waters cover the sea?" Men have always been looking for

THE LEAVEN

"the power of God" to be manifested in some crude, superficial way, not realizing that the personality of Jesus is the power of God. Thus when He appeared after His resurrection, His disciples asked, "Lord, wilt Thou at this time restore again the kingdom of Israel?"[1] And replying, He declared it was not for them to know the times and the seasons; they had the wrong idea of God's power; that power was not to be shown in divine pyrotechnics, but it was to operate, as leaven, *through them;* "But ye shall receive power and be witnesses unto Me unto the uttermost parts of the earth."

Another aspect of the operation of God's power in Christ is seen in the *secrecy* of the leaven's working. The change in a man's nature when he comes to know Jesus is, in a manner, unconscious. Just as when you associate with a strong friend you are changed to become like him, all the while thinking it is of yourself you are changing by your own volition. You do not think of yourself as doing, liking, and willing things because your friend does, likes, and wills them; but you suppose you thus act because you wish to. He has percolated secretly into your *desires* and *tastes*, and changed them, or ever you were aware. The heart has spies out to detect all

[1] Acts i. 6-7.

other forms of attempt to control it; law rouses opposition, argument combativeness, wealth self-respect, and fear suspicion, but personality steals in and captures the heart with the heart's consent; this works with, the others against, you.

Thus is Christ called not only the "power of God," but also "the wisdom of God."[1] The divine wisdom is apparent more in the way His personality has conquered than in all other exhibitions of Almighty intelligence. There is more shrewdness, judgment, perception, and foresight shown in the operation of Jesus than in any other of God's works that we can see. The law was a form of God's power, but it lost its force and had to give way for a better motive. Therefore came this new display of wisdom, "Immanuel, God with us," which men thought foolish, and which a hundred times they have proclaimed as dead and gone, but which to-day is the most vital power in the human race.

There is no danger in the fullest use of this power. The use of other ways to influence men is accompanied with extreme difficulty, and has had most lamentable results. Ecclesiastical authority has made heresy and rebellion, arguments have created infidels, wealth and social advantages have produced hypo-

[1] 1 Cor. i. 24.

THE LEAVEN

crites. But the personality of God in Christ shining in and through men has done good, only good, nothing but good. Not that church organizations, books of Christian "evidences," and the hope of a better social standing are bad motives; they are bad only when taken in themselves, when there is no supreme Christ-person in them.

The kingdom of God is like leaven also in its *silence*. We naturally turn to things that make great noise for our symbols of power. This is our childishness. All noise is waste. The real power of the lightning's bolt is not in the thunder, but in the electricity. What we hear in the roar of the locomotive or the trolley car is the friction and the offal of power; the real force of the steam and the electric current is intrinsically silent. So we call the army and navy the strength of the nation; but its real strength is in the sentiments of patriotism and heroism, and in the skill of hand and ingenuity of brain of its people. In like manner we have been deceived as to the real evidence of the power of the Gospel. It is not in the number of church members; it is still a mistake to "number Israel." It is not in the great endowments of Christian institutions and the revenues of the church. It is not in the laws. Church and law are not supports of the Gospel.

THE RELIGION OF TO-MORROW

The Gospel is the support of them. Take the personal influence of Jesus out of them and they would crumble like a mummy. It is the life that gives efficiency to the body, not the body to the life. God was not in the earthquake nor the storm nor the fire, but in the still, small voice. The potency of Christianity to-day is not in the great *works* Christians are doing, but it is in what Christians *are*. Our efficiency is not tested by our *volition*, but by our *condition*.

Leaven is also mysteriously *invisible*. No science has as yet explained how and why leaven changes the wort. Neither has any metaphysician explained how and why Christ renews the heart in His own image; yet both are indisputable facts. So you cannot tell the size of the church, and who are of Christ, and who are not; no man can read that new name save him that has it. The church is not bounded by its membership. For as a candle throws its beams into the darkness, so does the church "shine in a naughty world."[1] A little here and there, a subtle influence in press and legislature and business and society—who shall tell where the refracted rays of Christ's personality penetrate? He is filling earth with His Spirit as a rosebush fills

---

[1] "How far that little candle throws its beams!
So shines a good deed in a naughty world."
The Merchant of Venice, Act V., Scene 1.

THE LEAVEN

the garden with its perfume. In addition to "them that are His" how many feel His flavor, His warmth, His magnetism? As the light precedes the sun and the earth feels the god of day before he rises to beam upon it with his own face, so civilization, business, society, all human thought and imagination and conduct, are quickened and affected by the presence of "the Sun of righteousness" that has risen "with healing in his wings" full upon the heart and life of a few.

The reader of the New Testament has been struck by the fact, moreover, that leaven is made to illustrate the work of evil as well as of good.[1] The Jews ate unleavened bread at their feast of the Passover because leaven was a sign of the workings of heathenism, and the chosen nation should be kept untainted. Jesus warned His disciples to beware of the leaven of the Pharisees. In other words the kingdom of hell as well as the kingdom of heaven is like a lump of leaven, and the personality of God works precisely the same way in which works also the personality of evil beings. It is no new, strange method God in Christ adopts. "As by man came death, by man, also, came the resurrection from the dead." "As in Adam all die, *even so* in Christ shall all be made alive."[2] The

[1] Mark viii. 15.   [2] 1 Cor. xv. 21, 22.

terms of the new life are direct antitheses to the terms of the old life. Born in sin, born again from above; sin is death, Christ is life; sin is sickness, Christ came healing; sin is not outside, but within the very texture of the soul; Christ is to be formed within, not operating upon us from without.

Now, there are three ways in which evil affects me—first, personally and consciously, then through my environment; and again, by heredity. "Even so" Christ operates by His influence to save me.

Personally I am conscious of sin in the direct influences brought to bear on me by others. Sometimes I am pressed to sin by fear, fear of some loss or pain or of temporal unpleasantness or disgrace; "even so" I am induced to righteousness by the Gospel's elevating that fear from its action as a base and cowardly feeling and making it to be a noble and heroic emotion, as it is manliest of all things in a brave man yet to fear his own self-respect or the scorn of good men or the displeasure of God.[1] Fear of a low, sensual life is not a craven dread of the *consequences* of it, but a loathing and fleeing from its very self as a dreadful thing. Again, my imagination tends to lead me astray, being contaminated

---

[1] "Dowered with the hate of hate, the scorn of scorn, The love of love."   TENNYSON: The Poet.

THE LEAVEN

with unclean visions or conceiving for me forbidden pleasures; and "even so" Christ captures the fancy and sets it upon divine work, making it take pleasure in picturing the delight of being kind and helpful, filling it with anticipations of the joy I may work in sad men by my effort, and painting the glories of that place in the heavens He has prepared for me. Again, my habits are prone to become evil chains for my spirit; "even so" His work in the world has made churches by whose ritual and services I can form good habits, His Book preserves the law with its regulative moralities, and His own and His chief servants' examples encourage me in practicing religious routine and the arts of holy living, that thus custom may buttress my soul when mind and spirit are weak. But, most of all, evil affects me directly by arousing my bad desires, such as greed, ambition, jealousy, appetite, and the like. Now, he does not come among my desires to stamp them out, to make a desert of my heart and call it peace; but He comes saying, "What God has cleansed call thou not common";[1] there is no natural appetite nor propensity of flesh or spirit that is not holy; I am not to kill my flesh by starvation and mutilation; I am to master it. He says not, "Slay thy

[1] Acts x. 15.

heart," but, "My son, give *Me* thy heart."[1] He comes not to destroy, but to save life. He comes to set all the desires in order, to establish regulative harmony where was discord. Of loves He approves, so He but be the king of love in me. Eating and drinking are right, so they but be "unto the Lord." Ambition is holy, if it be His ambition—to serve. Avarice is right, if it be a desire to seek "not yours but you," not to be rich in taking goods from men, but in increasing good in men. So He descends into the very cellars and hidden wells of life, and where sin did abound His loving favor does much more abound.

But I not only am worked upon by evil directly, but indirectly, through my environment unconsciously molding me. There are millions sinful, not because they personally and deliberately choose to be so, but because their surroundings are such that they never have known anything else. They live under systems of caste and superstition; all around them lust is deified; cruelty is in the air they breathe; they suck in beastliness and sin with their mothers' milk. Therefore as sin thus is entrenched in environment, "even so" Jesus proposes to change and is changing that

[1] Pr. xxiii. 26.

THE LEAVEN

environment. As the kingdom of the devil has settled into vast institutions and governments and public opinions, as in China and the cannibal islands, so the kingdom of God "even so" develops great churches, civilizations, democracies. The condition of any man, even a bad man, born in the United States, where churches and English civilization and a free government make the atmosphere for him, is vastly better and more like Christ than the condition of a man born in Central Africa or Middle China, where he sees naught but cruelty, tyranny, lechery, and superstition: and that without touching the personal volition of the man himself. Where Christ's influence goes, laws and governments and customs and habits of life insensibly are elevated, giving the individual a better chance.

The third way evil works in me is by heredity, the most important of all, it is sometimes said. We can never decide whether heredity, environment, or personal volition is most responsible for our misdeeds. Perhaps it is a useless question; they all interplay; but the personal influence of God in Christ is working through all of them, and heredity not the least. Paul compares the two Adams, setting the one's work over against the other's. And whether we accept the modern scientific theory, that man evolved from the beast, or the view heretofore held by most churchly teaching, the comparison is good scientifically and theologically. That is, whether man's rise is a struggle to throw off "the heritage of the beast," or to rid himself of the taint of "Adam's fall," it amounts to the same thing practically. The gist of both ideas is the same; that I have inherited certain evil tendencies, whether evil as animalizing me or evil as alienating me from God, and that it is for me to lessen the power of these traits in me and transmit them in a less degree to my child.

Now, it is a historical fact that previous to Christ's personality getting a firm foothold in the world—that is, previous to the Reformation—no permanent progress was made by the race. There were spasmodic rises of certain nations into dignity and grandeur, such as among the Greeks and Romans, but the lapse into decay was speedy; whereas since Jesus has been everywhere preached by an open Bible as a risen Lord, there has been a general and world-wide progress of mankind.

Jesus emphasized the sanctity of marriage, the family life; and the family is God's institution for holding the new generation long enough in the lap of the old to rivet progress and make the advance in righteousness secure. No means is comparable to the family as a

THE LEAVEN

vehicle for transmitting personal influence. Thus it is the apparent plan of God not only to save the individual, but to save the human stock. The triumph of the Gospel is to be when men are born holy, even as they are now born in sin; when the personality of God in Christ is to be bred into them, coming as a power in the very blood. To this end looked the prophets, who declared that "My people shall be all righteous," and "They shall not teach, every man his neighbor, saying, know the Lord; for all shall know Me, from the least to the greatest." Through these ancient prophets the Lord declared that He would make a new covenant with His people, not like the old covenant on Sinai, that of outward rules and laws, "for this is the covenant that I will make, saith the Lord; I will put my laws into their mind, and write them in their hearts; and I will be to them a God, and they shall be to Me a people." Thus "Christ, the power of God," is to go on purging and clarifying the human stock, regenerating it by the same process by which it degenerated, flowing into it through the avenues of heredity until all men shall be born into the world like John the Baptist, "sanctified from their mother's womb."[1]

[1] "Before thou camest forth out of the womb I sanctified thee." Jer. i. 5. See also Luke i. 15.

THE RELIGION OF TO-MORROW

And now we begin to see the rational, scientific, common-sense view of the millennium, the second advent, the personal reign of Jesus on earth. As men misconceived the meaning of salvation and heaven and the resurrection, grasping the lower, the tangible thought, and missing the true and upper thought, so they have caricatured the millennium, conceiving it to be some theatric return of a bodily Christ in the clouds, to take place after the Jews' restoration to Judea as a nation, or after the world has gone on getting as wicked as it can, or after some mystical apocalyptic "time and times and a half a time," and all such literalistic artificialities. But the millennium is to come surely after the manner of God's working and Christ's Spirit. His manifest plan is by orderly development, not by spectacular cataclysms. The world is to be redeemed "even so" as in Adam it died. The personality of God in Christ is to work as leaven "until the whole be leavened." Not that the millennium is to come by breeding alone, but by heredity and environment and personal choice, even as sin has spread.

And what inconceivable majesty and vastness such a view lends to the whole idea of the work of the Gospel. We perceive the Christ entering the lists with evil and overcoming it by its own means. Being mani-

THE LEAVEN

fested to destroy the works of the devil, He is attacking wickedness by means subtler than its own. We sometimes despair at the lack of results in our work for Him. How few are converted by our preaching! Our churches and Sunday-schools and colleges, how unsatisfactory their effect seems to us! How many are the forces of the wicked! How many are the hypocrites among us! How evasive, yet how potent, are the lusts of the flesh and the more dangerous weaknesses of the spirit! How vast the great heathendoms that still enslave and imbrute men! What intellect, what social prestige stands over against the simplicity of the Gospel! How dominant are the great perversions of His truth! How selfishness and tyranny and greed have invaded business methods! In a word, how great are the kingdoms of the "prince of this world!" And what can we, who have naught but the preachment of the Gospel, avail against the prestige and resources of this immense display?

But when we rise to see God working according to the programme of Jesus we begin to see wherein is our hope of victory. It is in the personal influence of God; and that is shown in the testimony, the personal influence of His followers. Thus Christ, the Captain of our salvation, is not a whit behind the evil one. Is wickedness sly? It can creep into no corner of the heart, no depth of desire, where the Spirit of Him that made the heart cannot find and slay it. Is our imagination debauched by the profligate glories of sin? Sin can unroll before the mind no visions like unto those things which "eye hath not seen, nor ear heard, neither hath it entered into the mind of man to conceive, but which God hath revealed unto us by His Spirit which He has given us." Do evil friends contaminate us? No man nor woman has been given such power over us as He has given to the gentle mother whose songs have lulled our infant slumbers and whose prayers cling like changeless dew to our memory, songs and prayers of the dying love and risen power of our God. Are the immense institutions of men, their governments, their society, their business practice, corrupt and corrupting? As proud icebergs melt before the glow of the tropic sun, so shall they disappear before the invincible gentleness, the triumphant warmth and purity of the Sun of righteousness whose streaming light has in it the potency of Almighty God. Are we tainted by heredity? No taint of earthly parentage is of force to annul our original heredity from the Father when the Christ shall raise us up to be heirs of God and joint-

THE LEAVEN

heirs with Himself. Through this Man, who is the fullness of the Godhead bodily, radiates the personal influence of God to the earth; secretly as the leaven, strangely as the wind, tenderly as a shepherd, irresistibly as destiny, He is drawing all men unto Himself. "Christ the power of God! Christ the wisdom of God! Wonderful, Counselor, the mighty God, the everlasting Father, and the Prince of Peace! Of the increase of His government there shall be no end, to order it, and to establish it, with judgment and with justice from henceforth even forever."

"O the depths of the riches both of the wisdom and knowledge of God! How unsearchable are His judgments, and His ways past finding out!

"For of Him, and through Him, and to Him, are all things; to whom be glory forever! Amen!"[1]

[1] 1 Cor. 1. 24; Isa. ix. 6; Rom. xi. 33-36.

SUGGESTIONS

In propagating His religion Jesus did not use argument, for His religion is not a theory; nor force, for His religion is not an organization; nor fear, for His religion is not a superstition; but He used personal influence, for His religion is a Life.

Personal influence is a force that increases geometrically in proportion to the number of those who share it.

Public opinion is nothing but accumulated personal influence.

No other force than personality can change even the desires.

All other forces work against you, personal influence with you.

All other forms of effort to make Christians are accompanied with danger, except the form of personal influence.

Church and law are not the support of the Gospel; the Gospel is the support of them.

The aroma of Christ has worked wonders for the world, even as the taste of Christ has done for the elect.

The influence of Jesus descends even into the hidden wells of our life.

Christ's influence reforms not only individuals but institutions, giving the individual a better chance.

Christ also cleanses the channel of heredity.

God grows things; men make things.

We well say "Personal Devil," for there is no devil but personality.

One's personal influence alone remains in the world as the net result of all he has done.

CHAPTER XI

HELL

The Bible was not Given to Reveal "Last Things," nor Future Events; not to Gratify Curiosity, but to Reveal the Laws of God's Personal Influence

"What is that to thee? Follow thou Me!"—JESUS, John xxi. 22.

"Heav'n but the Vision of fulfill'd Desire,
And Hell the Shadow of a Soul on fire."
OMAR KHAYYAM, *Rubaiyat*, Stanza 67.

"There is no reason, indeed, against our believing anything clearly *revealed in Scripture;* but there *is* reason against going beyond Scripture with speculations of our own. One of the many evils resulting always from this, is, that we thus lay open Christianity to infidel objections, such as it otherwise would have been safe from."—WHATELY, *Corruptions of Christianity*, p. 210.

"While Johnson and I stood in calm conference by ourselves in Dr. Taylor's garden, at a pretty late hour of a serene autumn night, looking up to the heavens, I directed the discourse to the subject of a future state. My friend was in a placid and most benignant frame of mind. 'Sir,' said he, 'I do not imagine that all things will be made clear to us immediately after death, but that the ways of Providence will be explained to us very gradually.' I ventured to ask him concerning the doctrine of future punishment. JOHNSON: 'Sir, . . . some of the texts of Scripture upon this subject are, as you observe, indeed strong; but they may admit of a mitigated interpretation.' He talked to me upon this awful and delicate question in a gentle tone, as if afraid to be decisive."—BOSWELL, *Life of Johnson*, Vol. III., p. 135.

CHAPTER XI

There are few qualified to form correct notions about the future state of the wicked, because long ages of heated controversy have set prejudices firmly in most minds by the biting mordant of partisan spirit. If one is determined that he will hold his present opinion true, no matter what may be said, it will be manifestly time wasted to read this or any other writing which treats upon the subject. Theological disputes ranging through generations have, however, considerable value to the person who is seeking truth alone; they prove to him[1] that neither side can be wholly wrong, else so many sensible persons would not continue to choose it, and that neither side can be wholly right, else so many would not have rejected it; and still further, that the whole controversy itself cannot be an essential and pivotal element in our religion, else God would not have left it so that intelligent and pious men could hon-

---

[1] Perhaps it would be more exact to say "they make it appear extremely probable to him," than to say "they prove to him," for the variations of error, of course, have no value to locate the truth.

estly have had such variant views; and further yet, that the real, true view will never be discovered by either party gaining a complete victory and routing the other, else it would have been done long ago, but that the truth will finally appear, as indeed it has appeared in most such debates, from the subsidence of controversial war, and from the perception that after all both sides had somewhat of truth, and that they were separated, not by the wrong logic of the one and the right logic of the other, but because they stood upon different *points of view.*

There are two parties to the dispute as to whether the wicked will suffer forever. The one insists that if they do not so suffer the very heart is cut out of the Gospel. They make this question a test of orthodoxy. They think that to abate one mite from the eternity of the wicked's woes is to let down the gates to the presumptuous lawlessness of men; it is to make divine justice a farce. If this party be called extreme, the opposing party have often proved themselves none the less so. They have insisted that to make God out as capable of allowing His creatures to finally continue in misery is a barbarous notion; that all who hold to it are ignorant literalists, and that none except those who believe God's mercy will at last make all men happy

HELL

ought to be allowed to open their mouths in this enlightened day.

Now, in one respect, at least, both of these factions are wrong, in that they are trying to settle a question by reason (or, to be more exact, by *à priori* reasoning), which *in the nature of the case* can only be settled by a divine revelation. Nobody knows and nobody can possibly ascertain, by arguments drawn from that extremely limited sphere of God's operations we in this world can observe, what is going to take place a billion years from now. If God intends for us to know, He will tell us, and tell us certainly in clear language. Therefore the question must be decided entirely by the Bible; and as anything can be proved by a person coming to the Bible with a ready-made opinion, as he can pick out here and there texts to substantiate any view, we must call to our aid the only two reliable interpreters of the Bible—*i. e.*, common sense and the Spirit of Jesus.

Opening the sacred volume and reading over all that is said upon the subject of the sufferings of the wicked, we find, first, that as far as the Old Testament is concerned, there is no reference to their punishment in the next world at all. The old dispensation was entirely temporal. The woes pronounced were to overtake the rebellious in this life;

the extremest penalty for any violation of law was death. The author of Hebrews sums up that criminal code by saying, "He that despised Moses' law died without mercy."[1] While there may be hints or suggestions of calamity beyond the grave, Moses and the prophets never plainly declared it, and they spake understandingly enough when they wished.

It was Christ who "brought immortality to light." It is when we read the New Testament that we gain all our distinct information about the future state.

Now, before we read, we must remind ourselves *why* we read the Bible at all. We read it to find out what we do not already know or to confirm or correct what we do know. Certain things are revealed to us by the light of nature, or natural moral instincts; whatever harmonizes with these instincts and approves them may be lightly treated by the revelators, relying upon our own natures not to doubt them; but whatever is contrary to those natural convictions of mankind, and is utterly different from them, we must expect to be set down in a most unmistakable way. The natural feeling of men is that a sinner ought to suffer; but no one will say that we naturally think he ought to suffer forever. Hence,

[1] Heb. x. 28.

HELL

if God *intends to convey* to us the latter piece of information we shall find it plainly stated in such form as to leave no room for reasonable doubt. As, for instance, on the contrary, the conviction of immortality is natural, and always in some form or other has been a belief of every religion; therefore Jesus says of this, "If it were not so, I would have told you."[1] And we may well say that if He purposed to tell us that the wicked are to be eternally punished He would have told us explicitly.

Taking up, then, our New Testament, and marking carefully all parts that bear upon the fate of the wicked, we are struck first of all by the fact that the article of faith in question—that is, that the wicked are to be shut up in a hell of torment forever after they die—is nowhere didactically, categorically stated in plain terms. If it is there, it is there not because Jesus or His apostles said so distinctly, but because of an *interpretation* we put upon their words. If we read those words with that idea in our minds to begin with, we shall indeed find not a few texts that agree with it, but the idea itself is not originally revealed in the Scriptures. And knowing as we do that all false religions reveled in hells for the torment of unbeliev-

[1] John xiv. 1.

ers, we can readily see that the idea itself came into men's minds from outside—that is, from heathen or rabbinical sources, and established itself in Christian theology by its remarkable agreement with certain figurative language in which the fate of the evil persons is spoken of.

We are struck next with this feature of the language used in treating of this matter; that it consists in a *variety* of *illustrations* or *figures*, such as Gehenna (the valley near Jerusalem where refuse was burned), an unquenchable fire, an undying worm, outer darkness where there is wailing and gnashing of teeth, everlasting fire prepared for the devil and his angels, or such woe as that it had been better had the man never been born.[1] Now, common sense at once tells us that these figures cannot *all* be *literally* true, for they are contradictory; and the only way in which they can be understood as true *at all* is to construe them as different *illustrations* of some one *hidden* reality. Furthermore, the God who inspired the Scriptures surely inspired the *mode* in which they convey information; and

---

[1] Gehenna, Matt. v. 22, 29; x. 28; xviii. 9, etc. Everlasting fire, Matt. xxv. 41. Fire that shall never be quenched, Mark ix. 45, etc. Worm dieth not, Mark ix. 44-46 only. Outer darkness, Matt. viii. 12; xxii. 13; xxv. 30. Wailing and gnashing of teeth, Matt. xiii. 42. Fire prepared for the devil, xxv. 41. Better never been born, Mark xiv. 21. Tormented in flame, Luke xvi. 24. Lake of fire, Rev. xx. 14. Lake of fire and brimstone, Rev. xxi. 8. Second death, Rev. xxi. 8.

HELL

it is evident that it was the manifest design of Jesus *not* to *reveal* the place where the wicked are to go, neither the details nor the duration of their suffering, but to *conceal these very points*, while He disclosed the *general nature* of their fate.

There can be no figures or symbols, however, unless there is some reality to correspond with them. And the real fact that fits all these pictures is that to persist in evil will surely bring upon one boundless misery. Like a carcass in the Gehenna field of offal, he will cut himself off from the society of the good; his anguish will be such as can only be described by fire, outer darkness, weeping and wailing, and gnashing of teeth. No one can read the words of Jesus and the writings of Paul without gathering that the condition of those who neglect so great salvation is something infinitely tragic. Not only would Jesus not have used such lurid figures when He referred to the fate of the wicked, but He never would have been so terribly in earnest; He would not have so agonized in Gethsemane nor have so died upon Calvary, had not that *from which* He came to save men been pitiable and revolting in the extreme. Because Jesus did not *detail* the circumstances, fix the *duration* and locate the *place* of the evil ones after death, it is the most wretched perversion of a logical conclusion to hold that He did not *at all* say they were to suffer, or that He said they were to suffer lightly.

But it may be said, all this is not the point at issue; we all agree that the wicked will suffer, but some of us contend that this suffering is everlasting and some that it is not. To this the full and complete answer is that the Scriptures do not didactically state whether the suffering of the wicked will be endless or not. This is proved to common sense by the very fact that the controversy over this point has been so long waged. And as there is no criterion by which to settle religious controversy except the Scriptures, and as this dispute hinges upon differing interpretations of the Scriptures, there is very little prospect of its ceasing, unless it dies out from sheer exhaustion.[1] In short, we *do not know* whether the wicked will persist in sin and sin's inevitable misery forever, and God *never intended to tell us.*

It is a great fault with many that they think it an evidence of weakness to say, "I do not know," whereas, it is as much a sign of accurate thought to clearly see what it is that you do *not* know, as it is to see what it is

---

[1] As John Fiske says, upon another subject: "It is not that the question which once so sorely puzzled men has ever been settled, but that it has been outgrown."—Destiny of Man, p. 16.

HELL

you do know. Many think they must either believe or disbelieve every point in religion; and as a consequence they range themselves upon one side of every question, as baptism, or bodily resurrection, or eternal punishment, and make up in partisan loyalty and controversial zeal what they lack in real information.[1] For, as a matter of fact, we are called on to believe only what is so plainly revealed that we know what it means. Belief without intelligence is intellectual prostitution; it is not belief, it is blind mental partisanship. As for what is *not* revealed we are not called upon *either* to believe or disbelieve; we are, if we wish to be honest, to say frankly we do not know, and to hold our judgment in *suspense* awaiting reliable information. This is the kind of *agnosticism* Christian people ought to cultivate; without it our sincerity will always be justly suspected.

Those, therefore, who say they believe the wicked will persist forever in evil, are wise above what is written. And yet one does not feel like utterly condemning this class, because the *motive* of their belief is a just and good motive. It springs not from cruelty, nor is it because they are fond of their belief, but it arises from the profound conviction of the exceeding sinfulness of sin; they do not wish

---

[1] In the same way they also take up political beliefs.

in any slightest degree to countenance the heresy that a man can be wicked and ever be anything else than unhappy. Their belief, then, receives the strength of their whole consent, not because God has so plainly revealed this point, but because they fear the *consequences* of any other belief, as they are under the mistaken impression that if they do not believe this they *must* disbelieve it, not perceiving that their true position is to simply say they do not know.

But there are few greater errors than to allow our belief in the truth to be in any wise shaped by our hope or fears of the consequences of the truth. This is quite sure to lead us astray. It is, really, a subtle doubt as to the morality of truth itself, and as such it is a doubt of God's goodness; for God is truth. It is putting out our hand to stay the ark. It is presumptuous; and when we come squarely to look at it, it is absurd. For the consequences of truth are not *our* affair; they are God's concern. All we are to do is to ascertain the truth as nearly as we can, and, having found out what is truth, then to believe it, knowing well that it is good. Truth does not need our assistance. We are not to fly, with our rash and unfounded self-made beliefs, to the aid of the eternal truth. Therefore, whatever may be the effect, let us man-

HELL

fully say we know not, when we do know not; and let us further assure our hearts that the *consequences* of leaving this matter unrevealed will surely be *good*, or else God would not have left it so. "He doeth all things well."

The converse is equally true. Those who insist that the wicked shall all be gathered into heaven are also wise above what is written. The Scriptures say not so; and they have elevated an inference of their own mind up to the level of God's revelation. Just like the other class they, too, are rushing to the *defense* of God, as though He needed defense. As the others think they vindicate God's justice, so these think they vindicate God's love. Surely both these parties are like Job's friends, of whom it is written: "Then the Lord answered Job out of the whirlwind, and said: Who is this that darkeneth counsel by words without knowledge? Gird up thy loins now like a man, and answer thou Me; where wast *thou* when I laid the foundations of the earth? He that reproveth God, let him answer it!"[1] God certainly designed the future for all men, both good and bad, to be hidden, as far as place, duration, and circumstance are concerned; and He intended only to make known the *general law* that the results

---

[1] Job xxxviii. 1-4; xl. 2.

of the life of Christ will be glorious beyond dreams, and the results of rejecting Christ will be the most terrible thing that can possibly befall. And who are *we* that we "add to the words of the Book,"[1] for fear enough is not written?

This view, that of candid ignorance upon the ultimate fate of men, is perfectly consistent with the general order of Providence as we observe it in this life. If that order is to be reversed, we may reasonably expect to find that fact unmistakably declared; but we do not find this. No man knows what the morrow will bring forth.

"Heaven hides from all the book of fate,
All but the page prescribed, the present date."

It is under such conditions God created man; intending him to use the *present* and to leave the future in his Maker's hands. The *laws* which govern the future He makes plain, as that goodness brings future peace, and evil future trouble; but the *kind* of peace or trouble, the *circumstances* or the exact *duration*, He does not disclose. Such is the nature of His moral government. And why think we it will be all different beyond the grave? We have a right to *infer* that it will be the same; the burden of proof rests upon those who insist that it will be changed.

[1] Rev. xxii. 18.

We find, then, that the New Testament reveals a *fact*, which is figuratively stated by Christ, and purposely so stated by Him as to preclude common sense from taking Him literally. Christ's method was story and picture. Paul's method was round, downright, didactic statement; and hence in Paul we find the fact definitely stated to which Christ poetically referred—to wit, that "God will render unto them that do not obey the truth, indignation and wrath, tribulation and anguish; and to every soul that doeth good, glory, honor, and peace,"[1] and that He will do this "in the day of revelation of the righteous judgment of God." That does not necessarily mean the commonly held day of judgment, but the day or time when the righteous character of God's arrangements *appear;*[2] for *now* wicked men often seem happy and good men wretched, His laws seem so unequal that many a fool thinks to be successful by defying them, but by and by it is absolutely certain that they will *see* that sin brings woe, and goodness joy, and *that* is "the day of the revelation of God's righteous judgment."[3] When that is to occur no one

---

[1] Rom. ii. 6-9.

[2] "Exposure, detection, disgrace; this is the worst part of punishment. But what can any exposure be in this world, to the revelations which may come hereafter when the secrets of all hearts shall be revealed?"—James Freeman Clarke.

[3] Rom. ii. 5.

knows, "no, not even the angels of God, but only the Father."[1]

All along the course of time men have been setting dates for God, and He has been disappointing them. If there is anything manifest in sacred history it is this law that God will bring His servants to joy and reward and the wicked to confusion, but *also* that He *specifically reserves* the method and time of so doing in His own counsel.[2] Abraham, Moses, and the other Old Testament saints, "all these died, not having received the promises"[3]—that is, the promises were not fulfilled as *they* thought they would be, but in a better way. And the apostles and early Christians fully expected Christ's bodily return to earth, but while Christ has returned as a spiritual power, they were certainly mistaken if they believed that He would return in bodily glory in their day.[4]

Let us therefore leave the places and other details of the future life where Jesus left them—in God's hands. To say it is not enough to let the matter remain so indefinite is to distrust God. "Take no thought for the morrow." Live right to-day and God is pledged for a bright to-morrow. But it may

---
[1] Matt. xxiv. 36.
[2] See the case of Jonah—Jonah ii. 10; iii. 1.
[3] Heb. xi. 39.
[4] F. W. Robertson's sermon on "The Illusiveness of Life" beautifully expands this thought.

HELL

be said, the future states are great incentives to right lives. That they are such is true; yet it is not the *fancies*, but the *facts* of those states that are *proper* incentives; the facts are woe and joy, the fancies are the place, time, and circumstances of that woe and joy.

A similar question is that of whether the heathen will be "saved" or not. This question is half removed when we recall the Scripture sense of salvation, which is not that of taking a man to a place called heaven. The other half of the question is removed when we remember that God's design in revelation was not at all to impart any information except such as bears upon the character and fate of those *to whom* the Bible is *addressed*. Now, the Bible is addressed, of course, only to its *readers;* it has absolutely nothing to say of the fate of others. It tells me *my* duty and destiny; and when I look within it to find the duty and destiny of any one else it only says: "What is that to *thee?* Follow thou Me!"[1] In other words, the Book of God does not impart purely speculative information; never gratifies mere curiosity. The fate of the heathen in the next world is distinctly none of our affair; God will attend to them. Those who say the heathen will all be damned because they did not believe, having never

[1] John xxi. 22.

heard, and also those who say the heathen will all be saved because God is good, are alike wise above what is written. The *true* belief is that we do not know what will take place between them and their Father hereafter; but we *do* know that their joy will be increased to an infinite degree both in this and the next life if we impart to them this grace of God's transforming influence we have received. The "nerve of missions," their motive, is not to hasten to save lost souls from the wrath of an angry God, but rather to hasten to impart unto them eternal life, because we love them as Christ loved us.

The case stands very much the same with the dispute concerning a second probation. Neither those who contend for this nor those who deny it can find a clear line of Scriptural teaching substantiating their position. And from this it is manifest that God did not intend for us to know. If He had, He would have told us. The importance of the present life is by Holy Writ impressed upon us by the fact that the future is unknown. That is *God's* way. Deeming that insufficient, we make haste to *add* our conclusions and inferences to the body of revelation; therefore to our theological fray has been "added all the plagues written in the Book."[1]

[1] Rev. xxii. 18.

HELL

But the view here stated will be met by two protests. One class of persons will say: "What! shall a man be given to understand that he may have hope, if he dies in his sins?" This class is properly jealous for God's justice, and suspicious of any form of doctrine that may contain the least implication that the rejection of Christ is not a fatal and dangerous thing. The other class will say: "What! shall we mourn by the coffin of our friend, who never had the Gospel strongly, attractively, and clearly put to him, as for one eternally damned?" This class is properly jealous for God's kindness. Let us answer both.

And first: Is there any ground of hope for one who dies in his sins? The supposition is that if such hope is entertained, it will lead men presumptuously to put off accepting Christ until the next life. Now we must be again reminded that death has no moral significance. Death as an event eternally settling and irrevocably fixing the moral condition of man is not clearly and unmistakably taught in the Scriptures. The idea is an outgrowth of that artificial Latin theology that made as much of the "last things"; exalting to an unwarranted significance the "day of judgment" and heaven as a place. It was not the idea of Jesus and the apostles to use the fear of death as an inducement for men to accept the Gospel. They taught it is fatal for a man to *be* in his sins, to live in them. If to die in sin was to be irrevocably lost, that certainly is a fact of most supreme and horrible importance, and Jesus and Paul could in no wise be excused for not stating it over and over again. But they did *not* so state it; we gather the doctrine from their *allusions*, and from single texts invariably selected from their course of argument or narrative about something *else*. For instance, the parable of the ten virgins[1] is explicitly said to relate to the destruction of Jerusalem, and the parable in Luke where those who knocked were refused admittance[2] contains no hint that the shutting of the door is *death;* and only in parables does this idea[3] occur even this much, never in Christ's didactic teaching. The author of Hebrews says: "As it is appointed unto man once to die, and after that the judgment";[4] but the gist of his argument is not that he is proving that man has only one trial, but that Jesus as the divine Lamb needed only *once* to die in order to perfect the remission of sins. It is not sound sense

[1] "*Then* shall the kingdom of heaven be likened unto ten virgins," etc., Matt. xxv. 1.
[2] Luke xiii. 25-30.
[3] That is, the idea of the *time when* the punishment of the wicked is to take place.
[4] Heb. ix. 27. The gist of the argument, in which this passage occurs, is: As a man has but one life, even so he needs but one sacrifice to purify that life.

to elevate these and similar illustrations, which are by-remarks, into a doctrine of the most fatal importance.

But, it will be objected, this opens the flood-gates to presumptuous sin; unless we teach that death is the fatal mark beyond which is no chance, unless it is only "while the lamp holds out to burn" that "the vilest sinner may return," the Gospel is simply powerless; the strongest motive is gone. To which it may be said that this is the wrong state of mind entirely in which to approach the study of truth; we should inquire solely what *is* truth, not what will be the *effects* of truth. If the views here given are correct and Scriptural, then it is *God* that we impeach; if not correct, then we should show that they are *not Scriptural*, and not that we think them dangerous.

But the fact is that they are *not* dangerous. The only difference between the doctrine here stated and that commonly held by vulgar theology is that *this* doctrine tends to alarm the sinner by a Scriptural fear of entering the future state an alien from God to face the *unknown* consequences of his sins, which the Scriptures only say will be "a fearful thing";[1] while *that* doctrine *adds* human inferences to divine fact, and seeking by adventi-

[1] Heb. x. 31.

tious aids to frighten the sinner, loses its force and brings itself into contempt. The one is biblical, reasonable, and germane to what we know of the orderly processes and methods of God; the other is extra-biblical, unreasonable, and artificial.

If, however, a sane view of the Bible sweeps away the traditional pictures of Paradise Lost and Dante's Inferno, at the same time it destroys the unfounded hope of those who "believe" in a future probation. If God had intended us to know that in the life to come we should have another opportunity, He certainly would have so stated. The Gospel plants no flag of hope over a sinner's grave. If we believe in a second trial, we are believing our own ideas, not God's. The dying, unrepentant sinner who expects his Maker to take him into bliss, is trusting utterly to a vagary of his own mind, and has not one promise of his Father upon which to stand as he enters the unknown life beyond.

So, then, we find both parties wrong for the same one reason; they stand on the same false premise, conceiving salvation to be chiefly an affair *after* death, and the sorrow or joy of the soul then to turn upon the *place* whither they are to go. Let us therefore erase all these unfounded speculations and curious inquiries, and see if there be not a reasonable

HELL

idea of the sorrows of the wicked, see if there be not an idea that harmonizes both with what we here observe of the operation of natural law and with the general tone and drift of the Scriptures.

The nature of sin is well known. It is at first pleasant, but as it progresses the pleasure decreases and the attendant difficulties and sorrows increase. The human spirit is so constructed that it can be permanently and increasingly happy only as it obeys the law of its being; that law is that it shall know God and live under His influence. The evil of the lust of the flesh, John says, is that it "passes."[1] The soul is a son of God, with all the eternal desires and boundless needs of its Father. Fed upon aught else than God, it writhes at length in divine hunger pains. One does not have to die to be in hell. Grant him five hundred years of life, with unwasting powers of body and mind, and he will run through the gamut of all that earth can give to satisfy within at least one hundred years; the last four hundred will be more and more filled with ennui, disgust, wretchedness, and at last a very hate of life and despair of joy.[2] To insure perpetual hunger deprive a man of nutritious food, and so long as he lives he will

---

[1] "And the world passeth away, and the lust thereof; but he that doeth the will of God abideth forever." 1 John ii. 17.

[2] As in the case of Solomon. See Eccl. ii. 1-11.

suffer; so pain will last so long as a soul is deprived of God, after the artificial stimulants of sin's pleasures have lost their effect. Death has nothing to do with it; for as long as the soul lives apart from God, whether on this or another planet, it will be wretched.[1] If the unrepentant sinner is immortal, his sufferings will be immortal.

But when the sinner finds, in the next world, that he suffers, will he not turn to God for pardon, and will God not forgive him? In answer to this, we can only say that there is nothing in the Bible by which we are warranted in believing that God will not freely pardon at any time any one who asks, that He would not even pardon Satan were he to repent. But we must not forget *what God's pardon is;* it is not a removal from His books of a sentence against us, not an artificial and statutory thing; but it is His entrance into a man by His influence and *thus* cleansing him, in which work the man must be willing and coöperate. And the reason why there is no ground to believe the wicked will turn to God in the life to come is not the artificial fixity of state imparted by death, but it is the nature of man himself. It is not the unwillingness of God, but the character of the sinner that

---

[1] "Fecisti nos ad te, Domine; et inquietum est cor nostrum donec requiescat in te."—Augustine (Thou hast made us for Thyself, Lord; and our heart is restless until it rests in Thee.)

HELL

holds no hope of future pardon. For sin is *cumulative* in its nature. Doing one wrong prepares us to do another. Rejecting God's influence makes us more prone still to reject it. It is of the very nature of sin that it "waxes worse and worse."[1]

We find this made plain by what we know of wicked men here. Go among the depraved and criminal classes; you will find misery enough, and squalor, wretchedness, and disease; but do these things operate to lead them to a pure life? Do they make their victims fly to the company of the good and pure? On the contrary, they breed only further despair and transgression, and morbidly inflame the propensities to evil; and these classes even give their *sufferings* as an excuse for their *crimes*, instead of looking upon them as reasons for forsaking crimes.[2] There is nothing redemptive in sin. Stripes and woe never regenerated a rogue, although they may have made him more careful as to the methods of his rascality. If such be the effects of evil and evil's punishment *here*, how can we look for any *different* effects *hereafter?*

What does regenerate a bad man? Love, hope, self-respect; and these impulses are aroused in him by God in Christ and in

[1] 2 Tim. iii. 13.
[2] The bad heart produces bad surroundings which in turn tend to further deprave the heart.

Christly men. Now, the almost inevitable consequence of sin is to destroy the very *belief* in purity and goodness. He doubts such things exist; or if he believes in them, he does not believe they can ever reach *himself*. Thus it is that the continuance in sin tends to block the *only* avenue of escape. The influence of God alone can save him; he closes against that influence more every day; and there is no ground whatever for believing that in the *next* world he will be different from what he is in *this*. If *here* he looks on Christian men and pure women as either hypocrites, or uninteresting, colorless weaklings, doubtless he will *there* continue in the same persuasion. Therefore, we are justified in thinking it extremely probable that the man who persists in sins here until death will persist in them after death, and of course his sufferings will last as long as his sin.

The two future states of joy and of misery do not depend upon an arbitrary decree of God, given for no reason that we can see except His own will, but they are consequent upon the very nature of the case. The law of the punishment of sin is not a law which is right simply because God says so, but it is a law just as gravitation is a law, working in the constitution and nature of things. Do we complain because it hurts us when we put our

HELL

hand in the fire, or that no one believes us after we have told many lies? These laws are not whimsical verdicts of a great judge, but flow naturally along the course of reason; so likewise flows the law that he who has the life of the Son of God in him ascends from glory to glory in his career, here and hereafter, while he who has *not* this life descends more and more into the deeps of wretchedness, emptiness, and distress.

Why, then, did not God make all men so they could be no otherwise than happy? Simply because He is good. To make His laws so that a bad man can forever be happy, would show Him to be a bad God. A moral being, a good man, could not look up to such a God as his ideal. The very nature of thought implies that if obedience and truth are to gain happiness, disobedience and wrong must merit unhappiness, else there is no moral distinction between the two. If both good and evil inherit the kingdom of God, then that kingdom is not a moral one. To efface the *effects* of good and evil is to efface all good and evil themselves, and also to efface the distinction between them.

But why did God make men *capable* of evil, and so of suffering? If He made them capable of being sons of God, He must have made them also capable of refusing to be sons. If God made man *at all*, a being able to love Him of his own free will, it follows by the very nature of thought that He must have made man able to refuse to love Him. Otherwise man would simply have been a machine or a beast; for if he moves by *will*, he must be able to refuse by will.

But will God allow the major part of the race to thus persist in evil? To think so would be to limit the power of God's influence. As there is nothing in the nature of *sin* to warrant us in believing the impenitent sinner will ever be converted hereafter; so also there is nothing in the nature of *God* and His *limitless resources* to warrant us in believing that a large number of His sons will continue forever in sin and alienation from Him. But we must always bear in mind that *both* of these convictions are from our *own* reasoning—what God will actually do we must leave to Him, for He has not chosen to tell us.

Above all things we should never forget that there is no spirit of retaliation in God corresponding to our own feeling represented by that word. He is always and ever kind, just, and forbearing. The Old Testament figures of speech of God's vengeance, His whetting His sword, His fury, and the like, are widened and elevated by Christ's teachings and His personality, which show that

HELL

while the old prophets correctly apprehended the *fact* of the woe awaiting the wicked, they did not understand the *spirit* of that fact. We must clear away from our minds, along with much other theological rubbish, the notion that God has the slightest vindictiveness in His disposition. When it is said He will punish the wicked we know that He cannot inflict injury upon them merely to gratify a passion of resentment.[1] We know this, because surely Jesus was a perfect representation of God, and in Jesus we find no such feeling. He had that spirit which beareth all things, hopeth all things, and endureth all things, which returns good for evil. If He spake harshly to the Pharisees, He only warned them of the fate they were bringing upon *themselves*, and never showed the slightest sign of bringing injury upon them in return for their treatment of Him.[2] To suppose that He was acting as He did, all the while intending some day to return and pay back His persecutors in full vengeance, rejoicing in their burnings because they had offended Him; to suppose Him praying upon the cross for the Father to forgive them, and yet harboring a

---

[1] Vengeance, ekdikesis, means primarily vindication. God will *show* to the sinner and to all that the apparent prosperity of evil was a delusion and a snare.

[2] The point is, that while, as the Mover of universal law, He will bring upon them calamity, yet He will not do so as a Person seeking to sate His ire.

THE RELIGION OF TO-MORROW

plan of future retaliation—such suppositions have only to be put into words for us to see how absurd they are. When the Scriptures speak of divine "wrath" and "punishment," these terms must be understood in the full light of all that Jesus said and did and was. "No Scripture is of private interpretation";[1] that is, all texts must be read in their relation to the whole. And, above all, no one can understand the Bible without reading it in the spirit of Jesus. No text must be received apart from the light His face sheds upon it. His character and personality are a qualification upon every word of the Book.

This being true we are sure that the sufferings of the wicked will in the next world be viewed by the Deity in no spirit of gratification arising from glutted resentment; but He will view them there, as Jesus did here, with infinite sorrow and sympathy. His judgment will be just, tender, and merciful. If any suffer, it will be because for them suffering is the best, wisest, most beneficent thing that can happen. God does not hate sinners; He loves them, and will love them to the end. If there be souls in hell, He loves them also; for His love plays upon all. If they continue there in sin and sin's torment, it will be only because His infinite and ever-present loving

[1] 2 Pet. i. 20.

HELL

Spirit can find no opening in hearts shut and barred against Him. Over against the abode of lost souls stands not a furious and vengeful Monarch; but a pitiful Father, echoing His own cry upon earth: "O Jerusalem, Jerusalem, thou that killest the prophets and stonest them which are sent unto thee, how often would I have gathered thy children together, even as a hen gathereth her chickens under her wings, and ye would not!"

The sum of what has been here said, therefore, is that God has simply revealed that the reception of the Christ-Spirit's influence into the soul sets it upon an order of life increasingly joyous and full of glory, and that the neglect or refusal to receive this influence results in increasing emptiness, distress, and woe. Whether or not the wicked will eternally continue in sin, and hence in sin's sorrow; where they will go to; what is the nature of their torment; how long it will continue; whether or not they will repent and be saved after death; whether they are inherently immortal or will eventually be annihilated—all these are *speculations*, and form no part of the distinct divine revelation; we may think as we choose about them, provided we do no elevate our opinions into divine decrees. And, mainly, whatever sorrow comes upon the evil ones is the direct, natural result of their own deeds and character, and not an arbitrary or statutory infliction of penalty by an incensed Judge.

When we penetrate into the reason and ground of this revelation, and ask why God did not clearly show us the heavenly mansions and horrid pits the good and bad respectively are to inhabit, we shall see that this reason and ground lies in the fact that the motive power by which the Gospel proposes to save men is not the hopes and fears of rewards and punishments, but God's own personal influence. If heaven and hell were to be our incentives, surely God would have set the one shining invitingly in the sky and the other burning terribly and openly upon earth, where we could all see them. Why has He removed them to the distance, veiled them, only alluded to them in figures of speech? The profound reason is that what is done for pay can only affect conduct, but not character. Expectation of reward or fear of stripes may regulate, but cannot develop man. Now, as we have said, the manifest intent of God is not to coerce us into any form of conduct, else His whole dealings with mankind are a stupendous failure. Neither is it to rescue us out of one place into another place, for if this is His plan, it has succeeded poorly, for only a small fragment of the race has been

HELL

saved in the orthodox sense. But the reasonable supposition is that His design is to develop, uplift, and finally ennoble men to be His sons; and toward this end all history tends.

> "One God, one law, one element,
> And one divine, far-off event
> To which the whole creation moves."

Now, this sort of an object can only be attained by a change in the whole character of man. His very nature must be regenerated. This, in turn, can only be accomplished by a potent influence — to wit, the influence of God. If, every time we sin, bodily pain would strike us at once, we would develop a right instinct, but not a right character. When we sin we see a possibility of temporary pleasure in it, and we are thrown back upon our principle and intelligent reflection to find the power that shall restrain us from it. Because the Ruler of men allows the wicked to prosper and the righteous to suffer for a time, drives mankind to discover and act upon the great underlying laws and principles of action. By so doing we are not trained to be oxen, keeping the road because we know that to turn aside means a blow of the whip, but we are educated to rely upon ourselves. Thus the individual conscience is developed, for we would need no conscience if rewards and punishments were immediate and certain. The will is trained, for an open and apparent hell and heaven would render the will unnecessary. The judgment is strengthened, for the judgment would have no scope if calamity came swift and sure for every misdeed. Therefore we perceive that the very *perplexity* we so cry out against, the *ostensible* frequent success of evil and apparent failure of good temporarily, is *purposely* ordained by a Father who would raise up sons to be manly and self-reliant. "Thy gentleness hath made me great." And we further perceive that the veiling of the future state is of His design who would have us learn to do right because we have right characters, and not because of hope and fear. Hope and fear, to be sure, are *partial* aids, and so the objects of hope and fear are *partially* revealed; but they are not to be the principal motive, and so the future states are not explicitly shown.

The chief, main, dominant motive for right life is to be the presence of God in our midst, the influence of His personality upon us. So, also, the chief agent to keep us from sin is to be the revulsion toward and hatred of sin because of its antipathy toward God and that character which God's personal influence works in us. If heaven and hell were set forth in the Book of God's revelation as dis-

HELL

tinctly as they are drawn by traditional theology, they would largely interfere with and set aside the operation of God's influence.

Therefore we conclude, that as God's purpose is to develop His sons into the right kind of life, and not to drive nor bribe slaves into a certain future city, He has declined the use of rewards and punishments as a main incentive, revealing them only as general divine laws, and in Jesus Christ has substituted, as a better motive, His own personal influence. Reward and punishment constitute the very heart and motive of the law, but of the Gospel Jesus Christ is the heart and motive— Jesus Christ, "who is made, not after the law of a carnal commandment, but after the power of an endless life. For the former commandment has been disannulled because of its impotency and unprofitableness, for it developed nothing to perfection; but the bringing in of a better hope did, by the which we draw nigh unto God. For if that first covenant (of rewards and punishments) had been effective, a second would have been unnecessary. But, finding fault with the former, He saith, Behold the days come, saith the Lord, when I will make a new covenant, enter upon different relations, with My people; not according to the covenant that I made with them of old, when I led them out of Egypt, because they continued not in My covenant. But this is the new covenant, saith the Lord; I will put My laws into their mind, and write them in their hearts, and I will be to them an immanent God and they shall be to Me a people. And they shall not teach every man his neighbor, and every man his brother, saying, Know the Lord; for they shall all know Me, from the least to the greatest. The law and its motives were a schoolmaster to bring us to Christ; but now that He is come, we are no longer under a schoolmaster. Stand fast, therefore, in the liberty wherewith Christ hath made us free, and be not entangled again with the yoke of bondage."[1]

[1] Heb. vii. 16, 19; viii. 7-11; Gal. iii. 24, 25; v. 1.

SUGGESTIONS

Most theological disputes are settled by subsidence.

It was not the purpose of the Bible to reveal the ultimate eternity, but the immediate eternity.

It is as much a sign of intellectual accuracy to see clearly what it is that you do not know, as it is to see what it is you do know.

Partisan zeal is usually in inverse proportion to information.

It is as much our duty to refuse either to believe or to disbelieve what is not revealed, as it is to believe the truth or to disbelieve error.

Christian honesty is based upon a liberal supply of Christian agnosticism.

Unless the Scriptures explicitly state the contrary, we have a right to assume God's moral government will be the same in the next world as in this.

Forever men set *dates* for God, and God disappoints them; but men have never discovered a *law* of God which He repudiates.

The Bible is addressed only to them that read it.

God is the only source of joy; to live apart from Him is hell.

There is nothing redemptive in sin or its penalty.

If the sufferings of the wicked do not make them turn to God here, we have no reason to believe their sufferings will make them turn hereafter.

The hell of sin is that it destroys belief.

Every text of Scripture must be read in the light of Christ's face.

Rewards and punishments can regulate, but not regenerate.

CHAPTER XII

LIFE IN THE HEAVENS

God's Personal Influence upon His Eternal Sons

"Then felt I like some watcher of the skies
   When a new planet swims into his ken;
Or like stout Cortez, when with eagle eyes
   He stared at the Pacific, and all his men
Look'd at each other with a wild surmise,
   Silent, upon a peak of Darien."
KEATS, *On First Looking Into Chapman's Homer.*

"I should know that what I have said is truth, had I the confirmation of an oracle; but this I will affirm, that what I have said is the most likely to be true of anything I could say."—PLATO, *Timæus.*

"When I consider Thy heavens, what is Man that Thou art mindful of him?"—DAVID, Ps. viii. 3.

"Beloved, now are we the Sons of God, and it doth not yet appear what we shall be; but we know that when He shall appear, we shall be like Him."—JOHN, 1 John iii. 2.

CHAPTER XII

If stress has been laid heretofore in this writing upon the erroneous views concerning the life hereafter, it is not to be supposed that the intention has been to minify the importance of the hope of a glorious life beyond, nor in any way to mar the precious and tender anticipations of the joy there awaiting us. The imagination cannot possibly indulge in fancies so sweet that the reality itself will not be sweeter. But the error has been that many of those Scriptural expressions which were given to show us the beauties of a present life in Christ have been transferred to allude to a future existence. However, after removing from the life to come all those descriptions that more properly apply to a present Christian experience, there yet remain a sufficient number and quality of revelations concerning the home beyond the grave to convince us that it is indeed delightful above compare. This chapter is added, not only to trace the probable effects of the endless influence of God upon undying spirits, but also to indicate a form of thought concerning our everlasting life that may be more consistent with common sense and the present state of our knowledge of the universe—a form, it is conceived, infinitely grander, more entrancing, and more attractive than the old forms.

It must always be kept in mind that all our speculations as to the career of the deathless soul in eternity *are* speculations merely, except that we know that if one is in Christ it will be well with him. We know that for the spirit of one who is Christ's there is a certainty of joy beyond. The writer of this essay does not wish to commit the very mistake he criticises in others.

The apostles were very careful not to indulge in any rhapsodies touching what they would do in the next world. Socrates allowed his fancy to run on before and depict the pleasure of his meeting with old friends and with great master minds; and many other philosophers and many uninspired religious teachers have composed the most interesting fictions concerning the unknown future. But the Bible writers confined themselves, as if under divine restraint, from any such forecastings; and it is not unreasonable to presume they thus abstained from what they would naturally be inclined to do, lest they should lead men to suppose their conjectures to be positive revelations of facts. Paul

LIFE IN THE HEAVENS

speaks of the "prize," the "crown," the "rest," being "with the Lord," and "with Christ"; but nowhere relates, for instance, how he expects to enter the golden city, and the house he is to live in, with its gardens and all such things. He alludes to being caught up in the air when the Lord shall appear, and otherwise describes with something of detail Christ's second coming, but manifestly he did not mean what his words seem to make him mean—*i. e.*, that Jesus should appear in bodily glory in Paul's own lifetime; or else if he *did* mean that, we know he was mistaken. But we do not here discuss the second advent; the point is that all the circumstantial descriptions of final glory and wrath in the apostles' writings most probably are connected with the second coming of Christ, and not with the life of men after death. If there is an exception to this, it is in the Apocalypse; and of that book it needs only be said that the best scholarship and piety of the ages are still undecided as to its meaning. At least its holy city and river and tree of life and such incidents of description are certainly sacred figures whose real contents are unknown, except that they portray things lovely and most pleasant.

It may not be unnecessary to insist here that whatever the joys of heaven may be, they are not to depend upon the kind of place it is, but upon the kind of people in it. Wherever there is a God-filled man there is heaven. If all men were like Jesus, this earth would be as good a place as another in which to spend a million years. All God's places are good; it is sin only that turns any of them into a hell. Give me love and wisdom, my Master's presence, and the touch of one dear hand, and why should I care whether I walk golden streets or live upon this earthly ball?

And yet it is impossible to prevent men from creating pictures of what is to come beyond death; and such pictures are not only harmless, but they may be helpful, provided only that we do not forget that they *are* but *pictures* of our own making, and provided that we do not get to pinning our hopes of happiness *upon them* instead of upon *God*. For that is the very essence of idolatry; to look for joy and help from any scenes or circumstances God gives us, instead of looking alone to *Him*. It is trusting in created things, not in the Creator. It is enough for us to know that we are to be "forever with the Lord." All other joys flow from that. We are to take all lesser pleasures simply on *trust* from Him. The reunion with friends, the bright scenes, and other delights, we know are safe in His keeping. The blessed assurance we have

LIFE IN THE HEAVENS

upon our entrance into the unknown is that our Father's hand is in ours and that "He will freely give us all things." If any think h s is too vague and colorless, they have the wrong spirit toward the Father. It is not His promises, nor what we think to be His promises; it is He that our trust hangs upon.

Keeping ever in mind, therefore, that all our theories concerning the circumstances of the next life are only attempts to give *form* to the general *fact* that we shall inherit supreme joy because we are God's sons and joint heirs with Jesus, there is no harm, but there may be much real helpfulness, in imagining the place and manner of our future life. Some fifty thousand human beings, it is said, go every hour as a colony from earth into the unknown.[1] It is of most absorbing interest to inquire whither they go; for they take with them the fondest love of us who are left behind; they are still united to us by the ties of affection and friendship. Hitherto we have had two kinds of ideas concerning their destination. One notion is that they go to some paradise or intermediate state, there to await the general resurrection. This view finds its support in bending many varied kinds of Scripture allusions to fit a preconceived theory of one great "general assizes" called

[1] Dr. O. W. Holmes.

"the day of judgment." And this theory in turn sprang from the general idea of making salvation a getting safe into a place called heaven. But it is a mere supposition and arbitrary interpretation of indistinct texts to hold that God keeps all souls in waiting-rooms until a final great day, after which the present universe shall be destroyed and two new cities appear, called heaven and hell, into which respectively shall go the good and the bad.

The second notion is that God, Christ, and the angels now live in a city or country called heaven, somewhere in the skies, and the souls of good men at death go to that place. These souls come out at "the day of judgment," but simply as a matter of form, for they receive the verdict of acquittal and immediately go back to their celestial residence. This view also rests upon literal interpretations of conflicting prophetic imagery.

It is to be regretted that one cannot put aside these notions without seeming to be indulging in wanton iconoclasm. They have so long been the set form of Christian thought that to intimate that they are incongruous and self-contradictory appears cruel. They have been embodied in some of the greatest literary masterpieces of the world. It is in the garb of these conceptions that Dante,

LIFE IN THE HEAVENS

Milton, and Bunyan have spoken to the heart and hope of mankind. Many of our favorite hymns are filled with these figures of the truth; the "sweet and blessed country," the "sweet fields of Eden," the city whose "glittering towers outshine the sun," and "Jerusalem, my happy home," are woven into the very fabric of our religious sentiment. And there is no necessity of tearing them out. One can still sing these songs and read these poems, with a full appreciation of the feeling they express; if he has not put them away by proving them false, if he feels that they are still deeply true at heart, that he has filled them full and run them over, if they are no longer *large* enough to contain the new conceptions of glory. They express the poetic genius of a former age seeking to embody in the words and visions of that time the thought about heaven. It seems, therefore, that the time is ripe for a new poet, who shall bathe his wing in higher fields of ether than were known to Milton or Dante, who shall express the enlarged outlook of our time, even as they expressed the narrow outlook of theirs: just as we need a new Pilgrim's Progress that shall narrate the adventures of Christian, not running away from a lost world to a holy refuge in the sky, but running after the world to save it and bring it to his own abounding heavenly life. The kind of concepts in which such a poet might indulge I shall endeavor to outline—a heaven of heavens infinitely more sublime than the holy city of mediæval thought.

There are some who cannot hear without alarm of any change in our religious ideas. If the Bible is true, they say, it must be fixed. If there be any change, it must be away from the set and unalterable truth of Holy Writ. Now, our belief in the Bible is indeed a fixed thing, unchanging; yet the *degree* to which we *understand* the Bible must always enlarge with our growth in knowledge. If the Bible is a revelation of God, it is not fixed *behind* us, but *before* us. We are growing up to it. As our knowledge of science and the laws of nature increase, our interpretation of Bible revelations will alter, and we may be sure that if the advance of intelligence brings us nearer the truth of God in nature our new interpretations of God in the Book must be also nearer the truth. Instead of the increase of knowledge, with the progress of the race, impoverishing and limiting the ideas which we gain from God's Book, on the contrary it expands them to a remarkable extent. Our present world-view, due to the results of scientific research, gives to the language of Holy Writ meanings of which the prophets and

LIFE IN THE HEAVENS

writers themselves, doubtless, in many cases, were but little aware. "When I consider Thy heavens," sings the Psalmist, "what is man that Thou art mindful of him?" But the insignificance of man compared with the stupendous universe, which the sacred poet here intended to depict, is how much more striking in this day, when telescopes range the sky and reveal, beyond and above those hosts of heaven that were visible to the Hebrew of old, seas upon seas of worlds and systems of worlds fading away into infinite distance! Thus has science crowded the sacred writer's phrase with newer and truer meanings, hints and analogies, of which he never dreamed. So geology has stretched the six creative days of Genesis from a poor, theatric display of artificial power into a sublime drama of divine action, covering æons of time, moving with the measured tread of unhasting law, rising with the majestic dignity of a godlike growth. A word with a small meaning at the date of its utterance may be enlarged to become a most momentous expression by the discoveries of the explorers. Such a word is "the world"; for when the Master said, "God so loved the world," how limited was the notion conveyed to the disciples' minds and with how vague edges of distant barbarous lands! But now not only have millions of Chinese and islanders and North Americans been ushered into its contents, but also the whole concept of "the world" has been unified and woven together.

All this leads up to and illustrates the alteration necessary in our views of the life beyond. We believe as truly in heaven, and accept the symbols of it as given by the New Testament writers as implicitly as did Bernard of Cluny when he wrote of "those halls of Zion conjubilant with song," but we are compelled to abandon many of the conventional trappings and appurtenances which he and those of his time deemed essential. What *helped* them *hinders* us in getting a helpful view of the future life. When all thought the earth to be flat and the sky to be its star-punctured semispherical cover, they could only conceive of heaven as one place, a city or land on the other side of this lid, and they supposed that some day the city would come down through the blue canopy to receive us. Thus did they understand the mystic poetry of the Revelator, and thus only perhaps *could* they understand it. But we know now there is no such lid. A heaven becomes the heavens. The canopy, on being approached with a lens, extends away into measureless reaches of space. We *must* adopt a new form for our thought, or stultify our own intelligence. Is it possible to find such a form which shall be as true to

LIFE IN THE HEAVENS

Scriptural imagery as was the old, and at the same time square with our present knowledge of the universe? In order to indicate such a form, let us assume, merely as an hypothesis, some such theory as this:

The earth is the breeding-ground from whence God intends to populate the whole universe. After death the soul goes to that place God has prepared as its home. This, in brief, in our present state of knowledge, seems a rational view of the future estate. Let us examine into its reasonableness.

And first, let us ask ourselves why God made so vast a system of worlds. Of course, we can never fully know God's counsel, but as His sons we are justified in studying His deeds. Knowing God, as we do in Jesus, we know Him to be a sentient, loving personality. Jesus taught us to call Him Father. Now, if He be a Father, His sons are dearer to Him than all His possessions. A mechanic takes pride in the locomotive or watch that is the product of his skill; but more does he care for his little child, and he only makes his handiwork for his child's sake. So God, looking abroad upon all the immense and inconceivably great works of His hands, "the moon and the stars which He has ordained," still would say, "The Lord's portion is His people." Rather would He destroy them all, wondrous as they be, than that any harm thereby come to "one of these little ones." If men *are* the sons of God, destined in the ages of the future to become "*like Him*," then He surely could not have made the universal frame for any *better* reason than to furnish dwelling-places for His children. The mightiest works of the Creator are none too fine for the use of them that have a right to look up and say, "Our Father, which art in the heavens."[1]

It may be objected that such a view gives an unwarranted importance to man. Infidelity, curiously enough, makes two criticisms upon the Christian scheme: one, that it makes man too small, humiliates and prostrates him; the other, that it makes him too large, occupying too much of the Almighty's care; which two criticisms we might quietly leave to devour each other. But *size* has nothing to do with *importance*. Because a man only weighs a hundred pounds is no reason for saying he is not worth more than a planet weighing a trillion pounds or so. A father standing by the bedside of a dying baby would give all his broad acres and monster buildings for the life of that little fragment of human flesh and spirit. Even so the great cities are insignificant as compared with the

[1] The word is plural in the Greek.

LIFE IN THE HEAVENS

humanity that built and inhabits them. Man is not the largest of the animals, yet has he "dominion over every living thing"; the lion and the elephant flee before his face. Worth is to be measured by soul and intellect. It is "the spirit in man" that endues him with such importance.

We rarely suspect what is implied by endowing man with immortality. As an unending being man must have something unending with which to employ his energy. God has provided him here with two things to do which meet this requirement: the first is to complete God's unfinished work, the second is to study it; and these two tasks would be exactly that which would furnish him hereafter with an inviting career. We find here that the Creator gave us an unfinished earth; there are swamps to drain, lake borders to beautify, deserts to irrigate, and marble quarries to transform into temples and statues. As He made a garden, but put Adam in it to tend it, so He put the race upon earth to be its gardener and bring all its rough readiness into complete order. This is what supplies the legitimate work of man, and this kind of work is never irksome when undertaken merely for its own sake. That we should toil for bread and clothes, doing our stint merely for wages from another man, was not the original design, and that sort of labor is very properly called a "curse." We are to labor as the child plays, for the delight of it. One who grasps the meaning of the tendencies of human progress can already see how Christ is redeeming us from this curse-work. For Christ's influence produces civilization, civilization makes machinery, and more and more is machinery taking all the manual labor, the lifting and drudgery, away from human hands; and we may confidently expect that by and by machines shall do all the disagreeable slaving, leaving men to be simply the superintendents directing the tireless potencies of steam, electricity, and heat.[1] With a proper system of distributing wealth, all the products of the earth necessary to sustain the life of the race in abundance, and even luxury, could be raised by a few persons, and by their working in an agreeable manner, while the rest of mankind could pursue higher aims, such as the adornment of the planet. Thus is Christ "taking away our curse" and making of the earth a play-ground; for play differs from work in this, that play is exertion undertaken solely for the pleasure of it,[2] while work is exertion which we do not like, undertaken for the sake of securing by it a remoter pleasur-

---

[1] See Bulwer's "The Coming Race."
[2] Bushnell, "Work and Play."

LIFE IN THE HEAVENS

able end. And therefore may we not suppose that God brings His sons into existence, in order that in them He may see Himself reflected (for a loving Being must desire to be loved), and calls the race to the divine employment of being His partner in creation, going forth through all the worlds of the heavens to add the finishing touches of habitable and homelike beauty and order to the spheres that He has made? And can man aspire to a higher destiny than thus to lay his hands upon the universe God has prepared for him, and looking up into the unclouded face of his Maker, to say, "My Father worketh hitherto, and I work"?

Secondly, an immortal spirit like man must have something that shall eternally occupy his intellect. As the body finds its health and pleasure in activity, so must the mind have its field and task. Therefore has the Father put within His marvelous creation rich and toothsome laws and problems in the investigation of which the mind finds its purest delight. The observation of nature, the study of the sciences, is fit to be the permanent occupation of the life to come. To many this may seem quite uninviting, for they conceive scientific research to be dry and hard. But the mere drudgery of science, the classifying and compiling, is not minded by those who have tasted the intoxicating cup of real scientific work. It is the most entrancing and prophetic of all callings. For, as Bushnell says, "we find that a certain capacity of elevation or poetic ardor is the most fruitful source of scientific discovery; for what are the laws of science but the ideas of God—those regulative types of thought by which God created, moves, and rules the world?" Thus will we be engaged throughout the endless ages in the only mental occupation which we can imagine to go on in increasing delight without end; in stretching out our minds upon the glorious framework of creation, its laws, its harmonies, and its relations, exclaiming in sacred rapture to Him who ever abides in us, "O God, I think Thy thoughts after Thee!"

We should not suppose our employ hereafter to consist only in singing psalms and shouting hallelujahs. The common notion that in heaven we shall be engaged in purely religious exercises all the time is not an agreeable one, simply because man was not intended for this. Our natures are so made that a place "where congregations ne'er break up and Sabbaths have no end" does not attract us. Yet many, under the impression that this is to be our sole future occupation, strive to live that sort of life here. From much

LIFE IN THE HEAVENS

religious teaching one would gather that his Christian life is not what God would have it unless, as much as his struggle for bread will permit, he be always engaged in singing, praying, testifying, listening to preaching, or reading the Bible. But the invariable result of giving one's self wholly to religious thought is morbidity and unhealthy spiritual life. Temperance is the rule, also, in religion. While some may be called upon to give themselves almost wholly to religious exercises, such is not the normal life. In emergencies, upon certain occasions, it may behoove us to lay aside all secular matters and concentrate ourselves upon church work. But that is not the typical Christian life. We are created to plow, to sow, to reap, to build, to explore, to study, to laugh, and to play. The right Christian life consists in doing these things like children of God, and not like cats and dogs. Religion, in fine, is the spirit in which work is to be done; it is not a work to be done. It is not something to do, it is the way in which we are to do all things. Religion is the *tune;* "earthly" business is the *words.* When men have lost the tune or are off the key, it is proper enough that some of us should devote ourselves wholly to setting them right; but the Father never intended the race to be finally forever humming "songs without words." The most wholesome kind of Christianity is not that of priests, preachers, and deaconesses, but that of housewives, merchants, artists, students, and especially little children. Excessive religiosity is as dangerous as any other kind of excess and is as fruitful as any in insanity.

Engaged thus in the everlasting career that shall continually employ the faculties of the mind and of whatever body the spirit may take unto itself, we must not forget that such a being will ascend ever higher in *development*.[1] If man is "fearfully and wonderfully made" now, what will he be when endless time has removed every barrier to his progress? After ten thousand years of unimpeded development the meanest boor will become as much more magnificent in his personality than a Goethe here, as such a Goethe living now would be above an African slave. What amazing possibilities does eternity open before the mind! How rich may it become in wisdom and knowledge, how skilled in the perception of the truth! What possibilities of artistic attainment are also thus disclosed! Art also shall be an employment, for it is the representation and interpretation of the works of God. Doubtless the germs of all that any man has become lurk in each soul of the

[1] Bushnell, "The Power of an Endless Life."

LIFE IN THE HEAVENS

whole race. Given unending time, the basest and lowliest men may outstrip Beethoven and Michael Angelo; playing also upon what new instruments and painting with what new colors! Well might the Psalmist cry, "I said, ye are gods!" and John, "It doth not yet appear what we shall be!" And who knows but that Michael and Gabriel, the angels and archangels, the seraphim and cherubim, are but human souls elevated by the orderly development of eternity's long years to that supernal dignity and radiance wherein they stand? Endow a human being with eternity, and what is not possible? May we not hope that at last God will look upon our own full-grown souls, glorious with His glory, reflecting back the very fullness of His love and beauty, and thrill with gratitude and pride because of His children? "He shall see the travail of His soul and be satisfied."

If it be objected that Tellus is too small a planet to be given such supreme significance, and that this view is but reviving the fallacy of the ancients that earth was the center about which all the heavenly host stands; it may be answered that making the earth to be the center of *spiritual* interest for the universal people does not in any degree imply that it is the *physical* center of the universe; and again that God surely must begin somewhere if He is to people His spheres at all, and it is as reasonable to suppose He begins at Tellus as at any other planet or star.

As to the matter of time, God is in no hurry; it is only man who frets and is impatient; and what matter if it be many millions of years before all the habitable worlds are full; what matter, indeed, if they never be full at all, many being reserved as parks or playgrounds, many others being central suns merely to give light and heat to their surrounding populated planets, others still, being like our moon, worlds grown old, and others being worlds yet in process of preparation? Geologists tell us the earth is yet young, so that for millenniums yet to come it will continue to send forth these colonies out into "the republic of God" in the heavens.

There is another singular way in which this theory sheds light upon the coherence of the Christian scheme of thought. Has it not always seemed a little strange that the Almighty should go to so much pains to save this little world; that He should send His "only begotten Son" to this planet? For, if other worlds be peopled, it is not unlikely that similar demands would be made upon His love by them. And why is the *man* Christ Jesus called His *only* begotten Son? Is there any other hypothesis than the one

LIFE IN THE HEAVENS

here suggested that makes this reasonable? But if the other worlds be filled with the humanity of this, if they all be linked together as one human stock, if by incarnating Himself into this race He became one with the whole population of the heavens, *then* our idea of the incarnation is not out of proportion. At once He entered into and identified Himself with His *whole* people.

Touching this is another fact, that while Jesus was "very man" during His life, He is also explicitly described as *still remaining a man* after His resurrection. After rising from the grave He showed Himself to His disciples; He urged them to feel of His hands and side, saying, "Hath a ghost flesh and blood?" for they thought He might be an apparition. And He ate fish and honeycomb. And that His life continued to be the same, and that death was simply *nothing at all*, except a change in the bodily substance, is shown by His still expounding the Scriptures on the way to Emmaus, just as He did in His earthly life, and by His taking up the thread of His relations with Peter where it had been dropped upon the fatal night when the impulsive apostle denied Him, and asking thrice, "Simon, son of Jonas, lovest thou Me?" so that His whole personality thus still persists. Carried to its logical conclusion, what does this mean? It means that God's identity with this race is more than a figure of speech. If Christ is very man, God is very man. If God is man, man is of God. Humanity is thus elevated to most imperial significance. We begin to get glimpses of what Christ meant when He prayed the Father: "As Thou, Father, art in Me, and I in Thee, that they also may be one in Us. And the glory which Thou gavest Me I have given them; that they may be one even as We are one; I in them and Thou in Me." Thus did He lift in intercessory prayer that face which brightens the air of Paradise; thus did He raise those arms, by which also He made the worlds, and bind together in indissoluble and awful unity (the plain meaning of whose words we hardly dare believe), the Father, the Son, and the many sons, all by the Eternal Spirit.

Now, if we be sons, all things are ours. Look, therefore, to the star-sown deeps, filled with worlds each as glorious as this, and know that they are yours, all yours, by direct inheritance from your Father! Is this too great? To say so is to misapprehend a human soul. Instead of being too great, it is the only idea that has ever been large enough to measure up to the wants and possibilities of man. You think you can fill a man! There is a hungry, ragged street urchin; try to fill him; he wants—a dinner. Give him dinner and breakfast and supper, and assure him of these every day; is he satisfied? No; now he wants clothes, then a little knowledge, then more knowledge, then to rule his ward, then he wants a whole nation, then the world itself; and thus go on with that insatiate soul, smitten with eternity-hunger, pouring into it lands, houses, oceans, continents, honors, riches, pleasures; and what do you get from him? A distressed cry for more.[1] For you have tried to fill a soul with one planet when it will hold galaxies. The human spirit alone can contain and use a universe, and therefore has the God who made the universe given it to the only being that would know what to do with it.

It may not be trivial to remark also that Christ's asseveration, "In the resurrection they neither marry nor are given in marriage,"[2] acquires a cogency from the theory here proposed that it gains from no other hypothesis. Ours alone, then, is the generative planet. The function of physical reproduction not only supplies inhabitants for the universe, but it lays the foundation for the family, and introduces man to the divine feeling of love, which, purged from all fleshly grossness (be-

[1] Carlyle, "Sartor Resartus."   [2] Matt. xxii. 30.

cause there is to be no reproduction hereafter), is the tie among heavenly intelligences. To incorporate Himself into the race the Father must needs come to the reproductive planet.

Why, then, is it either useless or sacrilegious to endeavor to modify our ideas of the Scriptures' meaning to conform to the known facts science has discovered? The Bible glows with a new light when it is interpreted by the best results of investigation. The forms of thought concerning a future life that once enraptured saints on earth several hundred years ago, are not attractive to an intelligent man now, because they do not fit what he knows to be the construction of nature. Abandoning all the pure, divine joys of art and science and creative work, to dwell forever in one cubical city crowded with souls, and there to be occupied entirely in religious services, all this appeals not to a wholesome, normal man, but only to a sickly instinct reveling in a literalistic interpretation which is as distorted as it is unsound.

The spacious firmament has always been the most prophetic spectacle the Creator has revealed to men. It thrilled the ancients, it humbled Immanuel Kant, it convinced Napoleon of God. It has peculiarly lifted the lives of men, as though some strange force in it

LIFE IN THE HEAVENS

drew humanity upward, away from their fellow-animals, as though its silent voice touched that in them which other creatures do not possess. Can it be pure absurdity to suppose that the sympathy and yearning of celestial humanities form no insignificant part of the force that makes the sky the majestic, yet mute, herald of Almighty God?

"The heavens declare the glory of God:
And the firmament showeth his handiwork.
Day unto day uttereth speech,
And night unto night showeth knowledge.
They have no speech nor language,
Yet without these is their voice heard.
Their influence is gone out through all the world:
And their words to the end of the world."[1]

Best of all, when we view the heavens as our destination, we get a better grasp of the home idea of the life to come. Thus are we not all to be huddled into one great city where the endearing and domestic affections are to be swallowed up in religious ardor. Each man goes to his own people. "I go to prepare a place for you," said Christ.[2] If He was merely returning to that abode of angels from whence He came, how could He be said to be preparing a place? for that was already prepared. But He went to make ready a particular place for them especially, as He pre-

[1] Ps. xix. margin.   [2] John xiv. 2.

pares other places for others. Even Judas "'went to his own place.'"[1] The Bible's terms do not require us to think of but *one* place for all. "In My Father's house are *many* mansions."

Coming into this world we find a place prepared; a mother's breast whereon to lean, and a father's willing hands to shield and help us.[2] Going into that world it is not out of reason to presume that there, also, those departed loved ones, bright with the increment of divine days and years of growth, shall meet us with smiles, welcome us into some dear *home*, and instruct our feeble understandings, our wayward will, and our undisciplined heart in the new life. Home is the sweetest of words. Because one place is peculiarly mine argues not that all other places are inferior; that some friends are especially my own only makes me the more charitable to strangers. Yonder, too, is a home—not, like this one, a moving tent, no continuing city, but a house eternal in the heavens.

The men of old peopled the firmament with constellations, fantastic forms of departed heroes; was this a foreshadowing hint of the truth that the exaltation we feel when we stand beneath the starry dome is not only the natural wonder at something vast and great,

[1] Acts i. 25. [2] Clarke.

LIFE IN THE HEAVENS

but also the yearning of our hearts in response to the down-shining eyes of them

"That we have loved long since,
And lost awhile"?

Go forth, therefore, beneath the unmeasured deeps of heaven, and from thence drink in THE PERSONAL INFLUENCE OF GOD, and of all saints. It is infinitely tender and consoling to imagine that perhaps even now as you stand there gazing upward at the friendly stars that wink at you in strange yet familiar beckonings, upon some one of them a little colony of emigrants, who sailed from the port of death and took with them all the brightness and zest of life, stand waiting for *you*. Even now, mayhap, your eyes behold the "home, sweet home," where shall be restored to you

"The touch of a vanished hand
And the sound of a voice that is still."

SUGGESTIONS

The imaginations touching the future life may be helpful, provided we remember they *are* imaginations.

The time is ripe for a new Dante and a new Milton, who shall read the imagery of the Bible in the light of modern information.

The Bible is a fixed book, but fixed before us, not behind us.

Every scientific discovery is a new parable of God.

The pictures of heaven that helped the mediæval saint may hinder us.

The universe is none too fine nor great for the sons of God.

Christ takes away the curse of work thus: Christianity makes civilization, civilization makes machinery and altruism, machinery does the drudgery, and altruism will distribute the fruits with justice.

An eternal spirit must have an eternal task.

An eternal intellect must have eternal problems.

Religion is not a work to be done, it is the way in which work is to be done.

Religion is the *tune*, earthly business is the words.

With eternity, the meanest boor may become an archangel.

Perhaps at last God may be proud of us.

God values us, not for what we are, but for what He intends to make of us.

By the incarnation God identified Himself with the population of the universe.

Christ was "very man"; He is still "very man"; and Christ is "the fullness of the Godhead bodily"; from these premises we hardly dare draw the conclusion.

APPENDIX

Extract from Whately, "On the Abolition of the Law"

(See note 1, p. 54.)

APPENDIX

Extract from Whately's Essay, "On the Abolition of the Law," in "Difficulties in the Writings of Saint Paul," p. 148.

The simplest and clearest way, then, of stating the case with respect to the present question is, to lay down, on the one hand, that the Mosaic law was limited both to the nation of Israelites and to the period before the Gospel; but, on the other hand, that the natural principles of morality, which (among other things) it inculcates, are from their own character of universal obligation—that is, on the one hand, "no Christian man (as our article expresses it) is free from the observance of those commandments which are called moral," so, on the other hand, it is not *because* they are commandments of the Mosaic law that he is bound to obey them, but because they *are* moral. Indeed, there are numerous precepts in the laws, for instance, of Solon and Mahomet, from a conformity to which no Christian can pretend to exemption; yet, though we are bound to practice almsgiving and several other duties there enjoined, and to abstain from murder, for instance, and false-witness—which these law-givers forbid—no one would say that a part of the

APPENDIX

Koran is binding on Christians since their conduct is determined, not by the authority of the Koran, but by the nature of the case.

If men are taught to regard the Mosaic law (with the exception of the civil and ceremonial ordinances) as their appointed rule of life, they will be disposed to lower the standard of Christian morality by *contenting themselves with a literal adherence to the express commands of that law;* or, at least, merely to enlarge that code by the addition of such precise moral precepts as they find distinctly enacted in the New Testament. Now this was very far from being the apostle's view of the Christian life. Not only does the Gospel require a morality in many respects higher and more perfect in itself than the law, but it places morality universally on higher grounds. Instead of precise *rules*, it furnishes sublime *principles* of conduct, leaving the Christian to apply these, according to his own discretion in each case that may arise, and thus to be "a law unto himself." Gratitude for the redeeming love of God in Christ, with mingled veneration and affection for the person of our great Master, and an exalted emulation, leading us to tread in His steps; an ardent longing to behold His glories, and to enjoy His presence in the world to come, with an earnest effort to prepare for that better world; love toward our brethren for His sake who died for us and them; and, above all, the thought that the Christian is a part of "the temple of the Holy Ghost," who dwelleth in the church, even the Spirit of Christ, without which we are none of His, a

APPENDIX

temple which we are bound to keep undefiled—these, and such as these, are the Gospel principles of morality, into a conformity with which the Christian is to fashion his heart and his life; and they are such principles as the Mosaic dispensation could not furnish. The Israelites, as not only living under a revelation which had but a shadow of the good things of the Gospel, but also as a dull and gross-minded and imperfectly civilized people, in a condition corresponding to that of childhood, were in few things left to their own moral discretion, but were furnished with precise rules in most points of conduct. These answered to the exact regulations under which children are necessarily placed, and which are gradually relaxed as they advance toward maturity—not at all on the ground that good conduct is less required of *men* than of children; but they are expected to be more capable of regulating their own conduct by their *own* discretion, and of acting upon principle.

When, then, the Mosaic code was abolished, we find no other system of rules substituted in its place. Our Lord and His apostles enforced such duties as were the most liable to be neglected, corrected some prevailing errors, gave some particular directions which particular occasions called for, but laid down no *set of rules* for the conduct of a Christian. They laid down Christian *principles* instead; they sought to implant Christian *dispositions*. And this is the more remarkable inasmuch as we may be sure, from the nature of man, that precise regulations, even though some-

APPENDIX

what tedious to learn and burdensome to observe, would have been highly acceptable to their converts. Hardly any restraint is so irksome to man—that is, to "the natural man"—as to be left to his own discretion, yet still required to regulate his conduct according to certain principles, and to steer his course through the intricate channels of life, with a constant, vigilant exercise of his moral judgment. It is much more agreeable to human indolence (though at first sight the contrary might be supposed) to have a complete system of laws laid down, which are to be observed according to the letter, not to the spirit, and which, as long as a man adheres to them, afford both a consolatory assurance of safety and an unrestrained liberty as to every point not determined by them, than to be called upon for incessant watchfulness, careful and candid self-examination, and studious cultivation of certain moral dispositions.

Accordingly, most, if not all systems of man's devising (whether corruptions of Christianity or built on any other foundations) will be found, even in what appear their most rigid enactments, to be accommodated to this tendency of the human heart. When Mahomet, for instance, enjoined on his disciples a strict fast during a certain period, and an entire abstinence from wine and from games of chance, and the devotion of a precise portion of their property to the poor, leaving them at liberty generally to follow their own sensual and worldly inclinations, he imposed a far less severe task on them than if he had required them constantly to control their ap-

APPENDIX

petites and passions, to repress covetousness, and to be uniformly temperate, charitable, and heavenly-minded. And had Paul been (as a false teacher always will be) disposed to comply with the expectation and wishes which his disciples would naturally form, he would doubtless have referred them to some part of the Mosaic law as their standard of morality, or would have substituted some other system of rules in its place. Indeed, there is strong reason to think (especially from what we find in 1 Corinthians) that something of this nature had actually been desired of him. He seems to have been applied to for more precise rules than he was willing to give, particularly as to the lawfulness of going to idol feasts, and as to several points relative to marriage and celibacy—concerning which and other matters he gives briefly such directions as the occasion rendered indispensable, but breaks off into exhortations to "use this world as not abusing it," and speedily recurs to the general description of the Christian character and the inculcation of Christian principles. He will not be induced to enter into minute details of things forbidden and permitted, enjoined and dispensed with; and even when most occupied in repelling the suspicion that Gospel liberty exempts the Christian from moral obligation, instead of retaining or framing anew any system of prohibitions and injunctions, he urges upon his hearers the very consideration of their being exempt from any such childish trammels as a reason for their aiming at a more perfect holiness of life on pure and more generous motives. "Sin," he says, "shall not have dominion over you; for *ye are not under the law, but under grace*"; and he perpetually incites them to walk "worthy of their vocation," on the ground of their being "bought with a price," and bound to "live unto Him who died for them"; "as risen with Christ" to a new life of holiness, exhorted to "set their affections on things above, not on things on the earth"; as "living sacrifices" to God; as "the temple of Holy Ghost," called upon to keep God's dwelling-place undefiled, and to abound in all "the fruits of the Spirit"; and as "being delivered from the law, that we should serve in newness of the spirit, and not in the oldness of the letter."

He who seeks, then—as many are disposed to do—either in the Old Testament or in the New for a precise code of laws by which to regulate his conduct, mistakes the character of our religion. It is indeed an error, and a ruinous one, to think that we may "continue in sin because we are not under the law but under grace"; but it is also an error, and a far commoner one, to inquire of the Scriptures, in each case that may occur, what we are strictly bound to do or to abstain from, and to feel secure as long as we transgress no distinct commandment But he who seeks with sincerity for Christian *principles* will not fail to find them. If we endeavor, through the aid of the Holy Spirit, to trace on our own heart the delineation of the Christian character which the Scriptures present, and to conform all our actions and words and thoughts to that character, our Heavenly Teacher will

APPENDIX

enable us to "have a right judgment in all things"; and we shall be "led by the Spirit" of Christ to follow *His* steps, and to "purify ourselves even as He is pure," that "when He shall appear we may be made like unto Him, and may behold Him as He is."

www.ingramcontent.com/pod-product-compliance
Lightning Source LLC
Chambersburg PA
CBHW032043220426
43664CB00008B/830